RETURNING TO YOUR FIRST LOVE

RETURNING TO YOUR FIRST LOVE

PUTTING GOD BACK IN FIRST PLACE

TONY EVANS

Renaissance Productions

MOODY PRESS

CHICAGO

ISBN: 0-8024-7908-1

3 5 7 9 10 8 6 4

Printed in the United States of America

*This book is gratefully dedicated to
Lois, my first earthly love,
whose faithfulness, patience,
graciousness, support,
and loyal love
have been the foundation
of my life and ministry.*

*"You are altogether beautiful, my darling,
And there is no blemish in you."*
Song of Solomon 4:7

CONTENTS

FOREWORD

I f the Lord Jesus Christ were to come to your house or
mine and sit down with us, what do you think He would
say?

I believe one of the first things He would ask is, "Do
you love Me?" That's the question the resurrected Christ
asked Simon Peter three times at their seaside breakfast
(John 21:15–17). Peter had denied the Lord at His crucifixion, and he needed to be restored.

Jesus undertook that restoration by bringing Simon
back to the basic issue: "Do you love Me?" The Savior
wasn't satisfied until He had zeroed in on the issue of Peter's love for Him and gotten the right answer. Only then
did Jesus release Peter for ministry: "Feed My sheep."

The lesson Jesus taught Peter—and the lesson the
Holy Spirit wants to teach us—in this marvelous passage
is the fundamental lesson that devotion precedes duty.
One reason this is important is that we so often get the
order reversed.

If we had been in Jesus' place that day by the seashore, most of us would have asked Simon Peter an entirely different set of questions. We probably would have asked him if he was truly sorry for what he did in denying Christ, and if he had confessed his sin and been forgiven.

Or we might have started off by asking Peter if he was still serious about being a disciple, if he still wanted to be a member of the team. The more devotionally minded among us would have quizzed Peter about his personal life, making sure he was spending time daily in prayer and study of the Scriptures.

And the service minded among us would probably have made sure Peter knew what his spiritual gifts were and was plugged into a ministry in which he was exercising those gifts.

But Jesus did not ask Peter about any of these things. Did Jesus not care about Peter's spiritual condition and future service? Of course He did. But Jesus knew that unless Peter's service was motivated by intense love for Him, it would lead to duty without devotion, practice without passion.

That's also true for you and me, by the way. Our love for Christ is so foundational that Jesus Himself called it our "first love" in Revelation 2:4. Here in the first of His messages to the seven churches, Jesus Christ tells the church at Ephesus that all their doctrinal purity and hard work could not compensate for what they had left behind: their "first love" for Him.

Dr. Tony Evans points out that Jesus Christ takes this issue so seriously that unless we put our love for Him in first place where it belongs, nothing else we do for Him really matters. That's why I appreciate *Returning to Your First Love* and am happy to recommend it to you.

Dr. Evans has done us all a service in focusing the biblical spotlight on the absolute necessity of keeping our love for Christ as the central passion of our hearts. Any earnest Christian knows how easy it is to become so absorbed in doing things for Christ that we forget to cultivate our love relationship with Him.

In his own provocative way, Dr. Evans helps us correct this imbalance. He begins by showing us how we can get turned off the right road and leave our first love. Then he offers us some very biblical and practical ways to get back on the right road.

This book is stimulating and challenging, and it goes right to the heart of the matter and speaks to us in language we can understand and apply. *Returning to Your First Love* is a welcome and much-needed book for the church and for individual Christians, and I pray that God will bless its truths to your heart.

CHARLES STANLEY
Atlanta, Georgia

PREFACE

o professional basketball players, rebounding is an art form. Some players are considered highly valuable for their rebounding ability alone.

Why is rebounding such a valuable art in basketball? Because those guys miss a lot of shots! The ball doesn't go in the hoop. It bounces off the rim or caroms off the backboard. The winners are those who get the rebound and take another shot.

That's true in the Christian life too. All of us take bad shots. We know where the hoop is and we have the ball, but somehow the two don't meet. The issue I'm concerned about is not so much the missed shot, but the rebound: what you do to get up and get back in the game.

Let me put it in other terms. If you have allowed something to replace your first love for Jesus Christ, there has been a missed shot somewhere. But the game isn't over. You can rebound, you can regain that first love for

Christ and still come out a winner in the game of life. That's what Christ wants you to do.

Jesus said the greatest commandment is, "You shall love the Lord your God with all your heart, and with all your soul, and with all your mind" (Matthew 22:37). Love for God has always been first on His priority list. God not only wants our duty, He wants our devotion.

If there were any doubt about this, the risen Lord erased it when He aimed pointed words to the church at Ephesus:

> I know your deeds and your toil and perseverance, and that you cannot endure evil men, and you put to the test those who call themselves apostles, and they are not, and you found them to be false; and you have perseverance and have endured for My name's sake, and have not grown weary. But I have this against you, that you have left your first love. Remember therefore from where you have fallen, and repent and do the deeds you did at first; or else I am coming to you, and will remove your lampstand out of its place— unless you repent. (Revelation 2:2–5)

What an amazing passage of Scripture this is. When Jesus Christ looked at the church in Ephesus, He saw a lot of good things. He saw good works, He saw hard work, and He saw continuing work. These folk were not lazy. They were diligent in the things of God. They had even endured persecution and hardship for the sake of Christ's name. So far so good.

When Jesus Christ looked at the church in Ephesus, He also saw doctrinal soundness. These believers could sniff out false apostles and false teachers because they knew their theological facts. They knew the Scriptures. The truth was important to them. Any pastor has to love a group of people like that.

In fact, there was only one area where the Ephesians had let things slip. Something had gone wrong, and it was this: the duty that was the result of devotion took the *place* of devotion. The Ephesians had left their "first love," their love for Christ Himself. They were efficient in their Christian lives—but they were *coldly* efficient. Somewhere along the line, the warmth and excitement of their love for God had grown cold and lifeless.

Well, you say, three out of four isn't bad. They had good deeds, they served God with endurance, and they were sound in doctrine. They just needed to work harder on the love thing.

Is that what Jesus Christ told them? No! He said, "Without your love for Me being what it ought to be, nothing else you do really matters. Unless you return to the love you had for Me at the first, I'll remove your church's lampstand from its place!"

God never meant for our duty to replace our devotion. That makes the issue of our first love so important that it's worth taking this and the following chapters to talk about it. I want to do this under two headings which will take us from where we are to where we want to be.

Unfortunately, since we are fallen, redeemed people living in a fallen, *un*redeemed world, there's a lot around us and even within us that can cause us to take our eyes off Christ and lose our "first love" relationship with Him. We face some formidable enemies: the world, which according to John includes "the lust of the flesh and the lust of the eyes and the boastful pride of life" (1 John 2:16), and that old lion the devil (1 Peter 5:8).

So in part one we'll talk about some things that can rob us of the priority of our love for Christ, and the consequences of allowing this condition to continue. This is part of the picture, because Jesus gave such a strong warning to the Ephesian church that we have to realize what we're risking if we don't put God back in His rightful place in our lives.

The second part of the book is the fun stuff, where we talk about regaining our first love. The outline for this is taken from Revelation 2:5, where Jesus told the Ephesians to remember, repent, and redo. This section is heavy on application, but all along the way I'll be giving you ideas for putting the truth we're learning into practice. Let's get started.

WITH GRATITUDE

I want to say a special word of thanks to my friend Philip Rawley for his excellent editorial help in the preparation of this manuscript, and to Greg Thornton, Cheryl Dunlop, and the entire Moody Press team for their continued commitment to biblical integrity and technical excellence.

PART ONE

LEAVING YOUR FIRST LOVE

CHAPTER ONE

THE CANCER OF CARNALITY

If we went back twenty-five years and did away with all of the country, pop, and rock songs that deal with someone leaving his or her lover, the list of available tunes would probably be cut in half. One that would definitely have to go is the seventies hit song by Paul Simon, "50 Ways to Leave Your Lover."

Judging by the music our secular culture keeps churning out, one would have to conclude that we are in a love crisis and have been for quite some time. The world's crisis is twofold. First, no one seems to know how to keep love alive, how to keep the flame lit, the fire burning. Second, everyone seems to be stepping out on his or her true love.

Well, I can testify that the church has a love crisis too. We have a hard time keeping our first love in its rightful place. The title of this book suggests that it's possible for us Christians to leave our first love. Jesus Himself said so to a group of Christians in the church at Ephesus (Revelation 2:4).

So we've got a problem. As I suggested in the preface, because we are very imperfect people in an imperfect world, it's easy for us to get our priorities messed up. And the place where we often mess up is in getting our eyes and hearts off Christ and on something else. It's called leaving your first love, and there's only one remedy for it. It's called returning to your first love.

Now, if you've ever been lost, made a wrong turn and left the road you were supposed to be traveling on, you know you've got to return. In fact, if you're like me, you *want* to return to the right road once you see you're going the wrong way!

But before you can get back to where you're supposed to be, you've got to see where you are, figure out how you messed up to get where you are, and retrace your steps. If it's possible to leave your first love, and Jesus said it is, we'd better identify and deal with the attitudes and actions that can get us off track. That's what I want to do in these early chapters.

The first of these love-stealers is the spiritual condition the New Testament calls carnality. Whether it's in our individual lives, our family life, our church life, or our life in society, a lot of what is wrong with us is attributable to our own carnality.

God has too many children who are not really sure whose family they want to be a part of. They're trying to step out with Christ and the world at the same time, which leads to unanswered prayer, emotional and physical weakness, loss of peace, loss of joy, lack of stability, and all manner of ills.

Now don't misunderstand me. I am not insinuating that every time a Christian has a problem, it is because he or she is carnal. But I am suggesting that far too many of us are having far too many failures because we are carnal and are half-stepping with the gospel.

What does it mean to be a carnal Christian? Simply stated, carnality is that spiritual state where a born-again Christian knowingly and persistently lives to please and serve self rather than Christ. Paul explains the concept of carnality in 1 Corinthians 3, which we will consider below.

A GENUINE CHRISTIAN

The first thing I want to note is that a carnal Christian is a genuine Christian. When I say carnal *Christian*, I mean just that. I am not talking about those who have never come to Christ. You can't leave your first love for Christ if you were never properly related to Him in the first place. So when I talk about a carnal Christian, I have in mind a born-again believer.

Did you know it's possible to be on your way to heaven and yet be of little use to God on earth? It's possible to receive the Lord Jesus Christ as Savior and yet come to the place where you refuse to submit to His lordship. That's the picture of the carnal Christian: someone who is on his way to heaven but has compromised his life of faith on earth.

Many people think they are carnal Christians when they are not Christians at all. Some think they have backslidden when they've never *front*slidden! If you've never trusted the Lord Jesus Christ alone for salvation, then you need to be born again (John 3:1–7). You need to repent of your sins and be saved, to entrust your eternal destiny to Jesus Christ, who paid for your sins on the cross. Carnality is not your problem if you're in this category.

Sometimes we see a person who professes to have been born again but who is now living a Christian lie. It's easy to say this person was never a Christian. That's possible. But it's also possible that this person is a genuine Christian who has grown lukewarm and has become a failure in the faith.

This is so because Christians have a two-fold relationship with God. Just as it is possible to be legally married without enjoying the intimate fellowship that marriage should bring, it is also possible to be truly married to Christ but not enjoying the fellowship that ought to be part of our salvation.

That a person can be a Christian and be carnal is clear from 1 Corinthians 3. Paul says in verse 1, "And I, brethren, could not speak to you as to spiritual men, but as to men of flesh, as to babes in Christ."

Please notice that Paul addressed these people as brethren, as being "in Christ." Brethren are part of the family of God. And if you are in Christ, you are a Christian. Yet in this chapter, Paul is going to chastise his readers because even though they were brethren (part of the family) and in Christ (genuine Christians), they were failing spiritually.

Back in 1 Corinthians 1:2, Paul opened his letter to this church made up largely of carnal Christians by writing, "to the church of God which is at Corinth, to those who have been sanctified in Christ Jesus, saints by calling." The Corinthians were people set apart for God's purposes. They were saved, sanctified brethren, members of the family. Yet they were carnal, living as if Christ were not the object of their love at all, let alone their first love.

There are many illustrations in the Bible of people who committed themselves to God and then became abysmal failures. I think of Saul, the first king of Israel. He was the Lord's anointed ruler, chosen to lead Israel (1 Samuel 10:1). Yet here is a man who because of rebellion against God wound up using witchcraft and ultimately committing suicide. Saul became suicidal because of his rebellion against God.

Saul's successor, David, lived in a state of carnality when he not only committed adultery with Bathsheba, but committed murder and then tried to cover it up until Nathan the prophet confronted him (2 Samuel 11–12).

David's son Solomon was a great king. The first ten chapters of 1 Kings tell us how wonderfully committed he was. When he had a chance to ask for anything his heart desired, Solomon prayed, "Don't give me riches, give me wisdom" (1 Kings 3:2–15). And there are few prayers in the Bible as great as the prayer of Solomon when he dedicated the temple (1 Kings 8:22–53). He was a man committed.

But the Bible says in 1 Kings 11:1, "Solomon loved many foreign women." What an understatement for someone who wound up with 700 wives and 300 girlfriends on the side! These women "turned [Solomon's] heart away after other gods; and his heart was not wholly

devoted to the Lord his God" (v. 4). If that isn't a description of leaving your first love, I don't know what is.

No wonder that by the time Solomon wrote Ecclesi-
astes, his theme was the emptiness of life. When he left his
first love and entered into a life of carnality, all Solomon
could talk about was the meaninglessness of life apart
from a dynamic relationship with God because he had become a carnal saint.

The list could go on and on. Later in 1 Corinthians,
we read about a man who was living with his stepmother
in an incestuous relationship. Although Paul pronounced
severe judgment on this man in expelling him from the
church, the man may well have been a believer who needed severe discipline to bring him to repentance and restore him (5:1–5).

My point is that getting saved ten years ago doesn't
fix you spiritually today. God gave you new life, but you
must live the new life He gave you in order for it to be
meaningful. It is possible to be a spiritual victor yesterday
and a spiritual disaster today. Unless we keep short accounts with God, unless we live this Christian life day by
day in a dynamic walk with Him, it is possible for us to be
spiritual failures.

A STAGNANT CHRISTIAN

Second, the carnal Christian is a stagnant Christian.
Look at 1 Corinthians 3:2–3a: "I gave you milk to drink,
not solid food; for you were not yet able to receive it. Indeed, even now you are not yet able, for you are still
fleshly."

A carnal Christian is one who has been saved for a
period of time, yet is demonstrating little or no spiritual
development. One of the things that dismays me is the
number of Christians who come to church week after week,
month after month, and year after year, but who are making no progress even though they are still performing.

They still commit the same old sins in the same old
way. They still refuse to think biblically, to relate to God
as He demands. But they are in the same seat (you can
predict it) every Sunday morning. In fact, no one else had

better sit in their seat. They're still performing, but they're wrestling with stuff they should have been able to overcome long ago.

ABC Saints

Paul says the thing that marks carnal believers is their inability to eat solid spiritual food. In other words, they are not able to get into the deeper things of God. They're what I call ABC Christians.

Most of us would be insulted if someone gave us a book that started out, "A is for Apple. Apple is a fruit that grows on trees. A is for Apple." We would be offended if we turned to the next page and read, "B is for Boy. Boy runs after ball. B is for Boy." Then, "C is for Cup." You get the idea.

You would say, "Hey, I've already been to kindergarten. I'm way beyond this stuff." You learned your ABCs when you were four or five. Now you are able to understand sentences and clauses and prepositions and adverbial phrases and various other grammatical constructs. You have graduated way beyond kindergarten subjects. You put in the time necessary to learn and grow.

But we all know people who have not used their time to learn. They dropped out along the way. They stopped educating themselves and so today, even though they are adults, the best they can give you is "A is for Apple."

The way to develop your ability to read is by reading, not by wishing you could read, hoping you can read, or even praying for the ability to read. If you want to learn to read, you've got to practice reading. And if you want to become a spiritual Christian, one whose first love is in its rightful place, you have to do the things necessary to spiritual growth. You cannot remain stagnant.

Stalled Saints

When I was in Lagos, Nigeria, recently, a group of us were in a taxi cab when it stalled. We couldn't move. My first night in Nigeria, and I have to get out and help push a car.

Well, we discovered the driver's gauge wasn't working and he had no gas. He was trying to take us somewhere with no tiger in his tank. We got some gas and poured it in the tank and finally got the car to go because the engine had been fed.

In other words, air alone wouldn't do. That car had two holy men and two holy women in it, but it wasn't going anywhere because what was required was gas and anything less wouldn't do.

Many of us want to give God everything but what God requires. We want to offer Him a little of this and a little of that, but our spiritual engines don't roar because we are not giving what God is requiring: a committed life, using the time we have for spiritual development.

Unfortunately, there's another chapter to my Nigerian taxi experience. Just as we were about to enter a highway, the cab stalled again. I got out, and we pushed the car into a gas station, where it stalled permanently. So on my first night in Nigeria, I was on the street having to thumb a ride with my hosts.

Because that taxi stalled, we were not able to progress toward our intended destination in a timely fashion. We were held back.

Many times Christians are carnal because they are stalled. They can't move forward, no matter how hard they spin their wheels, because they are stuck in a rut. They have by their own choice failed to move from milk to solid food.

They still measure the success of their spiritual life by how well they were entertained, not by how much truth they were exposed to. They want to feel good even when they aren't learning anything. They want someone else to give them the Word. They never learn to pick up a knife and fork for themselves.

You can excuse a baby who does not have the capacity to eat on her own yet. But once you're grown up, you are supposed to be able to feed yourself. These Christians in Corinth had not done so. Like the people described in Hebrews 5:11, they had become "dull of hearing."

This word *dull* was used of a mule. Carnal Christians have become mule-headed, stubborn, refusing to learn and apply the truth of God, which stalls their spiritual development. This suggests a third characteristic of carnality.

A FLESHLY-MINDED CHRISTIAN

The carnal Christian is a fleshly-minded Christian. Let's look back at 1 Corinthians 3:3, where Paul says: "You are still fleshly [carnal]. For since there is jealousy and strife among you, are you not fleshly, and are you not walking like mere men?"

Now Paul gets to the heart of the matter. Carnal Christians have developed a mind-set of disobedience. That is, they are willfully living in sin, being controlled by the old person they used to be rather than by the new person they have become.

No Christian has to be carnal. We are talking about a decision of the will here, not an occasional lapse into sin. Everyone sins. No one is perfect. A person who falls into sin is not necessarily a carnal Christian.

Rather, carnal Christians have a spiritual mind-set, a way of thinking, that seeks to gratify themselves rather than please Christ. Paul uses the idea of flesh here to mean that capacity all of us have to serve and please ourselves. The thing that makes the flesh the flesh is that it pleases us.

Think of the sins that are most tempting to you. The thing that makes them appealing is that they gratify you. They make you feel good. They appeal to your senses. That's the flesh.

But when God saved us, He saved us to serve Christ. We can never rise above our carnality until we change our focus from being fleshly-minded to being spiritually-minded. To fully understand this, we need to look at the four types of people Paul mentions in this section so we can see how the carnal Christian fits into the equation.

The Natural Person

The first type of person is described back in 1 Corinthians 2:14: "A natural man does not accept the things of the Spirit of God; for they are foolishness to him, and he cannot understand them, because they are spiritually appraised."

I was talking to a brother one day and he said, "Yeah, I'm a natural man."

That may be a compliment to him, but according to the Bible that's really not something to be proud of. A natural man is another way of saying a non-Christian, an unbeliever. A Christian is supposed to be supernatural. A non-Christian does things naturally. A non-Christian's mind-set is that it's OK to do something if everyone is doing it, because it's only natural.

Notice the two main traits of natural men and women. First, they don't welcome spiritual things. Unbelievers will go along with spiritual things only so far. They don't want God's truth to control their lives.

A second trait of natural men and women is that spiritual things seem like foolishness to them. They can't grasp the truth of God. That is, they do not have the capacity to interact with spiritual things. Unsaved people don't welcome the things of God because they don't know what to do with them. They don't know how to take the things of the Spirit and make sense of them.

Therefore, issues like spiritual death and spiritual truth are not very important to natural folk. They want to talk about everything but spiritual things. The natural man can understand science and mathematics and other disciplines, but he can't understand and he doesn't appreciate spiritual reality.

It's like the man who is at a friend's house watching television when a great movie comes on. The friend has a small television, so this man says to himself, *Hey, I want to see this movie on the new big-screen television I just bought.*

So he races home and turns on his new big-screen television. But he can't find the movie he wants to see. He starts channel-surfing. The picture is sharp. The sound is great. But there's no movie.

You can probably guess what was wrong. This guy didn't know that his friend had cable television, which gave him the ability to pull in a signal from the outside. The second man had a bigger and better television, but he couldn't receive what his friend received because he didn't have cable.

The unbeliever can't link into the divine frame of reference no matter how expensive his equipment is or how much power or prestige he has. He has no access to God. Many non-Christians have a lot to show of this world's stuff, but they can't get the spiritual picture because they don't have the connection.

The Spiritual Person

The second type of person Paul describes is found in verses 15–16 of 1 Corinthians 2: "But he who is spiritual appraises all things, yet he himself is appraised by no man. For who has known the mind of the Lord, that he should instruct Him? But we have the mind of Christ."

Notice the reference to the mind. The spiritual person is the mature Christian who has learned to think like Christ thinks. The mind is key here because it is the channel through which you collect the data by which you operate.

Everything you do in your life, you do because your brain tells you to do it. Without your brain, nothing else works. It is the channel that controls your motor functions, your speech, and all the other functions. When your brain dies, nothing else can work.

What the brain is to the body, the mind is to the soul. So Paul is saying that a spiritual person has learned to think God's thoughts. He has reached the point where he consistently—yet not perfectly—appraises, evaluates, or examines life from God's perspective.

Now let me ask you a question. In your decision-making, your planning, your whole orientation to life, do you regularly raise the question, What does God think about this? If you do not, it is because you are not a spiritual person yet. A spiritual person thinks like Christ.

One of the things that marks a spiritual person is spiritual perception. Spiritual people are able to connect present decisions with future consequences because they are mature. Immature people don't make that connection. They just live for the moment.

My children, especially my younger ones, don't talk about saving. They don't even bring it up. But they talk a lot about spending. I give them some money and it's gone. That's because their maturity level doesn't allow them to see long-term, only short-term.

Maturity, though, says I've got to look at the future instead of only at the moment. The spiritual person perceives things from the divine vantage point, not just from the immediate circumstance. He has the ability to discern. She has divine insight.

Babes in Christ

Paul's third type of person is described for us at the beginning of chapter 3 in 1 Corinthians:

> And I, brethren, could not speak to you as to spiritual men, but as to men of flesh, as to babes in Christ. I gave you milk to drink, not solid food; for you were not yet able to receive it. (vv. 1–2a)

Now we are talking about infant Christians, people who are brand new to the faith. They simply have not been saved long enough to become spiritual.

That may sound confusing, because some new Christians take off and soar spiritually from the day of their conversion. They appear to be more spiritual than some of the old hands. When I say a baby Christian cannot be spiritual, I mean he cannot be mature. A baby Christian can be a Spirit-controlled Christian, to be sure. But he cannot be mature, because maturity requires time.

Notice that Paul attaches no blame to these people for their immaturity. You don't condemn babies for being babies. That's all you can expect them to be. So when he talks about "babes in Christ," he's talking about Christians who are in kindergarten because they haven't had time to get to college. They haven't had time to develop simply because they are young.

When I was in Nigeria, I needed help because the people would be speaking another language and I wouldn't know what was going on. So I often had to say to my host, "What is he saying?"

I was new to that environment. I could not be expected to speak or understand the Nigerian language. There was nothing wrong with me. That's the way it is with infant Christians. They are new to the environment, so they don't know the walk and they don't know the talk. If you are a brand-new Christian, don't get frustrated because you are not mature. Just let the Holy Spirit control what you have and He will make it into more.

The Carnal Person

Now we are back to where we started. We've come full circle, because the fourth type of person is the carnal Christian, described at the beginning of verse 3: "You are still fleshly."

That word *still* is the key. There has been ample time for spiritual growth. But carnal Christians are still living in light of their old patterns of behavior. They have slipped back into their old fleshly ways of doing things. They aren't that different anymore.

You probably made some great changes when you first got saved. But after the initial burst, it's easy to stagnate and then start to backtrack. If you're not careful, you start doing some of the things you gave up when you first got saved.

When that happens, you put up a spiritual facade so that when people look at you, they think you are something. But if they were living with you, they would know you are something else! You dress holy. You wear holy cologne. You've got a holy smile. But none of that can hide the fact of arrested spiritual development.

In the case of the Corinthians, Paul had known them for about five years. Now he was writing to say, "You folks are five years old and not walking. You're still on pablum. You're five years old and making no progress. You are going through the spiritual exercises but you are half-stepping."

One of the ministers at the church I pastor in Dallas is Dr. Sonny Acho, who's from Nigeria. In conversation he will often switch back and forth between English and his native dialect. I don't know what he's saying to me. I get worried. He could be fomenting a revolution and I would never know it!

Dr. Acho gives me enough English to let me know he can speak it, but then he gives me enough Nigerian to let me know he's not about to let me in on everything he knows. So I often say when he does that, "You've got to speak English around me."

Well, that's what a carnal Christian is like. He speaks Christian, but then he lives another dialect. He says, "Praise God! Hallelujah! Amen!" with his lips, but he speaks a different language with his life.

So of the four types of people Paul describes in 1 Corinthians 2–3, the carnal Christian is the only one who isn't acting the way he's supposed to act. You can't expect a natural person to act any way but natural, you can't blame a baby for being immature, and you can't fault a spiritual Christian who's growing like he should. But the carnal man is disappointing because he's had time to grow and yet has become stunted in his growth.

A REBELLIOUS CHRISTIAN

This brings us to our final point: The carnal Christian is a rebellious Christian. Paul says in 1 Corinthians 3:3b–4, "Are you not walking like mere men? For when one says, 'I am of Paul,' and another, 'I am of Apollos,' are you not mere men?"

Have you ever said, "I'm only human"? That's non-Christian talk. That's "mere men" talk. Have you ever said, "Everyone does it"? More "mere men" talk.

Paul says to the Corinthians, "You are acting just like everyone else, like the unbelievers around you. You are not acting like the new men and new women you were created to be. You are doing the things non-Christians do."

Refusing to Submit

What were these carnal Christians doing? In this chapter Paul cites their jealousy and strife concerning various human leaders. They were taking sides, pitting one leader against the other. And in chapter 5 we discover that they not only tolerated a shameful case of incest, they even took perverse pride in it.

In Galatians 5, Paul talks about immoral living, impure activity, envy, strife, and idolatry. He calls these things the works of the flesh. He is saying that when Christians adopt these patterns of behavior, it is because they are rebellious. They are refusing to submit.

We have all seen children who get rebellious when they go through their teenage years. It's not that your teenage son doesn't understand your statement, "Clean up your room." It's that he now thinks he is grown. He thinks he pays the bills. So he says, "I'm not going to clean up my room!"

Now you've got a rebellion problem. So you tell him once again to clean up his room, and he still doesn't do it. That's rebellion. Your son is acting unlike you have trained him to be, so you have to deal with his rebellion.

So it is with a Christian who has been saved for some time but is living after the pattern of the flesh. It's not because he can't help himself. Let's get that straight. It's because he refuses to help himself, because the carnal life is a decision of the will.

Now I realize people have problems that need to be worked on. I know people can get themselves trapped in all sorts of problems and bondage. But what I am saying is that these sinful patterns are either precipitated or perpetuated by willful decisions a person makes. A Christian is never a helpless pawn in Satan's hands.

Playing in the Dirt

If you see a little kid playing in the dirt, you don't give it a second thought because kids play in dirt. They try to eat dirt. They scrub themselves in dirt. Dirt is a toy to a kid.

When you see a twenty-one-year-old man playing in the dirt, rubbing himself with it and trying to eat it, you have a serious problem on your hands. But the only difference between the child and the man is time. By the age of twenty-one, a person ought to know that dirt is not a toy.

Well, we have too many Christians who have been saved too long still playing in the dirt spiritually and having fun with it. We could understand if they were brand-new baby Christians who didn't yet know that dirt was something you don't play in.

But Christians can't be exposed to the truth of God week after week and month after month and not know mud when they see it. God isn't just trying to keep us out of the dirt pile. He wants to show us something so much better that we'll never want to play in the dirt again.

The dirt this world offers can only look good to a Christian who has left his first love and needs to return. My challenge to you right up front is to evaluate your life and determine whether you are natural, not saved; spiritual, seeing things from God's viewpoint; brand-new, a baby Christian; or carnal, not living like the new person you are in Christ.

If you discover that carnality best describes you, I urge you to return to your first love, Jesus Christ, today.

RETURNING TO YOUR FIRST LOVE

Although the second half of the book is heavily focused on application, I want to give you ideas at each step along the way to help you in this all-important matter of regaining your first love and keeping Christ at the center of your heart. Here are some ideas to get you started:

1. If after reading this chapter you realize that you are what Paul calls "natural" in that you've never been saved, you can deal with this eternal issue right now. Simply acknowledge your sinfulness before God (see Romans 3:9–10, 23). Believe that Jesus Christ, God's Son, died to pay for your sins on the cross and arose from the dead to save you (Romans 5:8; 10:13). John 1:12 promises that "as many as received Him, to them He gave the right to become children of God, even to those who believe in His name." You can know the joy of forgiveness and eternal life.

2. Perhaps you would have to admit that, to use our earlier analogy, you turned off the right road somewhere and left your first love behind. The important thing now is that you realize what happened and you want to retrace your steps. Tell God about it. Ask Him to forgive you and set you back on the path of spiritual growth. He is eager to do that, just like the father watched the road for his son to return (see Luke 15).

3. Since the path to carnality is marked by a series of choices and decisions, maybe you need to start making better choices. Remember that one mark of spiritually mature people is that they see the long-term consequences of their decisions, not just the immediate, and they act accordingly. Are you about to make a decision that may need more prayer and reflection in light of what we have discussed? If at all possible, postpone it until you can say you have God's mind on it! Talk with your pastor or a mature Christian if that will help you get perspective.

4. The Christian life is a supernatural life. Therefore, as others look at us they ought to see something that can't be accounted for in purely natural terms: our love, our peace, our joy, our generosity, etc. Ask yourself this question: Is there anything about my life that can't be explained except by the power of the Holy Spirit working in me?

CHAPTER TWO

(HOKING THE WORD

We are talking about "habits of the heart," attitudes and actions that can cause us to leave our first love for Jesus Christ. In this chapter I want to talk about a love-stealer that is very crucial but may not be readily apparent: an inappropriate response to the Word of God. When my love for someone is not what it should be, my interest in what he or she says is not what it should be.

For this I want to turn to the words of Jesus Himself in Luke 8, where He tells a story that Luke calls a parable, a story that uses the known to explain the unknown.

Jesus took things that people understood in order to communicate things that His listeners wouldn't normally understand. In this case, He used the physical to explain the spiritual, and Luke says in verse 4 that a huge crowd came together to hear Jesus teach.

The people loved to hear Jesus teach. They loved the way He could take normal everyday things and turn them into great spiritual truth. That's exactly what He did on this occasion.

THE PARABLE OF THE SOWER

Jesus told a story about a farmer, a sower, who went out to sow his seed (v. 5a). This farmer didn't have all the farm technology we have today that cultivates the ground, spaces out the seedlings, and creates those straight rows you and I see when we fly over or drive by a modern farm.

In Jesus' day seed-sowing was all done by hand. A farmer put his seeds in a bag and draped the bag across the neck of a donkey. He walked the donkey along a path that was on the side of his farm or plot of land where he wanted to cast his seeds. He reached into his bag, pulled out a handful of seeds, and threw them onto the land.

The seeds would go here, there, and everywhere. The idea was to so saturate the land with seed that the farmer was sure to get the kind of productivity he wanted. This is the basic picture Jesus had in mind when He said that a sower went out to sow his seed, which fell on four different kinds of soil.

The Soils

Some seed fell on the side of the road, where "it was trampled under foot, and the birds of the air ate it up" (v. 5b). This seed didn't even make it. It slipped through the farmer's fingers, dropped on the ground. He stepped on it, and it stuck to his shoe. As he walked a little farther, it came off his shoe. The birds saw it, came and took it away, and ate it.

Some other seed fell on rocky soil (v. 6). This was a thin layer of soil with rocks, stones, and grit underneath. As a result, the seed grew but withered because it had no moisture. It couldn't get down deep enough to suck moisture from the ground in order to feed its growth. The soil couldn't sustain life.

Jesus continued: "And other seed fell among the thorns; and the thorns grew up with it, and choked it out" (v. 7). Evidently the thorns grew up faster and stronger than the plant, and there were so many thorns that they choked the life out of the plant.

Finally, Jesus said in the first half of verse 8, there was "other seed [which] fell into the good soil, and grew up, and produced a crop a hundred times as great." This soil had the right balance. It was rich with nutrients and produced the desired result.

That was the end of the parable, so Jesus delivered the punch line: "As He said these things, He would call out, 'He who has ears to hear, let him hear'" (v. 8b).

Now Jesus knows we have two ears. But He also knows it's possible to have two ears and *not* hear. So what He is saying is, "Pay close attention!" When a teacher says that to you in class, you know exactly what he means. He's saying, "You'd better make sure you understand what I just said, because you're going to see it again on the exam."

The Question

That being the case, what had you better do if you don't understand what your teacher just said? That's right. You had better raise your hand and ask him to explain. That's what Jesus' disciples did in verse 9: "His disciples began questioning Him as to what this parable might be."

In other words, they were saying, "Jesus, we don't know what in the world You are talking about. A sower went out to sow. We got that. But what are You trying to tell us?" This is very important because of the astounding statement Jesus made before He explained the meaning of the parable:

> To you it has been granted to know the mysteries of the kingdom of God, but to the rest it is in parables, in order that seeing they may not see, and hearing they may not understand. (v. 10)

Jesus then proceeded to explain the meaning of the parable. Why? Because the disciples asked Him to!

The crowd just came along for the ride. The crowd liked Jesus' stories. They liked the way He could put phrases together. They liked hearing Him talk in a way that ordinary people could understand. They loved His ability to pontificate on the excellencies of divine truth.

In other words, the crowd loved listening to Jesus. But they never got around to asking the all-important question, "Jesus, what do You mean?" They were satisfied with data, not with understanding.

There's an important principle here, which is this: Your ability to perceive divine truth is related to how much you want to know. If you are satisfied with a story here and a story there, a good feeling here and a good feeling there, you won't fully understand all that God has for you in His Word.

If you are satisfied just to show up at church on Sunday, if putting in an appearance is the bulk of the benefit you get from being under the sound of God's Word, then you will leave empty. You will miss a lot of what God wants to do for you, the benefit He wants to bring to you. You will be an anemic Christian.

This is what was happening in Luke 8. The people loved to hear Jesus preach, but by and large they didn't love *Him*—at least not in the way we're talking about in this book. Since Jesus was not their first love, His Word was not their first concern. Just listening to a preacher— even if it's Jesus Himself—is never enough. We need to go on and ask, "Jesus, what do You mean?" Let's do that now.

THE FAILURE TO RESPOND

In answer to the disciples' question, Jesus began to explain His parable:

> Now the parable is this: the seed is the word of God. And those beside the road are those who have heard; then the devil comes and takes away the word from their heart, so that they may not believe and be saved. (vv. 11–12)

Jesus says the first response to the Word is illustrated by the seed that fell beside the road. It never took root in the person's heart. It's just lying there on the road. The devil, represented by the bird that flew in and took the seed, comes by and snatches away the Word so that people in this condition don't become Christians. They can't leave their first love for Christ because they never loved Him in the first place.

THE SHALLOW RESPONSE

The next one is the "rocky soil" (v. 13), the shallow soil with stones and rocks underneath it. These are the ones who, "when they hear, receive the word with joy." Now when the Bible uses this terminology, it always refers to salvation (see 1 Thessalonians 1:6 and Acts 17:11 for two good examples).

So once He hits verse 13, Jesus is not talking about non-Christians anymore. He is now talking about the different ways Christians respond to the Word. These people receive the Word joyfully—that is, they get saved. But they "have no firm root; they believe for a while, and in time of temptation fall away."

These are Christians who truly get saved but who do not develop in their faith. They remain spiritually weak— baby believers. Because they don't go deep into the things of God, when trouble shows up, when trials hit, they want to run. They want to renege on their commitment to walk with God.

Don't Blame the Seed

Let's be sure of one thing. This has nothing to do with the seed. God's Word is complete, all-sufficient. The Bible says of itself, "The word of God is living and active and sharper than any two-edged sword, and piercing as far as the division of soul and spirit, of both joints and marrow, and able to judge the thoughts and intentions of the heart" (Hebrews 4:12).

So the seed is not deficient. The Word of God is sufficient to raise in your life a crop of spiritual vitality, victory, power, and tenacity. Everything you need in order to be all that God wants you to be is already given to you at the point of receiving the Word. That's why James 1:21 urges us to receive "the word implanted, which is able to save your souls."

Jesus is saying that when you receive the seed of His Word, you have all you need to become all God wants you to be. But the first example in His parable makes clear that some Christians don't allow the seed to take root. The Word does not get deep into the soil of their hearts.

Your Response to Trials

How do you know when your life is in this condition, when your response to God's Word is not what it should be? One way you know is that when trouble shows up, you want to run. When adversity hits, you back up. God lets you know whether you are spiritually strong by bringing adversity into your life.

Notice I did not say God sends adversity so *He* can know how spiritual you are. He already knows what you are going to do. The test is for your sake, so you can see whether your "amens" on Sunday are as real as you thought they were when you said them.

It's sort of like trials in a marriage. Your commitment to your marriage cannot be tested on the honeymoon. It's too early. There hasn't been enough time for enough stuff to come down yet. Your commitment to your marriage is seen when everything is going wrong, when it seems you married the opposite of the person you thought you married when you said, "I do."

That's when the husband finds out that his wife doesn't always look like he thought she would look when he married her. And she finds out that he only gave up televised football temporarily. The depth of a commitment is determined when people run into the trials of life.

Jesus says people like this with no deep roots tend to fall away when the going gets tough (Luke 8:13). Instead of digging deeper into the things of God to find out how to deal with the trial, how to overcome the problem, they want to run. They want to get out of it. They don't want to be identified as belonging to Christ. Their love for Him is seriously withered.

That's why Paul told his would-be traveling companion John Mark, "You can't go with me anymore because you have fallen away. I'm out here risking my life and you are going to put my life on the line. You can't come with me" (see Acts 15:37–40).

Paul was saying that Mark's roots didn't run deep enough. They were in the wrong kind of soil. His heart was not wholly committed to the Lord. Thankfully, in Mark's case he got a second chance through Barnabas and eventually made good as a disciple.

You Have to Go Deep

Salvation is free. Discipleship is expensive. You can get to heaven for nothing, courtesy of the cross. But it costs a lot to get heaven down to you. God has already given you, free of charge, eternal life. But to get eternal life operating in history demands the price tag of loving commitment.

You must be committed to Jesus Christ, and that means you must have roots that run deep. The only way your roots can run deep is for you to make the proper response to the Word of God; to go deeper into the things of God and to take seriously the application of His Word in your life.

The difference between a victorious Christian and a defeated Christian is that one has allowed the root of the Word to go deep into the soil of his life, while the other is living on the topsoil and not putting down deep roots. The difference is not that God has favorite kids. He is available to give every Christian the same level of victory.

The only way to get deep roots is the knowledge and application of the Word. I can tell you right now whether you are on your way to deep roots. Is the only time you are in the Bible the hour or two you show up on Sunday?

Well, you are not going far. Imagine a person eating only a Sunday afternoon meal, even a big one, and not eating the rest of the week. By about Tuesday he's going to be in trouble. One meal can't last all week long.

It's the same with our spiritual nourishment. If there is no passion to learn and apply the Word, no desire to discover what the Word says about the situations we face, we will become malnourished and emaciated and unable to handle trials when they come.

And they *will* come, make no mistake. Jesus said so in verse 13. He spoke about them as an accomplished fact. It's not as if spiritual Christians don't get trials and carnal Christians do. If you're a Christian, you get trials. The issue is whether trials get you. Your response to the Word determines whether you are victorious or defeated.

No Christian has to live a defeated life. Yes, you will have problems. Yes, you will have moments of failure. But if you are being whipped day in and day out by the world, the flesh, and the devil, you may have a root problem. The problem is you've got rocky soil so the root doesn't go deep.

A Strong Foundation

Lasting growth comes only by the application of God's Word. But you can't apply what you don't know. So Jesus says to us, "He who has ears to hear, let him hear." The seed of His Word is being scattered, but not everyone receives it equally. Some people ignore and trample it. Others take a little bit and they grow a little bit. But as soon as trouble comes, they are going to collapse because they didn't go deep with it.

By the way, you have to go deep *before* trouble comes. It's too late to go deep when trouble is present. It's a fundamental issue of life. If you want to be able to handle life's difficulties, you need to grow deep first. It's called laying a strong foundation. In Luke 8 Jesus is dealing with the foundation of life. That's why if you are a new Christian, the most important thing you can do is get the basics of the spiritual life. You've got to get the basics so you can lay a strong foundation and grow.

Foundations aren't pretty. When was the last time you went foundation hunting? You don't go foundation hunting, you go house hunting. You want to see the house: the windows, the layout, the size and shape of the rooms.

Well, all that's moot if the foundation is on sand. You must have a solid foundation. Then you can build anything you want on it because you are solidified. "Rocky soil" Christians need deep roots, a strong foundation.

CHOOSING THE WORLD OVER THE WORD

In Luke 8:14 Jesus moved on to explain to the disciples the third kind of soil in His parable:

> And the seed which fell among the thorns, these are the ones who have heard, and as they go on their way they are choked with worries and riches and pleasures of this life, and bring no fruit to maturity.

These people have itsy-bitsy apples, itsy-bitsy oranges, and itsy-bitsy pears. That is, their fruit doesn't grow to full size. The group we just looked at barely get started. They are baby Christians. These folks are more like teenage Christians. But their response to the Word is still inadequate.

We know they have grown some because they have some fruit. The problem is that their fruit doesn't mature. I remember when I was sixteen and wanted my father to let me start having adult privileges. I would remind him, "Well, Dad, you know I'm almost a man. Two more years, I'm going to be a man. So you might as well let me start practicing some of this stuff now."

My dad would say, "When you start acting like a man, then you can do some of this stuff." What he was saying was that I was in between the worlds of childhood and adulthood, and I needed to get straight which side of the fence I was on.

That's the problem with the people Jesus described in verse 14. They are producing some fruit, but it's not maturing. It's not ripening and enlarging the way it should. The reason for this stunted growth, according to Jesus, is that these believers are being choked.

Choking Yourself

What He means is that some Christians have mixed-up priorities. Because of this, their spiritual lives are entangled in things they shouldn't be messing with.

Look at what Jesus says can choke a Christian: "worries and riches and pleasures of this life." Did you know that when you make this world—its money, its fun, its concerns—the engine that drives your life, you are committing spiritual suicide? Jesus says, "It chokes you!"

If you've ever choked, you know there's nothing funny about it. You can't breathe. And if you choke long enough and hard enough, you will die because something has cut off the oxygen that is necessary to give you life.

This is serious stuff. When you allow the concerns of this life to take priority over the concerns of the kingdom of God, when you replace your first love with love for this world, the Bible says you are putting a choke hold on yourself, cutting off your own spiritual oxygen.

Many Christians are cutting off their spiritual esophaguses. Their lives are so crammed full of wrong priorities that the flow of God's blessing, God's power, God's deliverance, and God's enablement is cut off. Many Christians are suffocating spiritually. They say, "I can't breathe. I'm miserable. I'm depressed. I don't have any joy!" Why? Because they are choking themselves. Every time God tries to send some spiritual fresh air through, the flow gets choked off because the believer is too deep into this world; too much into getting money; too much into having fun. As a result, God's blessing is choked out.

Now don't get me wrong. There's nothing wrong with making plans for your kids' education or advancing in your career. Those are legitimate concerns. There's nothing wrong with wanting to be successful. Jesus is not throwing a blanket condemnation over everything enjoyable in life.

The problem comes when you are choked by the concerns of this life. That is, when they become so dominant in your life that they grab you by the throat and cut off your spiritual breath.

This Life's Cares

The key phrase here is "of this life." This is important because while we are to live *in* this life, God does not want us to be *of* this life. The Bible says we are to be in the world, but not of the world.

That's a fundamental distinction. On average, you are going to live in this world for about seventy years. So for those seventy years you will participate in the daily life and routines of this world.

But you are not to be *of* this world for those seventy years. That is, you are not to let the world set your agenda, determine your goals. You are not to be driven by the things that drive this world.

Many of us Christians are spending so much time being like the Joneses, we don't have time to be like Christ. We are spending so much time trying to meet everyone else's expectations that we never get around to being what God wants us to be.

And if we're not careful, we can spend our entire lives trying to please everyone else. Then Christ will meet us in the kingdom and say, "How in the world could you do that to Me? I loved you, gave My life for you, and made every provision for you, but you never got around to My agenda because you were trying to please everyone else." That's being of this world.

In terms of our love for Christ, this is a crucial point. We always hear that love is spelled t-i-m-e. It's true. A man can't tell a woman he loves her and then not spend time with her, finding out what she thinks, what pleases her, how he can fulfill her wishes and meet her needs.

No wonder the Bible calls it adultery when a believer falls for the world. Jesus Christ is to be the first love of our hearts. The Christian life is a love affair with Him.

Jesus said in Matthew 6:33, "Seek first [God's] kingdom and His righteousness; and all these things shall be added to you." We want to reverse it. We want to say, "Seek first all these things, and if you have any time left over the kingdom of God is available and waiting on you."

That is not how it goes. Whenever you choose to put the issues of this life ahead of the perspective of the kingdom; whenever the rule of this world (the Greek word for kingdom means rule or authority) takes precedence over the authority of God's kingdom, you have choked your spiritual life.

How do you know whether you are choking yourself? You say, "I'm concerned about my economic well-being. I want to be able to provide proper housing for my family and an education for my children. How do I know if I'm going too far?"

Well, let me suggest several guidelines from the Bible. In 1 Timothy 6:6 Paul says, "Godliness actually is a means of great gain, when accompanied by contentment."

Practicing Godliness

Here are two important tests in one verse. The first is, are you having to compromise God's Word to fulfill any of your goals? If you have to disobey the Bible to fulfill your desires; if you have to practice questionable ethics and surrender your moral values to get the things you want; if you have to do things that bring disrepute to God and His Word, you are not godly.

And if you aren't godly, you aren't serving the kingdom. And if you aren't serving the kingdom, then God is against you and you are choking yourself. So the first test is this: Are you compromising spiritually to accomplish your goals?

Experiencing Contentment

Paul's second test is this: Are you content where you are even though where you are is not where you want to be? You may want to do better. You may have lofty goals. That's fine. But godly contentment means that your joy as a child of God, your peace of heart and mind, and your inward happiness are intact despite your external circumstances. It means you are at rest on the inside while you wait for God to make a change on the outside.

Some of us are frustrated and irritated and exasperated because things are not the way we want them. But that's the reaction of a Christian who has forgotten he has a heavenly Father who knows what he needs and has promised to meet those needs. A Christian who is out of touch with God's Word has forgotten that nothing can take God's will away from him.

A person who is truly content may drive a Mercedes. I can hear someone saying, "Yeah, I'd be content too if I had a Mercedes." But the point is that if this person loses his Mercedes and has to go back to a Volkswagen, it's OK because in both cases he has a ride.

A content person may have a big house. But if he loses his job and has to go back to an apartment, he can handle that because he and his family still have a roof over their heads.

A person who possesses godly contentment can thank God for a T-bone or a hot dog because he has something to eat and he sees that God has met his needs.

I could multiply the examples, but you get the idea. Once you understand that you are fed and clothed and housed and protected by the grace of God, you can be content because you know that God has met your needs. He has been faithful.

The spiritual Christian has this attitude because he's under God. He wants to do better, but he's not letting it destroy his life. You can't escape Paul's point. If you are not content, you are not spiritual. Paul says God can make us content even when our circumstances aren't very conducive to contentment.

THREE THINGS THAT CHOKE US

So a fundamental question is, Is your passion to get ahead removing your passion to grow? Let's go back to our original text in Luke 8. In verse 14 Jesus named three things that choke us.

Worry

The first is worry. Did you know it is a sin to worry? No Christian should ever say, "Well, everybody worries."

That's an irrelevant statement, because everybody's not a spiritual Christian, which is the goal toward which we should be heading. Paul says in Philippians 4:6, "Be anxious for nothing." That is, don't be weary. Don't allow anything to so control your mind that it keeps you from functioning.

You say, "But I can't control what's controlling my mind." Sure you can, because Philippians 4:6 goes on to say, "but in everything by prayer and supplication with thanksgiving let your requests be made known to God."

Then verse 7 adds this promise: "And the peace of God, which surpasses all comprehension, shall guard your hearts and your minds in Christ Jesus."

The word *guard* means post a sentry, set up a watch around your mind so that when worry or anything else shows up, the sentry takes it out. If you will pray instead of worrying, God will set up a guard around your mind.

The idea is that every time you start to worry, you pray because you can't do both at the same time. You can either pray or worry, but you can't pray *and* worry. What God wants you to do is counter worry with prayer.

I'm not talking about having legitimate concerns. I'm talking about coming to the place where you can't function because you are immobilized by this thing called worry. Jesus says it will strangle your growth. Are you gagging on your worries?

Riches

The second thing Jesus named in Luke 8:14 is riches. When your love for money—not your *having* of money—supersedes your love for God, you'll start choking on your wallet.

How do you know when you love money more than you love God? When you have to choose between money and God, and money wins. That's when you know how much you love money. Jesus said you know what you love most by what you invest in (Matthew 6:19–21).

What are your spiritual investments? What do you give to the kingdom of God as opposed to the toys you buy for yourself? What money are you willing to lose because it's compromising your spiritual values? That's the issue.

When should we refuse financial gain? When it would damage the reputation of the kingdom. We can tell what our true first love is by the value decisions we make day in and day out, week in and week out.

Some people like to do something big for God once a year. I think of the folks who come to church on Easter Sunday. We have to have three Easter services at our church in Dallas. The "nod to God" crowd comes out that day and they are proud of the fact that they made it. They showed up for God. But the rest of the year, many of them are choked with the worries of this life.

Pleasure

Finally, Jesus said in Luke 8:14 that pleasure has a way of choking off a proper response to His Word. I don't have to tell you our culture is pleasure-ridden. We've got television to pleasure ourselves with and VCRs to tape the programs we miss. We don't want to miss out on any of the pleasure.

And if that bores us, we can go to the theater to see a movie on its first run before we see it later on television or tape it on our VCR or rent a copy at the local video rental store. It's a kind of madness our society is afflicted with. We heap up pleasure upon pleasure upon pleasure.

Whenever a person starts talking like this someone always objects that there is such a thing as legitimate pleasure, legitimate enjoyment of the arts or entertainment or whatever. I won't argue with that. That's not the part that concerns me.

But if you are watching so much television you can't open your Bible or get on your knees and pray; if you are having so much fun with your friends that you can't talk about spiritual things; if you can talk and joke about everything but never bring up Christ; if the Bible and the things of Christ would embarrass you in your social circle, something is wrong with your fun.

With stuff like "virtual reality" and other pleasure technology getting more sophisticated and more readily available every day, I'm afraid we haven't seen anything yet in our culture's insane pursuit of pleasure. Keeping our first love for Christ intact amid all this bombardment is going to be a real challenge, but we can do it in the strength He gives.

THE GOOD SOIL

Aren't you glad Jesus had one more category of people, one more kind of soil, to tell us about? Look at Luke 8:15: "And the seed in the good soil, these are the ones who have heard the word in an honest and good heart, and hold it fast, and bear fruit with perseverance."

These are the Christians who bear abundant, full-grown, lasting fruit. The first thing to note about fruit is that it always bears the character of the tree on which it grows. Oranges don't grow on apple trees. The character of the fruit always reflects the tree.

When you are responding properly to God's Word and your love for Christ is in its proper place, you are going to act, talk, look, and think more like Christ. It's inevitable, because Jesus is the vine to which you are attached (John 15:1–5). You are going to display His character.

A second thing to note about fruit is that fruit exists for the benefit of someone else. A tree never eats its own fruit. You've never seen an apple tree eating apples. Those apples are not for the tree.

One way you know you are growing spiritually is that other folks want to take a bite out of your life. They start saying, "I want to be like you. How can you help me become the kind of Christian you are?" Jesus said in Matthew 13:8 that the fruit of Christians like this would multiply thirty, sixty, and even a hundredfold. That is, the benefit of your life to others will just go on and on.

This is the result of a proper response to God's Word, of letting His Word do its perfect work in our lives. Believers who have gotten off track and left their first love for Christ produce only stunted, partially grown fruit. So it's critical that you and I decide we don't want to be like that.

You say, "Well, I'm bad soil. How do I become good soil?" You can begin simply by applying what you have learned of God's Word. It is the application of the Word that produces mature, lasting fruit in the Christian life. The application section at the end of this chapter has some ideas to help you.

One day an angel and a man were talking. The angel asked him, "What can I do for you?"

The man said, "Show me what the stock market will be one year from today so I will know how to invest and make a fortune."

The angel snapped his finger, and out came a *Wall Street Journal* dated one year in the future. The man noted which stocks would be high and which ones would be low. He was overjoyed.

But in the midst of his joy, a frown came upon the man's face and tears began to roll down his cheeks. He had turned the page and seen an article about prominent business people who had died that year. His picture was among the dead.

This life can only offer so much. We've just learned from Jesus how to live today in light of eternity. What will your response be to His Word?

RETURNING TO YOUR FIRST LOVE

J esus' parable of the seed—or more properly, the four soils—
is a vivid reminder that the way we respond to God's Word
makes all the difference. I hope the action steps below will help
you turn up the intensity in this area and stoke the fire of your
love for Christ:

1. One of the most easily accomplished, and most overlooked,
   growth exercises in the Christian life is simply *reading* the
   Word. Too often we neglect to pick up our Bibles and read
   them every day. One way you can remind yourself to read
   your Bible is to keep it out where you put your other reading
   materials: on the coffee table, by the recliner, in the kitchen,
   or whatever. Once you get in the habit of reading the Bible,
   you'll be hooked!

2. Approach your Bible as if it were God's love letter to you,
   because that's exactly what it is. Before you begin reading,
   ask the Lord to open your heart and help you make a heart
   response to what you read.

3. If you would have to honestly admit that the worries, riches,
   and pleasures of daily life are choking off your desire for and
   obedience to the Word, try this experiment for one week.
   Spend just one-half the amount of time in Bible reading and
   study each day as you spend reading the newspaper, watching TV, doing the bank balance, or reading other material.

   This exercise has a double benefit: You'll probably spend
   far more time in God's Word than you would in a normal
   week. You'll also realize how much time you are investing
   in the cares and concerns of this life, and where you may
   need to make adjustments.

4. If your true desire is to be the good soil Jesus described, tell
   Him so in prayer. Write in the fly leaf of your Bible the day
   you made the commitment to soften the soil of your heart,
   pull out the thorns, and deal with the choking effects of this
   world's concerns. Refer to that page often as you seek to live
   out your commitment.

CHAPTER THREE

GOING BACKWARD

I suppose nothing will cause us to leave our first love for Christ faster than going backward in our Christian lives, because Christ is always moving us forward. When our lives are marked by persistent spiritual regression, we distance ourselves more and more from intimate communion with Jesus Christ. That's where we get the term *backslidden*.

Whenever you see a Christian enter into a lifestyle of debauchery and sins of the flesh; whenever you see a Christian lose all meaning in life; whenever you see Christians shipwreck their faith (like Hymenaeus and Alexander, see 1 Timothy 1:19–20), you know it did not happen overnight. There was a pattern.

Have you ever ignored a warning sign and just kept on driving? You're in a hurry, and you don't want to believe the sign. You know deep down you're on the wrong road, but somehow you don't stop and turn around.

That's what we're talking about—Christians who ignore the signs and keep on going. There's trouble ahead if they don't get back on the right road.

I want to look at five warning signs along the road to spiritual regression. Each one is a little more serious than the previous one, which is as it needs to be. As you and I know all too well, warning signs are no help unless you read them and then do what they say. Otherwise, you wind up in the ditch or over the cliff. We'll be using the book of Hebrews as our biblical source and guide for this portion of our study. The believers to whom this author wrote were themselves on the "backsliders" road, so they needed warnings. We can learn a lot from them if we'll just read and heed.

THE SIGN OF NEGLECT

The first warning sign I see on the road of spiritual regression is found in Hebrews 2:2–3a:

> For if the word spoken through angels proved unalterable, and every transgression and disobedience received a just recompense, how shall we escape if we neglect so great a salvation?

Spiritually regressing Christians are characterized by the neglect of spiritual matters. The author of Hebrews is writing to a group of Jewish Christians who were going backward rather than forward in their faith, and he raises this fundamental question: "How shall we escape if we neglect so great a salvation?"

Passive Disobedience

To neglect simply means that there is a lack of interest. It's not that you are doing everything wrong. It's that you are doing little right. We are talking about passive disobedience here. It's not that you are messing up in the sense of going out and planning to do wrong, it's rather that you are not doing the things necessary to get you moving forward down the road.

If you are a student, you don't have to curse the teacher or be disruptive in class in order to fail. All you have to do is not study. That's passive failure. If you don't do the assignments, you fail.

When you see a marriage end in divorce, it doesn't always mean that someone committed adultery. It may mean that the husband has been stuck in front of the television too long. The dating has stopped. The compliments have ceased. No more doors get opened. Or the wife gives up and stops caring about the marriage and the home. Such passive, benign neglect opens the door to failure.

Some people are in bad health not because they have gone out and done things destructive to their bodies. It's just that they have neglected to keep up good health.

Taking Things for Granted

Some Christians begin to regress spiritually not because they have committed gross sins. But Satan has done just enough to keep them out of the Word. He's done just enough to keep them off their knees. All he's really done is cause them to neglect the things of God.

Why does it start that way? I think the answer is in the phrase "so great a salvation" in Hebrews 2:3. When you don't know what you have, you take it for granted. No one likes to feel taken for granted, because when that happens neglect soon follows.

A woman once told me concerning her husband, "He doesn't know what he has, and if he doesn't find out quick I'm not going to be around much longer."

She was saying, "He's taking me for granted. He's gotten used to having hot meals and washed clothes and ironed shirts. Now he just expects it."

A man may say, "My wife has gotten used to having a hard worker and a husband who tries to be sensitive and caring. I feel taken for granted."

God is saying, "Your salvation isn't just salvation. It's a 'so great' salvation." It's a salvation that cost God His Son and has given us eternal life. It's a salvation that has provided us with the enabling power of the Holy Spirit and the authority of God's Word.

Our salvation has provided us a home in heaven and eternal rewards. It's a salvation that answers our deepest need. It's a salvation that calms the hurting heart and restores the broken life. That's our salvation. How can we neglect so great a salvation as this?

Answer: We can't, not if we want to be spiritually healthy and growing. Let me tell you something. No one else in town is offering a salvation like this. No one else is offering a salvation this glorious. Nothing can compare with our salvation. How in the world can we neglect it?

So the first sign telling you you're on the wrong road and warning you to stop and turn back is the warning sign of neglect. The implication of the author's question in verse 3 is that we won't escape if we neglect our salvation. There is a price tag: the discipline of God (Hebrews 12). If your Christian life, your love for Christ, is suffering from neglect, you need to turn back.

THE SIGN OF SPIRITUAL INSENSITIVITY

The warnings we're studying in Hebrews are so strong that you might wonder if these people were really Christians at all. I don't think there's any doubt about that. The writer addresses them back in 3:1 as "holy brethren." There are many other similar references throughout the book. Hebrews is written to Christians who are heading down the wrong road.

That's important to understand, because as we go along we'll see the warning signs—and the danger of ignoring them—get even stronger. These things would not have the same implications for the Hebrews, and for us, if they were written to unbelievers. That's an entirely different subject.

With that in mind, let's consider the warning sign of spiritual insensitivity:

> Take care, brethren, lest there should be in any one of you an evil, unbelieving heart, in falling away from the living God. But encourage one another day after day, as long as it is still called "Today," lest any one of you be hardened by the deceitfulness of sin. (Hebrews 3:12–13)

Hard Hearts

I'm sure all of us have met people with hard hearts. We have a whole world of people today with hard hearts. When I hear the way people talk to one another and how often they say, "I don't care," those are expressions of a heart that is not sensitive anymore, that has become calloused.

How do we get a hard heart? According to the writer of Hebrews, we are duped into it by what he calls "the deceitfulness of sin." But that's no excuse, because in verse 12 he warns against allowing an unbelieving heart to develop in us.

An unbelieving heart is an evil heart because an unbelieving heart doubts God. When we doubt God, that opens the door for evil. Instead of turning to God, we begin to run from Him.

The context of this warning is interesting because back in verse 8 the author says, "Do not harden your hearts as when they provoked Me, as in the day of trial in the wilderness." He is saying, "If you want to understand what I mean, just look at Israel in the wilderness." During those years of wandering, the Israelites provoked God repeatedly by their unbelief.

Is there anyone in your life who provokes you, who intentionally does things they know are going to irritate you? Well, that's what Israel did to God in the wilderness. They provoked Him bad.

He turns a dry rock into a fountain, and they wonder where they are going to get their next drink of water. He feeds them with "corn flakes" from heaven, and they worry about where they are going to get their next meal.

And the greatest provocation of all happened when it was time to enter the land God promised to give them. They looked around and said, "We can't go in." They provoked God, and in the process they made their hearts harden.

The Trickiness of Sin

The Israelites' hearts were hardened because they were tricked by sin. Sin is tricky because it will get you to stop believing God and start believing Satan. One reason many of us are in the fixes we're in is that we have stopped believing God (an evil heart of unbelief) and started believing sin.

I know young people who are in jail today because they stopped believing mom and dad and started believing their friends. And when they started believing their friends they followed them right into prison, whereas if they had listened to their parents, they would have been fine.

God is saying to us, "If you would only listen to Me and stop listening to sin, your heart wouldn't be hard and you wouldn't be duped into a life going nowhere."

How do you know if you have been duped by the deceitfulness of sin and are becoming spiritually insensitive? Simple answer: if your sin is bothering you less and less. In other words, if you can go to sleep tonight with things in your life that would have made you sick a year ago, that's a sign of a hard heart.

When evil doesn't hurt you, upset you, and impassion you; when you get used to it; when you don't feel the pain anymore, something is wrong.

You might say, "Well, it's not that bad." But sin works like a woodpecker. The individual pecks may not seem all that bad. But when the job is done, you've got a hole in your tree. What God wants you and me to do is address the deceitfulness of sin because sin is tricky.

You see, sin doesn't tell you what it plans to do with you. Sin doesn't show you where it plans to take you. Sin always provides short-term gratification with a goal of long-term destruction. But you don't see the goal. All you see is the immediate pleasure.

Sin always starts by getting you to say now, "Ahhhhh!" But later on you say, "Oops!"

What God wants you to do if and when you sin is say to sin now, "Oops!" Then later on you can say, "Ahhhhh!"

God doesn't want you to be tricked by the deceitfulness of sin. He doesn't want you to be duped into taking the wrong road. But far too many Christians are being duped. They start off thinking a certain way, then talking a certain way. Before long they are watching things they ought not watch and being in places they ought not be until one day they are on the front page of the newspaper.

Now let me make sure you understand I am *not* talking about a person's eternal destiny here. If you have trusted Christ as your Savior, that has been settled forever. The issue on the floor is a Christian's effectiveness and witness in this life, which is the only place the devil can attack us.

Your parents or grandparents probably told you growing up, "Be sure your sin will find you out." Sin is a boomerang. If you don't get rid of it, it will come back to find you. But the more spiritual you are, the more sensitive you are to sin. When you do sin, it's painful. It causes an ache in your heart.

The air in a room looks fine until the sun shines through the window and you see the particles of dust floating around. If the light of Christ is not shining in your life, you will think you are living in a clean room. You won't see the dirt hovering around you. But when the light of Christ is shining in you, you are very sensitive to the dust of sin.

THE SIGN OF REFUSAL

A Christian who has left his first love for Christ and is regressing spiritually can not only become neglectful and insensitive toward the things of God. He can also refuse the spiritual diet he needs in order to grow. This is the third warning sign we see in the book of Hebrews to tell us we'd better turn back.

Again, we know the author is talking to Christians because in Hebrews 5:12 he makes a comparison between spiritual babes and the spiritually mature. That's an irrelevant statement if he is writing to unbelievers.

We need to begin at verse 11 to pick up the context of what the writer is telling the Hebrews:

Concerning him [Melchizedek] we have much to say, and it is hard to explain, since you have become dull of hearing.

> For though by this time you ought to be teachers, you have need again for someone to teach you the elementary principles of the oracles of God, and you have come to need milk and not solid food. (vv. 11–12)

The writer has just mentioned a wonderful and mysterious person named Melchizedek, whose priesthood preceded that of Aaron and was a type of Christ's priesthood. The writer has a lot more to say about Melchizedek, who had "neither beginning of days nor end of life" (7:3), but the Hebrews weren't ready.

In other words, he wants to take his readers into the deep things of God. He wants to explain to them just how great their "so great" salvation is.

Dull of Hearing

But then he realizes he's writing to the Sesame Street generation. They don't understand what he's talking about. Why? Because they have not grown. Because they have *refused* to grow. They are in a real sense refusing their salvation.

These Hebrew Christians were saying, "I don't need to know this. I don't need to understand that. I don't have to study that." They had become willfully rebellious against God.

That's kind of the way it works. You start off by neglecting the things of God, which eventually renders you insensitive, and then you get to where you don't want to know what you should know even when you can know it. The pattern becomes the natural movement and progression—or rather, regression—of your spiritual life.

The author says in Hebrews 5:11 that what he needs to say is hard to explain, but not because he as the teacher can't make it clear. It's because his readers have become dull of hearing. Notice he doesn't say, "You are dull of hearing," but "You have become dull of hearing."

In other words, the Hebrews had regressed spiritually. They were moving forward at one time, but now they needed to be put back a grade or two. The author says they had become mule-like, which as we learned back in chapter 1 is the idea behind the Greek word for *dull*. It has to do with slowness of perception, in their case due to moral laxness.

Now mules are not your greatest thinkers. They are not your most intelligent animals. They are kind of the dummies of the horse line. They're good for hauling loads on their backs, and some people ride them. But most of us would not choose a mule when it came time to ride for fun or exercise or whatever.

The Bible says Christians can become mule-minded. They can regress to the point that they are of very little value to the kingdom of God—not because God made them that way, but because they have become that way.

How does a Christian become dull of hearing? Well, according to verse 12 it's a choice. In the case of the Hebrews, the writer says, "You've become so immature spiritually, I can't feed you good Melchizedek meat. I've got to go back and give you some basic milk."

When adults can handle only milk, it's because there's an ulcer somewhere. I can tell you that if every sermon has to make you shout, you are a sick Christian. If every time you sit under the teaching of God's Word it has to make you feel good or it's no good, you've got a problem.

Some sermons are supposed to make you cry. Some sermons are supposed to arouse guilt or make you feel ashamed if there's something that needs fixing. Things like this happen when you get into the deeper meat of the Word of God. Many Christians are satisfied with milk because that's all they've ever tasted.

A Simple Test

You ask, "How can I know whether I'm a milk or a meat Christian? How can I tell if I'm progressing or regressing?" Well, one simple test is to ask yourself whether your understanding of the Christian faith still begins and ends with "Jesus loves me, this I know." In other words, are you feeding on and digesting the stronger stuff of God's Word, or is milk all you can handle?

In verse 12 the writer tells his readers that, by the time of his letter, they ought to be teaching others the deep truths of Scripture instead of having to be taught their spiritual ABCs. He can say this for at least two reasons.

The first is time. It's obvious that the Hebrews had been Christians long enough to gain some maturity. They were old enough spiritually to be on solid food.

But the passage of time alone is not enough. A second reason is found in verse 14: "Solid food is for the mature, who because of practice have their senses trained to discern good and evil." The word *trained* here is literally "gymnatized." It means you've been going to the gym for regular workouts. You've done some sweating to grow and develop in spiritual things.

There has to be effort put forth to grow in spiritual knowledge and insight. There has to be consistent, disciplined practice, just like you have to do to master any skill. In other words, these people should have been mature enough to teach spiritual truth to others because they should have been using their time to feed on and digest God's Word.

So we come back to the test. If you can open your Bible and explain God's truth to someone else, you're a meat Christian. If you can lead someone to Jesus Christ with your Bible opened up to the book of Romans, you are a meat Christian.

But if you as a husband can't answer any of your wife's questions about the Bible; if you as a parent can't answer your children's questions; if all you can say is, "Ask your Sunday school teacher," or "How do I know? I didn't go to seminary," it's because you are a milk Christian.

This is the test. If you can't help someone else understand the Word of God, you are a "pablum saint." You can only survive as long as you're getting milk.

Use It or Lose It

The point is this. Christians who willfully refuse to go deeper in the things of God don't use the Word because they don't know the Word. And as the old saying goes, "If you don't use it, you will lose it."

If you hear the Word of God but never practice it, you will eventually forget even what you have learned of it. You will hear a passage and think you never studied it. You will wonder whether it was ever taught because you have lost it.

Conversely, if you use it, you won't lose it. So the idea of moving from milk to meat is to learn what you need to learn and use what you learn so that you don't forget.

The problem with the Hebrews is that they made a different choice. I once sat next to a man on an airplane who told me, "Man, these women are getting to me. I just can't control myself. I'm married and everything, but I'm not sure God wants a man to have only one woman. That's just unnatural. I can't help myself."

Needless to say, he sat in the wrong seat because he found out that it's a choice he's making and for which he is accountable. You can change your choices. In fact, until you decide to change your choices, your choices will never change. No one else can choose for you. You must choose to progress and not regress in your spiritual life.

THE SIGN OF WITHDRAWAL

For this warning sign on the road to spiritual regression and the loss of our first love, we turn to Hebrews 10:23–25:

> Let us hold fast the confession of our hope without wavering, for He who promised is faithful; and let us consider how to stimulate one another to love and good deeds, not forsaking our own assembling together, as is the habit of some, but encouraging one another; and all the more, as you see the day drawing near.

These strong warnings are to Christians—unbelievers don't have hope to hold fast. You don't tell unbelievers to continue assembling together, because they don't have any reason to assemble.

Church Doesn't Matter

This is family talk, and it's a serious warning. One of the warning signs telling you that you are on the wrong road is when you don't feel that church matters much anymore. You don't feel like you need to be in the house of the Lord. You decide to become a member of Mattress Methodist or Bedside Baptist.

This is when you hear people say, "I don't have to go to church to be a Christian." While that's technically true, you *do* have to go to church to be a good Christian. Someone might say, "Of course you're going to say that. You're a pastor."

This isn't my idea. The Bible teaches that to be the kind of Christians God wants us to be, we need the dynamic fellowship, the dynamic motivation, the dynamic inspiration of the people of God. Not only do we need it, we need to give it to someone else.

Other folk live in this family too, and my place in the body is not determined just by whether I am hungry or I need something. It has to do with whether my neighbor is hungry or he needs something.

So those who don't share in the life of the church are only thinking of themselves. They forget about God and about other people. If they were looking at church as God's house, they would remember that God seeks our worship—reason enough to attend church whether or not we "get anything" out of a particular service. If they were thinking of the rest of the family, they would come and give not their leftovers, but their best because there are other people to be cared for.

Our job as members of the body of Christ is to "stimulate one another to love and good deeds" (v. 24). Your job isn't just to get blessed. Your job is to be a blessing.

Too many of our churches are plagued by people who only come to church to collect. "Where is mine today?" But they offer very little in the way of what God wants to do in the lives of others through them.

So Christians who are regressing don't have time to be with the family of God. It's not a priority. It doesn't kill them to miss church because it's no big deal.

The Blessing of the Body

But I trust you know what it's like to walk through those church doors with a broken spirit, with things going downhill, and have God lift up your face and then your spirit as the choir sings a song that reminds you, "He can make a way somehow." Or the sermon is just what you need for that hour. Or a brother smiles and puts a smile on your face.

No wonder God's Word says, "Don't stop assembling yourselves together." When you begin to do that, no one is around to hold you accountable. A New Testament assembly is more than just a meeting. It is a matter of stimulating one another to love and good deeds. It is relationship, life touching life. A fire won't last very long with just one log.

God saved you to be part of His body. Just as your finger can't work without your hand; your hand can't work without your wrist; your wrist can't work without your arm; your arm can't work without your shoulder; and your shoulder can't work without your body; so you can't be what God wants you to be by yourself.

Many Christians going down the wrong road are traveling alone. When you know a brother or sister who doesn't come to church anymore and there's no good reason, you can predict something is wrong. You need to say something to them, go after them, stimulate them to join the assembly.

THE SIGN OF REJECTION

A Christian who stays on the wrong road long enough and ignores enough warning signs will apostatize. That is, he will fall away from the faith, deny Christ, and wind up looking like the rankest of sinners.

Can a Christian regress this far? Can a believer get this bad? Absolutely. Now God's going to judge. God's going to intervene. He's not going to ignore it. The price tag for apostasy is staggering: all kinds of suffering and problems, and an untimely death if the person gets far enough down this road.

Beyond the Point

When a believer's problem is neglect, he can get help. When he is insensitive, I can help him. A believer who willfully refuses to grow can have a change of heart and put aside the milk. Even when a brother or sister withdraws from the fellowship of the church, he or she is not beyond help.

But when an individual gets to the point of rejection, the point of apostasy, it's too late. Now again, realize that I am not talking about the loss of salvation, but a tremendous loss of spiritual effectiveness in this life, possibly an early death, and a staggering loss of reward in heaven.

So this is very serious. Look at Hebrews 10:26: "For if we go on sinning willfully after receiving the knowledge of the truth, there no longer remains a sacrifice for sins."

This is not a pretty passage. If a Christian goes on sinning, having been warned time and time again, then not even the blood of Jesus can protect that Christian from the severe discipline of God. Some people have a problem with this. They say, "He can't be talking this strongly about Christians."

But even in this severe warning passage, he reminds his readers that they bore the reproach of Christ (v. 32). They were sympathetic to other believers who had gone to prison. They lost their own property while serving Christ and didn't worry about it because they knew they had great reward in heaven for their loss on earth (v. 34). Does that sound like any unbeliever you know?

If that's not enough, back in verse 29 he calls them "sanctified," set apart by the Spirit. And in verse 39 he identifies them as people who have saving faith. No doubt about it. He's writing to Christians.

"That's It!"

Now let me show you how bad it can get for a Christian when he or she ignores the warning sign of rejection. We looked at verse 26 above. It's a very sober warning, and it gets even more sobering in verse 27, which warns of "a certain terrifying expectation of judgment, and the fury of a fire which will consume the adversaries."

If we know better and yet we just keep on going down the wrong road, God is going to say, "That's it!" Now I don't know when God is going to say this in a particular believer's life. I don't have access to that information. But I know that if it gets bad enough He will indeed say, "That's it!"

At that point, God will have to treat His child like He would treat the pagans. The fire that will burn the adversaries is going to burn the sinning believer.

Older kids can push parents to drastic steps like this in the home. They can get so bad you have to treat them like you don't know them. You have to put them out because their behavior is destroying the family.

Well, God does the same thing. When you get this far, the only thing to expect is judgment:

> How much severer punishment do you think he will deserve who has trampled under foot the Son of God, and has regarded as unclean the blood of the covenant by which he was sanctified, and has insulted the Spirit of grace? (v. 29)

If you say, "I'm going to do what I want to do. Be what I want to be. Act the way I want to act. I don't care what God says. I don't care what the church says. I don't care what you say," then verses 30–31 are your epitaph:

> For we know Him who said, "Vengeance is Mine, I will repay." And again, "The Lord will judge His people." It is a terrifying thing to fall into the hands of the living God.

When my wife Lois really wants to get on our kids, she will say, "Wait until your father comes home." It's bad if Mama deals with you, but Lord have mercy if Dad does the disciplining. That's something of the idea behind these verses. The Christian life isn't a game. But too many Christians are playing with God.

HEEDING THE SIGNS

Now let me explain something. Many of us are going through crises because God is angry. Our joy and peace and power and finances and marriage and personal life and mental stability are going from bad to worse because we are on the wrong road.

We'd better pay heed to the warning signs and get off at the next exit, cross over the bridge, and get on the right road so God can give us back what He took before He takes it permanently.

This is serious stuff. What would you think of a doctor who, having found a tumor in your body, told you to take two aspirin and lie down? You'd think he was playing games with you.

What would you say to a fireman who saw your house on fire and said, "Well, it will burn itself out soon enough"?

You'd say, "Stop playing games with me. This is serious!"

How would you respond to a policeman who, upon seeing a group of boys beating up an elderly person, said, "Well, you know, boys will be boys"? You'd insist that the officer intervene on behalf of that elderly victim.

God is not playing games, but He *is* full of grace. As long as you are here, there is hope for change. "As long as it is still called 'Today,'" (Hebrews 3:13), you can turn around.

Have you ever ridden a bike with the wind blowing in your face? It's hard to make progress because the wind is resisting you. But if you simply turn the bike around, the same wind that hindered you will now help you. It will push you.

Many of us are struggling because we are going the wrong way and the "wind" of God's Spirit is blowing against us. But if we will change direction, that same wind will help us.

RETURNING TO YOUR FIRST LOVE

Because of the importance of these five warning signs and our need to do something about them before we pass the last one and plunge over a cliff, I want to give you a way to deal with each of these five areas:

1. Nothing cures the problem of *neglect* like a little gratitude. Maybe it's been a long time since you consistently said thanks to the Lord for your "so great" salvation and all the benefits it brings. To help you remember to be thankful, write the word THANKS on a 3 x 5 card and put it on the refrigerator, your desk, or wherever you will see it every day.

2. *Spiritual insensitivity* can be eased by brokenness and contrition of heart. Read Psalm 51, David's great prayer of confession and plea for cleansing, and make it your prayer.

3. If *refusal* to grow is a problem for you, determine today that you will put away the "milk bottle" and start feasting on some choice biblical meat, like the teaching on Melchizedek in Hebrews 7. Your pastor or your local Christian bookstore can recommend a number of good basic Bible study tools that will help get you started on the exciting, lifelong adventure of chewing and digesting God's Word.

4. *Withdrawal* from the fellowship of God's people is serious. If you aren't part of a Christ-centered, Bible-teaching church, you need to find one soon. Ask a friend for help if you need to. Visit a time or two. But don't treat it like window shopping, which you only do when you feel like it. Tell God you are serious about obeying this warning sign, and He will lead you to the fellowship of His choosing for you.

5. Finally, if you really believe that you have gone so far down the wrong road that *rejection* best describes you, I urge you to seek God in humble repentance while today is still here. You may also feel the need to seek help from a pastor or a trusted Christian friend. Do whatever it takes!

CHAPTER FOUR

FLESHLY LIVING

If you and I are going to keep our love for Christ in first place where it belongs, I know one thing: We are going to have to learn how to live by the leading and direction of the Holy Spirit rather than being led and directed by our flesh.

There's a very good reason for that. Several good reasons, actually. Paul gives us one when he says, "I know that nothing good dwells in me, that is, in my flesh" (Romans 7:18). No wonder he goes on to say, "Those who are in the flesh cannot please God" (Romans 8:8).

Another reason is in the primary text we will be considering in this chapter. "Walk by the Spirit, and you will not carry out the desire of the flesh" (Galatians 5:16). God's will for you and me is that we live above the desires and cravings of our fleshly nature. We cannot love Christ as we ought and love the flesh and all it stands for at the same time.

THE DESIRES OF THE FLESH

There are some things about the flesh you must understand. First, when the Bible uses the term *flesh* in discussing how we live, it means the unredeemed part of a person that wants to please self, that old pattern of life you had before you were saved, which may have been shaped by your family, environment, circumstances, social influences, or whatever. That's the flesh.

A second thing to understand about your flesh is this: If your flesh wants to do evil things, you can't help that. No, I didn't misspeak myself. I said if there is in your flesh a desire to be immoral, you can't help that. If there is in your flesh a desire to think evil thoughts, you can't help that.

You see, the flesh doesn't know anything but having bad desires. The Bible says that in your flesh and mine dwells no good thing. Our flesh, our old nature, is corrupted by sin. We inherited it that way from Adam. That's why, as we will see, what God condemns is not our having desires of the flesh.

This is where many people get confused. They say, "But I can't help desiring this." That's absolutely right. Your flesh has been trained to think and act a certain way and to have certain desires. When you received Jesus Christ as Savior, He did not kill the desires of your flesh.

You say, "Well, what difference does having Jesus make?" That is answered in Galatians 5:16, quoted previously. Jesus enables you not to fulfill, not to give in to, the desires of the flesh. Jesus Christ gives you the power to choose not to acquiesce to that desire you can't help having.

Being saved does not mean you don't have evil desires. Being saved means you don't have to fulfill the evil desires you have.

Dealing with the Flesh

When it comes to dealing with the flesh, some people say, "If you are saved, you shouldn't have those desires." But anyone who says he doesn't have them is lying. I have desires. You have them. Mine may not be yours. Yours may not be mine. But denying them doesn't help, because we know the flesh is weak.

We just read where Paul said there was nothing of any spiritual good to be found in his flesh. The flesh itself will always desire evil.

You say, "But isn't that desire what God condemns as sin?" No. Look at James 1:14: "Each one is tempted when he is carried away and enticed by his own lust." When an enticing temptation comes our way, our fleshly desire tells us to grab it. Something within us draws us to the temptation. But remember, being tempted is not a sin. There's no condemnation mentioned yet.

Let's go on to verse 15: "Then when lust has conceived, it gives birth to sin." Please notice that James doesn't call the fact of lust a sin. He calls the conception of lust a sin. Conception means you acted on that lust. You gave it life. There's an old saying that you can't keep a bird from flying over your head, but you can keep it from making a nest in your hair.

That's the idea here. What God is concerned about is your choice to let the bird make the nest. That is, you enter into sin when you decide to act on the desire that may have come without your control. It's at the point of *choice* that you either do or don't enter into fleshly living.

The Point of Sin

So the flesh has desires, but sin is when you act on them. A man may see a beautiful woman walk by or see a seductive picture, and his flesh responds immediately with a wrong thought about that woman. At that point, his desire is definitely luring him in the wrong direction, but God wants to know, "Now what are you going to do?"

If that man says, "I'm going to look. I'm going to play with this in my mind. I'm going to let my lust go where this temptation leads me," then he's entered into sin, because now he's made a choice to act on or enjoy his desire. The point of choosing is the point of sin.

So I've got good news and bad news. The fact that you have desires, you can't help. The fact that desires have you, you can help. It is this distinction that makes the Christian life possible. So while your past may have influenced your present, it does not have to control your present.

The War

Not that the flesh won't try to control you. Look at how Paul describes the war between the flesh and the Spirit in Galatians 5:17:

> For the flesh sets its desire against the Spirit, and the Spirit against the flesh; for these are in opposition to one another, so that you may not do the things that you please.

There is a war going on inside you. In fact, one of the ways you know that you are truly saved is that there is a war going on inside you.

If you can continue in sin without ever feeling a conflict in your soul, the problem could be that you are not truly saved. If you never have to battle to be righteous, it's probably because there is no Holy Spirit in you to fight against your flesh. An unsaved person can be constantly unrighteous and still be at peace. He can be unrighteous and be cooling out.

But that is impossible for a Christian. Like Jonah of old, you have to fight against God in order to become comfortable outside of His will. And even then, God will intervene at some point and interrupt your false sense of security. He did it in a dramatic way for Jonah. The prophet knew he was not going to be comfortable anymore when he hit that cold water!

So Paul says there's a war between your flesh and the Holy Spirit who lives within you. You may still commit the same sin you committed before you were saved. But you can't commit the same sin in the same way, because now that you are saved, when you sin all heaven breaks loose because there is a war on.

The effect of this war is given in the last phrase of verse 17: "So that you may not do the things that you please." In other words, you will want to do one thing, but you may wind up doing the opposite. Your flesh may say, "Go after that sin!" But because of the Spirit's influence, you don't do it.

Or the Spirit may say, "Go after that righteousness!" But because of the flesh's influence, you may not do what the Spirit tells you to do. The Holy Spirit can halt what the flesh desires to do, and the flesh can override what the Spirit desires to do. As a result, you and I are often self-contradictory persons. That's why we say, "I shouldn't have done that." We knew we shouldn't have done it. But we did it anyway, and we feel condemned because we did it. That's because we had to skip over the Spirit to pull off that sin.

If you don't ever have to do a hop, skip, and jump to pull off your desires, that means the Holy Spirit is not there. You have to do a lot of hopping, skipping, and jumping over Him to sin. If you are a Christian and therefore at war with your flesh, you've got to do a whole lot of conniving to get to that sin. You've got to go through a lot of mental gymnastics; you've got to go through a lot of justification to get to it.

So if you are a Christian, you are in a conflict, a war. Let's consider what happens when you yield to the flesh and how to avoid doing that, because the result of a fleshly lifestyle is that you will not please God and your "first love" for Christ will grow cold.

THE RESULTS OF FLESHLY LIVING

In verses 19–21 of Galatians 5, Paul gives three basic categories of sin that result from living for the flesh: sexual sins, superstitious sins, and social sins. This is not an exhaustive list, because he adds in verse 21, "and things like these." So no one can say, "Well, my stuff isn't on that list. I'm OK."

Notice how verse 19 starts: "Now the deeds of the flesh are. . . ." You can't do deeds without making choices. That's why counseling someone is a waste of time until that person gets to the place where he is ready to make a choice. It's not wasting time to move a person toward that choice, but until he gets there nothing will happen.

I could counsel a married couple for twenty years, but until that husband and wife are ready to make a choice, they will be stuck in neutral and not be able to move out in the victory God has already won for His people.

Sexual Sins

This is an obvious and dominating category when we talk about fleshly living. Paul says sins like these are evident. You don't have to do a lot of explaining to account for them. They are obvious.

Paul begins with "immorality," using the Greek word from which we get our English word *pornography*. This is a broad term that includes all kinds of immoral conduct: adultery, or illicit sex by married people; fornication, illicit sex by those who are not married; incest, sexual sin within a family; homosexuality, sexual activity among members of the same sex; impurity, filth of the heart and the mind; and sensuality, an open, shameless display.

This last sin, sensuality, is worth further comment. The Bible does not ever condemn being in style. It always condemns immodesty. There's nothing wrong with living up to the beauty you have. There's everything wrong with allowing that beauty to control you in an immodest way.

Some people try to be discreet in their sin. They hide and sneak around because they don't want anyone to know. But sensuality says you don't care who knows it and how much they see. I say all of this because sensuality is becoming the trademark of our culture, and it's wrong.

What you need to know about sexual sin is that God's attitude is the same regardless of which form the sin takes. We assign a hierarchy of nastiness to sin. When someone engages in the grossest form of sexual sin we can imagine, we say, "How could that person sink so low as to do something as nasty and dirty as that?"

When God sees a man with another man's wife, He says, "How could he sink so low as to do something as nasty and dirty as that?" When God sees men and women sleeping with partner after partner, He says, "How could they sink so low?" To God it all fits into the same category.

As I said above, our whole culture is built on eliciting from us a sexual response to the stimuli we see. These images, words, and suggestions appeal to our eyes and our flesh. There is an entire industry of men's clubs built on a woman's ability to captivate men and lead them to express their normal sexual desires in an illegitimate way.

A man once told me, "Dr. Evans, I have a weakness for women."

I said, "OK, you have a weakness for women. What are you doing about that weakness? What are you doing to guard against it leading you into sin?"

You see, having a weakness does not mean you have no control. You don't always have control over the temptations that come your way. But you have total control over whether you yield to them. That's why God gave you the Spirit.

Superstitious Sins

These are sins having to do with religion. In Galatians 5:20, Paul mentions idolatry and sorcery. Idolatry is worshiping anyone or anything other than God, putting something else ahead of God.

The Bible is clear on our priorities. First, we are to worship God. That's our number-one priority. That's why Sunday, the first day of the week, is the day of worship. That's why being in God's house ought to be a priority in your life. Worshiping God always comes first.

Second, we are to love people. Third, we are to use things. That's the order: worship God, love people, and use things. But we get it all mixed up. Instead we use people, love and worship things, and forget God.

How do you know if you are truly worshiping God? Well, Matthew 4:10 says that the way you know you are worshiping God is that you are serving Him. "You shall worship the Lord your God, and serve Him only" is the way Jesus put it.

What you serve shows what you worship. Is your life marked by serving God, or do you serve self? If you serve self, then you can't be serving God, because God is to take the dominant position in our lives.

Anything can be an idol. You don't have to go to some primitive tribe to find an idol. Some of our idols are parked in our garages. Some of us worship our homes. And a whole bunch of us worship our money. Some of us even worship our wardrobes. We get up every morning and conduct a worship service in front of the mirror. Every time we step out, it's as though we are saying, "Look at me, world! I'm here!"

This is not a matter of having transportation, a roof over our heads, or decent clothes. It is serving self, and you were not saved to serve self. That's idolatry. Idolatry occurs when anything takes a higher priority than God. When a man neglects his family in favor of his job, for example, it's job-worship.

Next, Paul mentions sorcery. Here's another interesting Greek word, *pharmakeia*, which you may recognize as the root of the English word *pharmacy*. When Paul talks about sorcery or witchcraft, he is including use of drugs, because the use of drugs was a main part of witchcraft then and still is today.

The most hideous feature of illicit drugs is not that they damage the body, but that they are a direct vehicle of Satan into your life. Someone who is hooked on drugs is hooked on much more than a substance.

A drug user is hooked on the Devil because drug use is tied into sorcery or witchcraft. In other words, a drug user opens himself up in a unique way to the domination of hell. Drugs are a vehicle Satan uses to ride into your life and entrap you in a lot of different ways.

That's why Satan always has a new drug. Every time people get used to one drug, a new one pops up that's cheaper and offers a better high. Crack cocaine can be bought fairly cheap, and it produces a quick high. But more than likely you will be addicted after the first try. A former star in the National Football League once said that he became hooked after just one experience with crack, and it shattered his life before he came to Christ.

There's always something new on the drug scene. Why? Because Satan always has his demons busy whipping up a new batch. And he has plenty of sinners who are ready to make sure anyone who wants it can get it.

By the way, before I leave sorcery let me say that reading and following your horoscope is as hellish as worshiping the Devil. Instead of asking people, "What sign are you?", we'd better be asking them, "Whose child are you?" The Bible condemns worshiping the creature instead of the Creator (Romans 1:25).

Social Sins

By now you're probably feeling like we're about as far from genuine love for Christ as we can get. It's a pretty ugly list, without a doubt. But I want us to understand what we can look like when we leave our first love and yield to the flesh.

We're not done with our Galatians 5 list, because in verses 20–21 Paul gives a long list of sins that have to do with how we relate to other people.

"Enmities" refers to hatred or antagonism toward others. You say, "But you don't know what they did to me. You don't know how they treated me, and my mama told me that what goes around comes around. You just can't let people do that to you."

Now you may have the fleshly desire to hate them. But remember Paul is talking about what you choose to do. That's why Jesus says, "Love your enemies" (Matthew 5:44).

Your emotions may say, "Hate them." But that has nothing to do with your decisions. Let me give you an extreme example. A husband may look at his wife and feel hatred. So he goes to a counselor and says, "I can't get rid of this feeling. Every time I look at that woman, my hatred grows."

So the psychiatrist or psychologist tries to help this husband get over that emotion. No, you focus on the choices he makes, what he decides to do. For now, that husband can feel the way he feels and still choose to do what's right.

I'm not denying the reality of an emotion. All I'm saying is it doesn't have to control our choices. And when we start choosing right, we will start feeling right.

But if that husband says, "I hate her and until I start liking her, I'm not going to love her," we will see him in divorce court because he is not going to make it.

The next item on the list is "strife" (Galatians 5:20), which is conflict that is a natural outgrowth of enmity or hatred. Then Paul lists "jealousy," which is the attitude that says, "I'm going to take you down because you have what I want. Since I can't have it, you aren't going to have it either."

This is the crab-in-the-barrel syndrome. Crabs will pull each other down trying to climb over each other to get out of a barrel. The result is no one gets out and they all get cooked. Jealousy says, "If I can't get to the top, I'm not going to be at the bottom by myself." This is a hideous sin that keeps people from reaching their full potential because other people do all they can to pull them back down.

The next social sin is "outbursts of anger." Here's a goodie. "He made me mad! I couldn't control myself, so I hit him!" Oh, really? You mean another person can force your pinkie and ring finger and middle finger and index finger to close? Another person can force your thumb to close, cause your arm to bend at the elbow and raise at the shoulder, and propel your fist forward at lightning speed? *Bam!*

No, another person can't do that. If you are a Christian, you have control over that. Paul says it's a work of the flesh, because one fruit of the Spirit is self-control (see v. 23). The Holy Spirit gives you the ability to contain yourself, to say, "I'm not going to do what I feel."

"Disputes" (v. 20) are arguments. "Well, she was arguing with me so I had to argue back." My philosophy is that someone else's anger doesn't have to make you look bad. It doesn't have to cause you to lose control. When someone wants to argue, I just invite him to have at it. Give me everything he's got. Say everything he wants to say. I listen, then when I think it's time I ask, "Are you finished, or is there more?"

"No, I'm not finished."

"Then go right ahead. Finish."

"You did this and this and said that. . . ."

"You're right. You finished?"

"I have one more thing. . . ."

"OK. Are you finished?"

"That's it."

"Great. Now can we talk about it?"

"We can."

Then Paul lists "dissensions [and] factions." These have to do with group conflict. Groups of people get together and take sides rather than taking truth and taking right. So they say, "Well, I'm for him."

If everyone was saying, "I'm for truth," we wouldn't be taking racial sides or class sides or cultural sides. If we were all living according to the Spirit rather than according to the flesh, we would all want to be on the Lord's side.

The final sins in this list are "envying, drunkenness, carousing" (v. 21). Envy is "the rottenness of the bones" (Proverbs 14:30 KJV). The word seems to suggest that we waste away as we look on what someone else has and want it so badly it kills us.

When drunkenness and carousing are used together, it usually means a public, brazen display of boisterous activity: rowdiness. Obviously, people who are drunk have lost control of their actions. Carousing has the idea of just being boisterous and loud without concern for others.

FLESHLY LIVING AND GOD'S KINGDOM

We noted earlier that even though this list is long, it's not exhaustive. But enough of the sins of the flesh are accounted for to warrant this very strong conclusion: "Of which I forewarn you just as I have forewarned you that those who practice such things shall not inherit the kingdom of God" (v. 21b).

This has caused a lot of confusion. Is Paul saying that those who practice such things aren't saved? No, we've already seen that Christians can get into the habit of practicing wrong. We have plenty of biblical illustrations of Christians who have gotten into very bad habits.

A Vital Distinction

The reason I believe Paul is talking about Christians who practice these things is the word *inherit*. This word is not used of unbelievers. Unbelievers who practice such things don't enter the kingdom. Christians who practice such things *enter* the kingdom, but they don't inherit the kingdom.

This is a very important distinction. There is a difference between entering the kingdom and inheriting the kingdom. When Israel was saved on the night of Passover and left Egypt, they were to go to the promised land, Canaan. This was called their inheritance in the Old Testament, the place God set aside for them to enter, enjoy, and benefit from—a land of milk and honey. It was to be a glorious life.

But because of their persistent sin and disobedience, what the New Testament calls carnality, the Israelites lost their inheritance. They forfeited long and productive lives. They never got to enjoy Canaan and the fulfillment of God's promises. They had to wander around in the desert.

The Question of Merit

There's one proof beyond all proofs that inheritance refers to believers missing out rather than unbelievers not getting in. Whenever the Bible talks about inheritance, it is always based on merit. Salvation is never based on merit, but always on grace. You are not saved because you earn it.

What proof do we have that inheritance is tied to merit? We've already seen this link in Galatians 5:21, where those who live for the flesh forfeit their inheritance in the kingdom. The tie is even more direct in Colossians 3:23–24:

> Whatever you do, do your work heartily, as for the Lord rather than for men; knowing that from the Lord you will

receive the reward of the inheritance. It is the Lord Christ whom you serve.

Paul can only be talking to Christians here because non-Christians don't work for the Lord. And even if they did, it would never earn them a place in heaven.

Our Inheritance

So our inheritance as believers is the reward God gives us for serving Christ. Therefore, Christians who persist in practicing fleshly living incur two losses. One is in this life and the other is in the life to come (see chapters 8 and 9 for a full discussion of this subject). The temporal loss is that they will not live full, productive lives.

That could come about in a lot of different ways. It could be a family tragedy, an early death, or not having needs met because God is disciplining. And even though Christians in this condition get into the kingdom, they will not enjoy the inheritance of the kingdom. They will not be granted the authority God wants to give them in the kingdom that is to come.

I love to go to the Texas State Fair here in Dallas because I love roller-coasters. And there's more food than you could ever eat. Now I usually get into the fair free because one of my church members gives me tickets. My admission to the fair is a gift paid for by someone else. So let's call the fair heaven.

Once I'm on the fairgrounds, there is so much to do: the rides, the circus, the games, an incredible array of exhibits. I could just go from one thing to another all day long. All of that is available to me simply because my entrance to the fairgrounds gives me access to it. I got in free because someone paid for my ticket. I wasn't denied entrance to the fair, and no one will ask me to leave. I can walk around all day and enjoy the exciting sights, sounds, and smells of the state fair.

But to enjoy everything the fair has to offer to its fullest, I need more than an admission ticket, because at the Texas State Fair, the rides and the food are not free. You have to buy coupons for them. So to fully enjoy the fair, what I need to do is "inherit" the fair. That is, I need someone to say to me, "Tony, this is all yours. Here are all the coupons you will ever need. Enjoy everything you see at no additional cost. You've been a faithful servant, and this is your reward."

All true Christians will enter the kingdom. They will be at the fair, if you will. And it's far better to be at the fair than to miss it completely. There's no comparison. But it's a terrible thing to be at the fair and not be able to ride. It's terrible to have access, but not be a full participant.

Look at it another way. Our oldest son, Tony, Jr., is prominently mentioned in the will Lois and I have drawn up, as you would expect. He's our son, and nothing can change that.

He can, however, be disinherited, even though he cannot be "de-soned." In fact, our will says if any of our children adopt a godless lifestyle from which they do not repent, then the blessings of our inheritance are to be passed on to the other children.

Tony, Jr., is my son by birth. But he is my *heir* by merit. Only by living a consistent Christian lifestyle can he inherit my "kingdom." The inheritance his father has waiting for him ought to motivate him to live right. You know what ought to motivate you and me to live right? The inheritance our Father has waiting for us!

RETURNING TO YOUR FIRST LOVE

Living to please the flesh is a losing proposition for any Christian, no doubt about it. It kills our joy and dulls our love for Christ, which is the bottom line of all that we're talking about in this book. Jesus said, "If you love Me, you will keep My commandments" (John 14:15). Here are some ways you can demonstrate your love for Christ:

1. Since we are immersed in a sexually explicit and illicit culture, we need to be constantly on guard. Maybe it's time for you to do one of those periodic inspections of what is coming into your home, making sure you aren't allowing sexual temptation to slip in over the television or through your front door.

2. The category of superstitious sins reminds us that many people in our culture, especially young people, are in bondage to evil spirits and satanic worship and all that goes with it. If you have a child, relative, or friend who is caught up in this, or if you want to guard your family, I recommend that you read an excellent Moody Press book called *Reclaiming Surrendered Ground*, by James Logan. It is full of biblical insight and practical steps you can take to protect yourself and your family.

3. Social sins take in a broad sweep of problems we can get into, mostly by the misuse of our tongues. If any of the things we discussed under this category is a problem for you, bring it to the Lord right now and ask Him to remove it. Also, if He reminds you of anyone whose forgiveness you need to seek, do it as soon as possible.

4. We know our flesh is weak, and we all have our unique weak spot. If you don't know where you are prone to fall, ask God to show you your particular weak spot, then go to His Word to find verses that fortify you against it. Commit them to memory so they'll be available to you when you need them. A Bible concordance can help you find these verses.

CHAPTER FIVE

THE FLESH VS. THE SPIRIT

This chapter is sort of a mirror image of chapter 4, where we looked at the problem of fleshly living and how it is another thief that steals away your first love for Christ.

In this chapter I want to go the next step and contrast the influence of the Holy Spirit with the influence of the flesh in the life of a Christian. You might call it part two of our study in this very important matter of dealing with the flesh.

This is so crucial and so much of the New Testament is devoted to the Spirit versus flesh war in all its forms that we could do a whole book on the subject. For now we will limit ourselves to two chapters. Here again the apostle Paul will be our teacher.

TWO CONTRASTING LAWS THAT SEEK CONTROL

We have within us two simultaneous laws or rules of conduct that are working at the same time to bring us under their control. Look how Paul begins Romans 8:

There is therefore now no condemnation for those who are in Christ Jesus. For the law of the Spirit of life in Christ Jesus has set you free from the law of sin and of death. For what the Law could not do, weak as it was through the flesh, God did: sending His own Son in the likeness of sinful flesh and as an offering for sin, He condemned sin in the flesh. (vv. 1–3)

Paul summarizes the two laws at work in us in verse 2. One is "the law of the Spirit of life," the ruling influence and control of the Holy Spirit. But there's another law at work in us, "the law of sin and of death." It's this other law that seeks to bring us spiritual defeat and ruin.

A Real-Life Example

Both laws are at work—or, better, at war—in each and every Christian. Now to understand how important this is, we need to understand how this war was affecting Paul. Paul was not your everyday Christian. He was the leader of first-century Christianity, the apostle to the Gentiles. He played a dominant role in communicating God's truth to us.

We have Paul's personal testimony of the battle between flesh and Spirit that he was enduring as a godly Christian. So if you are struggling with sin, don't feel bad. You're in good company because Paul, one of the greatest Christians who ever lived, struggled with sin too.

I said in chapter 4 that the desire to sin is not the problem. Our flesh has always had the desire to sin, and it always will. It comes with the territory. Paul felt that desire. We know this because of what he writes in Romans 7 by way of personal testimony:

For we know that the Law is spiritual; but I am of flesh, sold into bondage to sin. For that which I am doing, I do not understand; for I am not practicing what I would like to do, but I am doing the very thing I hate. (vv. 14–15)

Paul is saying, "I have this problem, and it's with me even now as I write to you believers at Rome. I feel the warfare of the flesh and the Spirit in my life, and sometimes I get caught in the tension of doing things I really don't want to do."

You know what it's like to be caught, don't you? You know you shouldn't do something, you don't want to do it, but you do it anyway. Afterward you say, "I wish I hadn't done that."

That's evidence of the two laws at work in you. Paul understood the nature of the battle, and he knew where the source of the problem was. So he continues in chapter 7:

> For I know that nothing good dwells in me, that is, in my flesh; for the wishing is present in me, but the doing of the good is not. For the good that I wish, I do not do; but I practice the very evil that I do not wish. But if I am doing the very thing I do not wish, I am no longer the one doing it, but sin which dwells in me. (vv. 18–20)

Do you realize the significance of what Paul is saying? He is saying you can't call on your flesh to help fix your flesh because there's nothing in your flesh that's salvageable. Your unredeemed flesh can't fix the problems in your life because your unredeemed flesh is the one causing the problems. You can't ask the problem-causer to be the problem-fixer.

This is the problem with much of today's so-called Christian counseling. It is often an attempt to get the flesh to fix the flesh, and it just won't work.

Paul says, "I have the right desire, but too often I do the wrong action." He says that even as he writes, a foreigner has taken up residence in his life. Paul calls it "sin which dwells in me" (v. 20). It's often referred to as the "sin principle."

The Sin Principle

This is that principle all Christians have within them that wants to rebel against the Word and will of God. That's why there's a part of you that really wants to do what God hates. Sin still dwells in you. It "hangs out" in you, and you can't get rid of it because it is has attached itself to your flesh.

Now you see why God will dispose of these old corruptible bodies and give us new ones made like His glorious body. God will not repair your flesh. In fact, your old body is only good for one thing: worm food. The Bible says that God is going to transform our bodies because the ones we have now have been contaminated by sin.

Stay with me because we're working our way back to Romans 8. But this section in chapter 7 is absolutely crucial to understand if we are going to grasp and appreciate what God has done for us. So let's wrap up Romans 7:

> For I joyfully concur with the law of God in the inner man, but I see a different law in the members of my body, waging war against the law of my mind, and making me a prisoner of the law of sin which is in my members. Wretched man that I am! Who will set me free from the body of this death? Thanks be to God through Jesus Christ our Lord! So then, on the one hand I myself with my mind am serving the law of God, but on the other, with my flesh the law of sin. (vv. 22–25)

What can we conclude from these verses? First, Paul is definitely a saved man here. "There's a part of me that wants to shout on Sunday, but there's another part of me that wants to be independent on Monday," he says. "In my heart, I know I want to please God. But in my body, I want to please myself. I want to feed my passions."

Notice that he calls this conflict a war. He says, "I, Paul the apostle, am not only living in a war zone, I *am* the war zone! Until I do something about me, the problem is just going to continue, because the problem is sin in me."

That's why you can't run from your problems. Wherever you run, your flesh will still be there. And you can't blame someone else for your sin, because it's your sin. No wonder Paul cries out, "Wretched man that I am!" If we're honest about our struggle with sin, this will often be our song too.

But praise God, this song has another verse. To Paul's question "Where am I going to find freedom to live a victorious spiritual life?" he provides the answer himself in verse 25.

So there you have it: two laws at work within you, two contrasting rules of life seeking to control you. Depending on whether the flesh or the Spirit is the controlling force in your life, you will either be a spiritual Christian or a carnal one.

A Higher Law

But the good news is that these laws are far from equal in power. The law of the Spirit is a higher law, because Paul says it has "set [us] free from the law of sin and of death" (8:2). That part of us that wants to rebel against God and please self has been overcome. Whenever that higher law is set free to work in our lives, we will see it supersede the law of sin and death.

It's like the law of gravity. This is a universal law—until you get on an airplane. Then something happens, because one day Orville and Wilbur Wright did some aerodynamic analysis and discovered a higher law. They found that a certain amount of combustion combined with a certain speed and a certain air flow allows people to transcend the law of gravity.

The Wright brothers didn't kill the law of gravity. They didn't eradicate it. They just rendered it inoperative by the operation of a higher law called aerodynamics. Now if that higher law ever stops working, if an airplane engine goes out, then the plane will come tumbling to the ground because the first law, the law of gravity, is not dead.

The law of sin and death is still around. It's at work. But when you combine the combustion of the Holy Spirit with the speed of obedience and the air flow of holiness, you are lifted higher to a new plane of spiritual life. So you ought to be rising higher, not living under the circumstances but soaring above them because the aerodynamic power of the Holy Spirit is at work in you, transcending the law of sin and death.

Have you ever seen a sidewalk turned inside out because a little acorn fell between the cracks? Now, an acorn can't move sidewalks. But when you set the acorn free to be what it was created to be, you no longer have an acorn. You've got an oak tree on your hands.

And when that oak tree begins to grow, it moves concrete because the law of the oak transcends the law of the concrete. When you accepted Jesus Christ, you received the acorn of the Spirit who wants to become the oak of your life to move aside the concrete of your problems. Why? Because as verse 3 explains, what the Law could not do, God did by sending His Son.

What the Law could not do is give you and me the ability to keep it. Now, the Law is good, meaning here the Law of Moses. Paul is actually using the word *law* in two different ways in Romans 7–8, and it's easy to get confused. The law of sin and death is the principle of sin within us, as we saw earlier.

But the Law of Moses came directly from God and is holy and just and good. The *New American Standard* text helps us distinguish these uses by using the lowercase word *law* for the sin principle, and capitalizing the word when talking about the Mosaic Law. That's a valid distinction, and I'm doing the same.

So the Law is good. "Thou shalt not commit adultery" is a good rule. The problem is with my ability to keep it. That's why the power of positive thinking can't work because you are asking yourself to keep the Law when there is no power in the Law to help you to keep it.

But what you cannot do, God did. He has provided you an internal motor, so to speak, to enable you to live up to the divine standard. Romans 6:6 says, "Knowing this, that our old self was crucified with Him, that our body of sin might be done away with, that we should no longer be slaves to sin."

If you are a slave to sin, it's slavery by choice. You don't have to be enslaved by the same sins year after year, because you became a brand-new person in Christ.

TWO CONTRASTING WAYS TO LIVE

The course or direction of your life as a Christian will depend on whether you are living under the authority of the flesh or the authority of the Spirit. Look at verses 4–7 of Romans 8:

> In order that the requirement of the Law might be fulfilled in us, who do not walk according to the flesh, but according to the Spirit. For those who are according to the flesh set their minds on the things of the flesh, but those who are according to the Spirit, the things of the Spirit. For the mind set on the flesh is death, but the mind set on the Spirit is life and peace, because the mind set on the flesh is hostile toward God; for it does not subject itself to the law of God, for it is not even able to do so.

Paul says, "If you walk according to the flesh, you will get the things of the flesh." These things can only dominate us when we go after them, when we allow them to usurp the place that Jesus Christ and the things of God should have in our affections.

Walking in the Flesh

When you leave your first love for Christ and start walking after the flesh, pretty soon you'll be walking like "mere men" (1 Corinthians 3:3). That is, you'll look just like the crowd because you're following the crowd and doing what everyone else is doing. When you walk with the world, the world sets the pace.

This is not saying that God empowers some Christians and doesn't empower others. You have the same Jesus and the same Holy Spirit every other Christian has. Even though you may have come from a worse background than some, the same God wants to impact your life.

But do you know what? You can't make a man walk. A man has to do his own walking. You can show him which road to take. You can say, "I'll help you." But you can't walk for him.

God won't make your choices for you. And God will not stop you from choosing in the same way He didn't stop Adam from eating and He didn't stop Eve from eating. What causes you to choose? Your mind. That's why Paul is saying, "Make up your mind" (see v. 5). You are walking the way you walk because you are thinking the way you think. If you want to fix your feet, fix your mind.

Let me give you a biblical example of this principle at work. In 2 Samuel 11, King David was out on his roof when he saw Bathsheba bathing. She was not just an ordinary person. We are talking about a bad mamma-jamma, a very beautiful woman. David looked and looked, and soon his heart and mind began walking in the direction the desire of his flesh was taking him. It wasn't long before he had his plans worked out.

The result of David's adultery with Bathsheba was personal and even national tragedy and disaster, which the following chapters of 2 Samuel describe. But the point is David could have fixed that mess before it ever got started if he had turned away and not decided to look and look and finally send for Bathsheba.

The grace of God is wonderful, and David was able to bounce back from that sin following his confession and repentance before the Lord. But that didn't change the fact that he thought the wrong stuff, acted on it, and was hurt by it.

A Battle for the Mind

The battle of the Christian life is a battle for the mind. Who will control your mind and the minds of your kids? Whoever controls the mind controls the feet. So if you are walking wrong, you are thinking wrong. Satan keeps working on your mind until your feet start turning in that direction.

That's the problem with believers who constantly feed themselves with junk and don't get fed with the Word of God. If you are constantly being inundated by godless music, godless friends, and godless amusements, all of a sudden things you used to think were terrible won't seem all that bad.

That's why in 2 Corinthians 10:3–5, Paul says we do not war against the flesh with the flesh. Instead, we tear down the strongholds and the imaginations and the false way of thinking of this world order because it's all in the mind.

The results of this are very interesting: "The mind set on the flesh is death, but the mind set on the Spirit is life and peace" (Romans 8:6). This doesn't necessarily mean that the Christian who is living for the flesh is going to drop dead. Death here is the opposite of life and peace—a spiritual impoverishment that sets in when the Spirit is not being obeyed.

In this condition you may be alive and well physically, but spiritually emaciated. Your spiritual life is ebbing away, and that leads to all sorts of emotional anxiety and depression, because your mind has been taught to focus on the flesh, and there is no peace, no joy, and no purpose in the flesh.

This is when Christians start doing the same things non-Christians do to find peace because they are not getting it from the Spirit. There's emptiness, lack of peace, and anxiety because they are cut off from the Spirit's life.

Walking in the Spirit

On the other hand, if you set your mind on the things of the Spirit, you have life and peace. You have purpose and meaning and joy, and you are content. When the Holy Spirit is in control, you say, "Lord, it's in Your hands. Things may not be where I want them to be, but it's where You have them so I'm going to be content with it."

You have a relaxed mental attitude and you are at peace. External circumstances do not govern your life. None of that really matters because you are at peace.

TWO CONTRASTING IDENTITIES

Where do you draw your identity from? Paul suggests two possible identities in Romans 8:8–9:

> Those who are in the flesh cannot please God. However, you are not in the flesh but in the Spirit, if indeed the Spirit of God dwells in you. But if anyone does not have the Spirit of Christ, he does not belong to Him.

Notice how Paul changes prepositions. Prior to this he has been talking about living *according to* the flesh. Now he talks about being *in* the flesh. Why? Because now he's not talking about how you are living. He's talking about who you are.

Every person on earth is either in the sphere of the flesh—that is, unsaved; or in the sphere of the Spirit— that is, saved. Remember, Paul's concern is Christians who are *in* the Spirit but who are living *according to* the flesh.

"First of all," he says, "let's get straight who you are." A lot of us are not acting like we should act because we don't remember who we are (see chapter 11). If you forget who you are, you are going to forget how you are supposed to act. One good reason for going to church every Sunday is to remind yourself who you are.

The first summer my wife Lois and I were married, we lived at 133rd and Lennox in Harlem. I was involved in a ministry there and we lived in an apartment over a church. We'd just been there a day or so when someone called and said, "May I speak to Mrs. Evans?"

Lois said, "Hold the line." Then she went looking for Mrs. Evans until it dawned on her that *she* was Mrs. Evans. She came back to the phone and in a different voice said, "Hello, Mrs. Evans here."

You see, she had forgotten her identity. A number of major changes had taken place in her life that year, among which was a change in her name. Her name had been Lois I. Cannings. But her name was now Lois Evans. She had a new identification.

Christian, do you know who you are? You are a child of God. You are a saint. You are sanctified. You are secure. You are part of the holy ones. You have royal blood flowing through your veins. That's who you are!

Stop letting Satan tell you, "You are a liar. You are an adulterer. You are a dishonest person." That's not who you are. Stop letting your friends tell you who you are. Most of us have too many friends trying to tell us who we are by telling us who *they* are, and telling us that if we don't accept their identity for us, then we can't be their friend.

Christian brother or sister, when Jesus died, you died. When Jesus arose, you arose. When Jesus comes back, you will rise to go with Him because that's who you are. So you and I must understand who we are in Christ. We have a new identity now. So Paul says in verse 11: "If the Spirit of Him who raised Jesus from the dead dwells in you, He who raised Christ Jesus from the dead will also give life to your mortal bodies through His Spirit who indwells you."

The same power that got Jesus up out of the grave is the power that will get you up out of that sin: up out of someone's bed you don't belong in; out of that unholy language you are using; out of that temper you can't control; out of that jealousy that's overcoming you; out of that contradiction you are living.

With that kind of power at work in you, you don't have to live a dead life. The Holy Spirit can turn the resurrection power of Christ loose in you.

TWO CONTRASTING OBLIGATIONS

The contrasts continue in Romans 8 as the apostle shows us that as Christians, we have an obligation to live a life of obedience rather than disobedience:

> So then, brethren, we are under obligation, not to the flesh, to live according to the flesh—for if you are living according to the flesh, you must die; but if by the Spirit you are putting to death the deeds of the body, you will live. (vv. 12–13)

Did you know that, as a Christian, you owe your flesh nothing? Your flesh hasn't done a thing for you.

Have you ever had people come to you and say, "You owe me this and you owe me that"?

People do this when their friends become successful. You know, you start making a little money and all of a sudden you owe them. Now, of course, they didn't help you while you were going through school. They didn't do anything for you during the hard times. But now that you are successful, you owe them.

That's what the flesh tries to tell you. The flesh says, "You've got to satisfy me. You've got to make me feel good right now. You've got to. You owe me."

But Paul takes a different view. "You are not obligated to the flesh," he says. "You are obligated to the Spirit. And when you obligate yourself to the Spirit, the result is that you will put to death the deeds of the flesh. You will start killing your anger and your immorality."

Starve the Flesh

I can hear someone saying, "But my flesh is so strong. It wants what it wants so bad." But that's only true because you keep feeding it. Do you know the only way to control the flesh? Starve it to death!

You've got to say, "You can't eat today, flesh! I know you want to eat bad language but I'm not going to feed it to you today. I know you want to eat more immorality, but I'm not going to feed it to you today. And I'm not feeding you pornography, alcohol, drugs, or pride either. I'm dead in Christ, so starve flesh, starve!"

To pull this off you may need some help. You may need some people around you who are going to stop you when you try to feed your flesh and say, "You know you're not supposed to be eating that." Whatever it takes, you've got to starve the flesh.

The irony of feeding the flesh is that it never gets enough. Why do you think people trapped in addictions and perversions have to keep going deeper and searching for more and more gratification? Because the flesh is never satisfied. It will gorge as long as you feed it. It will eat any kind of trash you give it. And if your flesh eats long enough, it will eat you!

But when you starve your fleshly life long enough, it will shrivel and die. Then, things you didn't think you could stop doing, you will stop doing. Habits you didn't think you could break, you will break.

Why? Because you don't feed them anymore. The reason the problem is getting worse for so many people is that they are feeding the flesh every chance they get. And so their sin is getting bigger and bigger and more and more controlling.

The life of the flesh is the death of the Christian. But the death of the flesh is the life of the Christian. When you kill the flesh, you live. When you feed the flesh, you die. You become "spiritually anemic" because you are now hostile to God. You are God's enemy.

Feeding the Spirit

If you are feeding your flesh, don't pray, because you are wasting your time. God is not going to answer your prayer so you can feed the flesh more. But when you live by the Spirit, you hear from God. You get peace even in the storms, and you see God working. You see power you didn't have before and victory you didn't think was possible, because you are feeding the Spirit.

The law of double jeopardy says you can't be tried twice for the same crime. Jesus has already been tried for your crimes, so you owe nothing to the flesh. Jesus has already pronounced judgment on it. Don't let the flesh try you again when it's already been pronounced guilty! You have no obligation to it.

TWO CONTRASTING LEVELS OF SONSHIP

Adoption was a big thing in the world in which Paul lived. He uses it to make an important point in Romans 8:14–15:

> For all who are being led by the Spirit of God, these are sons of God. For you have not received a spirit of slavery leading to fear again, but you have received a spirit of adoption as sons by which we cry out, "Abba! Father!"

In Paul's day, adoptions were viewed as entrance into great blessing and privilege. That is, adopted children had all the rights and privileges of adult children in the home even if they weren't yet adults. That was the nature of first-century adoption.

Paul talks about us as adopted sons and daughters in these two verses. But he begins by linking sonship with being led by the Spirit. Now, we know that not all Christians are being led by the Spirit at all times, because when we are walking according to the flesh, we are not being led by the Spirit.

It sounds like Paul is saying if you aren't led, you aren't a child of God. So we'd better find out what he means in verse 14. Let's start by asking, What does the Spirit of God lead you to do when He leads you? Well, in the context of this passage He leads you to put to death the deeds of the flesh. He leads you to kill the flesh.

So this much is clear. When the Holy Spirit is leading you to kill the flesh as you live in dependence on and obedience to Him, you are a son of God.

"But wait a minute," you say. "I thought I was already a son of God just because I'm saved."

Yes. But you can be a son without a son's benefits. Paul's not talking about your position. He's talking about your practice. He's dealing with the benefits of your position.

The Bible talks about this in a number of places. Jesus said that those who are peacemakers and those who love their enemies are sons of God (see Matthew 5:9, 44–45).

It's obvious that Jesus is not giving two conditions for salvation. You can't earn your way to heaven by making peace and loving your enemies. Instead, He's talking about acting like who you are, imitating your Father who adopted you. Revelation 21:7 talks about the overcomers being sons of God.

The Bible is saying that when you live according to the Spirit, you earn the benefit of crying, "Abba! Father!" When you are living by the Spirit, God is listening. He's saying, "I can't wait to talk to you, child!"

But when you live by the flesh, God says, "You're living like kids I don't know, like the ones who live down the street."

Abba means "papa." This is a term of great intimacy. When you are being led by the Spirit to put to death the deeds of the flesh, you can say, "My Daddy!" When you let the Spirit lead you to the place of holiness, you can come to your Father as a fully-privileged son who knows he is being heard.

TWO CONTRASTING LEVELS OF HEIRSHIP

Our final point is that Christians have contrasting levels of heirship based on their willingness to suffer with Christ:

> The Spirit Himself bears witness with our spirit that we are children of God, and if children, heirs also, heirs of God and fellow heirs with Christ, if indeed we suffer with Him in order that we may also be glorified with Him. (Romans 8:16–17)

All Christians belong to the family of God. So in that sense, we are all heirs. But not all Christians are "fellow heirs with Christ" or co-heirs. Please notice the condition tied to being a co-heir: suffering with Christ. Many Christians want to run from the cost of being a Christian. If you run from the cost, you are not a co-heir.

This is another way of coming at the same point I made in chapter 4 about our inheritance in the kingdom. I won't repeat that here, but notice again that Paul is basing his argument on merit. So we know he's not talking about salvation.

If he were, then according to verse 17 you'd have to suffer with Christ to be saved. That would put a condition on salvation, like we saw above with peace-making or loving your enemies. Salvation is by grace through faith. So we can lay that aside as the focus here.

What Paul is saying is that suffering brings you co-heirship in order that you might be glorified or honored with Christ. Second Timothy 2:11–13 helps us here:

> It is a trustworthy statement: For if we died with Him, we shall also live with Him; If we endure, we shall also reign with Him; If we deny Him, He also will deny us; If we are faithless, He remains faithful; for He cannot deny Himself.

If you died with Christ, you are going to live with Him. But if you are a committed Christian ("endure"), you get to reign alongside of Him. There will be many living in heaven who won't be reigning in heaven. They will get the presence of Christ, but not the glory.

The second half of verse 12 is the key. If we live a denying kind of Christian life, He will deny us blessings in time. And He will deny us the privilege of reigning with Him in eternity.

Some people think this verse means that God will deny us entrance into heaven. That's impossible given what Paul says in verse 13. If we are truly saved, we cannot lose our salvation, because God is faithful to keep His word even if we break ours.

But He's not going to be a fool either. If you are truly saved but you live a denying kind of life, He's going to deny you in your prayer life. He's going to deny you of your blessings. He's going to deny you of your desires, and when you stand in heaven, He's going to deny you of the position He had planned for you. But He remains faithful to His promise. That is, nothing can separate us from the love of God which is in Christ Jesus.

These are the contrasts of fleshly living versus Spirit-directed living; six good reasons to keep the flame of our first love for Christ burning brightly. Now that you know, there's only one question on the floor: Which do you choose?

RETURNING TO YOUR FIRST LOVE

Our choices regarding the flesh and the Holy Spirit are crucial to the kind of Christian life we live. Here are some ideas to help you choose wisely when faced with the contrasting choices of flesh and Spirit:

1. A good question to ask yourself is, "Am I feeding the Spirit in my life?" One way you can tell is to see what happens when you read your Bible, pray, or get in a conversation where the subject is spiritual things. Do these things feel strange to you? Are you comfortable or awkward in the Word, in God's presence, and among His people? Face those questions honestly, and you'll have a large part of your answer—and maybe a place to start turning things around.

2. It's important to have someone in your life who has your permission to say "You shouldn't be eating that" when you try to feed your flesh. If you don't have at least one other person—spouse, friend, coworker, fellow church member—to whom you are spiritually accountable, ask God to give you that person. None of us was ever meant to go it alone.

3. To help you remember and act on your new identity in Christ, memorize Galatians 5:24. Write it out and carry it with you so you can pull it out and work on memorizing it during those short "down" times we all have each day.

4. If you want to get a one-person praise service started, go back through this chapter and note once again the positive, Holy Spirit side of each of these six contrasts. You'll see what a wealthy person God has made you to be spiritually, and you'll have reason to praise Him.

CHAPTER SIX

TRYING TO GO BACK

Sometimes Christians consider throwing in the towel, turning around, and going back the way they came.

I think we would all agree that this is not desirable. But is it even possible for a Christian to do this? If it is, we're in trouble. That would mean a Christian could be lost.

But if it is not possible to turn back and be lost, then we had better put our finger on another love-stealer that could cause a child of God to consider leaving his first love.

To unravel this issue and get some answers, we need to turn to Hebrews 6. The recipients of this letter were considering turning away from Christ, their first love, and going back to Judaism because they found it much too tough to follow Christ. I guess they didn't know, to paraphrase my friend James Dobson, that sometimes love must be tough.

These Christians had lost the spark of their first love and gotten scared and confused. They were like a team that has suddenly forgotten all the plays the coach diagrammed in the locker room. So the author of Hebrews does what any good coach would do if he saw his team floundering. He calls a timeout.

A timeout gives a coach a chance to talk to his team and motivate them to get back out there on the court or field and do what they are supposed to be doing. So in Hebrews 6 the author says, "Timeout! What do you guys think you're doing? You're not following the playbook of God's Word."

He ended chapter 5 by telling the Hebrews that they were baby Christians who should be much further along in the faith than they were. They were struggling with things they should have gotten over a long time before. They still needed milk and not solid spiritual food (5:13).

So the contrast here is between spiritual maturity and immaturity (5:14). This understanding sets chapter 6 in its proper frame of reference, and I think it clarifies an interesting passage of Scripture.

CHRISTIANS WHO STAGNATE

When we come to Hebrews 6, we find the author drawing implications from what he said in chapter 5:

> Therefore leaving the elementary teaching about the Christ, let us press on to maturity, not laying again a foundation of repentance from dead works and of faith toward God, of instruction about washings, and laying on of hands, and the resurrection of the dead, and eternal judgment. (vv. 1–2)

He is saying, "These are the basic things that should have been taken care of early on in your Christian lives. What you must do now is press on, go forward, develop, move ahead. Stop being stagnant."

Pressing and Permitting

Many of us are not experiencing God's presence, power, and privileges because we have become stagnant.

Now, stagnation in the spiritual realm means more than just standing still. It means you are actually losing ground, going backward.

Since verse 1 talks about "elementary teaching," let's use a school illustration. Let's say you stagnate in the fifth grade. You never move on. The mere fact that you stay put means you're losing ground, because the rest of your class keeps getting further ahead of you. You are failing to keep up.

You can't put your spiritual life on hold. You can't tread water, because to do that you have to use the energy you should be using to propel you forward. Ultimately, you will tire out and go under. When Christians try to hold on to what they've got, they go nowhere. The Bible has a better idea: "let us press on" in our spiritual pilgrimage.

Notice the dynamic tension introduced in verse 3, where the writer says, "And this we shall do, if God permits." This actually is the key to the passage, because he suggests the possibility that God may *not* always permit us to go forward. Why does he say this?

There are two things that must always be at work if you and I are to move forward in our spiritual lives. We must do the pressing, and God must do the permitting. The divine and human elements must work in tandem in spiritual growth. We must press. God must permit.

If God doesn't permit, it doesn't matter how much you press. And if you don't press, God won't permit. Let me give another passage that brings these two things together, and then show what I think the writer means by these statements which are set in dynamic tension: "Work out your salvation with fear and trembling; for it is God who is at work in you, both to will and to work for His good pleasure" (Philippians 2:12–13).

Here's an Evans paraphrase of what Paul and the writer of Hebrews are saying: "God is not going to levitate your Bible off the shelf, open it for you, and let the Holy Spirit take a pencil and underline the verses you should read today.

"You've got to pick up your Bible. You've got to open up your eyes. You've got to engage your mind. But when you press your Bible open, God will permit you to learn, to grow and understand.

"God is not going to levitate you off your bed and bend your legs at the knee, forcing you to kneel. He's not going to cup your hands together for you, make your head bow, force your eyelids shut, and force your mouth open so you can pray.

"You must press against your bed to get up, press your knee down to the floor, and press your mouth open to talk to God. But when you do that, God will permit you to hear from heaven."

In other words, no pressing on your part, no permitting on God's part. The two must operate simultaneously for spiritual growth to occur.

The Cost of Commitment

But the Hebrews were stuck in spiritual kindergarten, so to speak. As I suggested at the beginning of the chapter, they had found it difficult to be committed Christians. It was hard keeping the flame of their first love burning brightly.

The more committed to Christ you become, the more difficulties you are going to face. A lot of people lie about this. They say, "Come to Jesus and you won't have any more problems."

That's a lie. When you come to Jesus and grow in Jesus, you are going to see more mess break loose than you ever imagined. Why? Because you have become an enemy of hell, and hell wants to shut you down. Some things are going to show up that you never dreamt of when you become a committed Christian. And at times you will be tempted to say, "I don't want this. I want to go back!"

Someone will say, "Well, it doesn't sound like Jesus loves us very much if He lets hard things show up."

Sure He does. That's the way love works. It's like marriage. The more committed you become to being the right kind of husband or wife, the more you have to be willing to have your rough spots sanded smooth. That hurts, but the rewards of a deeper love, intimacy, and ful-fillment in marriage are worth it. Otherwise, your mar-riage stagnates and begins to move backward.

Imagine a college student saying, "I didn't know I had to study all this. Give me high school again!" Of course there's more work in college.

You don't learn your ABCs just so you can recite them. The idea is to put letters and words and phrases together so you can read. You press on with your learning, because a greater challenge awaits you.

CHRISTIANS WHO FALL AWAY

Beginning in verse 4 of Hebrews 6, we encounter three verses that have caused a lot of confusion and a lot of difficulty. In light of what he has just said about press-ing on, in verses 4–6 the writer is going to explain why believers must press on in their faith. So let us press on: "For in the case of those who have once been enlightened and have tasted of the heavenly gift and have been made partakers of the Holy Spirit . . ." (v. 4).

The problem comes right away because some people read this and say, "These cannot be saved people. This has to refer to people who have just come close to salvation, who have only nibbled at it."

I want to tell you, such an interpretation is impossi-ble. It's popular, but it's impossible. I can prove it's im-possible by applying the discipline of biblical theology, so please allow me to do a few paragraphs of theological analysis here. I'll keep it basic.

True Christians

Biblical theology requires that before you go to the rest of Scripture to collect data on a particular topic (which is the work of systematic theology), you first find out what the author means by studying his own writings. So if the author gives you the meaning of his own terms, that's the meaning you must adopt.

This is important, because when you apply biblical theology to this text it opens up. Take the term *enlight-ened*. In Hebrews 10:32 the author writes, "But remember the former days, when, after being enlightened, you endured a great conflict of sufferings."

We know he's talking about people who were enlightened to the point of salvation because they suffered for their faith. Unbelievers don't suffer for their faith. They don't have any faith to suffer for.

But these people had suffered for Christ, and had even shared in their suffering with other believers in Christ (v. 33). If you need more evidence, earlier in chapter 10 the author called his readers "sanctified" (v. 10). Then he said that those who are sanctified are "perfected for all time" (v. 14).

There's no doubt that when the author of Hebrews uses the word *enlightened*, he is saying they were enlightened to the point of salvation.

What about the term *tasted*? Some people say, "There you are. They didn't eat the heavenly gift, they just tasted it. They nibbled it, but they didn't actually consume it."

But that definition won't work, for Hebrews 2:9 says Jesus Christ "tasted" death for all of us. Did He only nibble at death, never actually dying? If this word means that Jesus only got in the vicinity of death and never really experienced it, we're in trouble!

If you say to someone, "Girl, you ought to have tasted that food," you don't mean you nibbled on it. You mean you overate. You got all you could possibly get of it. That's what the author means in Hebrews 6:4. These people received all of God's salvation.

When it comes to the term *partakers* at the end of verse 4, it's easy to lay to rest any idea that the author is talking about unbelievers, people who just see part of the light and nibble at the corners of salvation.

I say this first because the author uses the word in 2:14 to refer to children partaking of their parents' flesh and blood, and Christ becoming flesh to die for us. Do your kids share only part of your flesh and blood, or are they 100 percent yours? And does anyone want to argue that Christ wasn't fully human?

Then, five times in Hebrews we find this word used to talk about what these people became partakers of when they got saved. It's an impressive list: a heavenly calling (3:1), Christ (3:14), the Holy Spirit (6:4), God the Father's discipline (12:8), and His holiness (12:10). They were believers!

Verse 5 adds that they have "tasted the good word of God and the powers of the age to come." We already know what this author means by tasting, and Hebrews 2:4 says the power of the coming age is the Holy Spirit's authentication of the gospel in your life. Any way you look at it, it's impossible for these people to be unbelievers.

Loss of Salvation?

But verses 4 and 5 of Hebrews 6 really aren't the problem. Verse 6 is the real "sticky wicket" of this text. The author says if Christians who have enjoyed all these divine blessings fall away, or apostatize, "it is impossible to renew them again to repentance, since they again crucify to themselves the Son of God, and put Him to open shame."

We have already established that he's talking to Christians, trying to get them to press on. But now he brings up the real possibility of Christians falling away, of going backwards to the point of dropping out of the faith. That's exactly what he is warning these Hebrew Christians not to do.

The best way to begin is by seeing exactly what the author says and then stacking that up against what people say this verse means. For instance, the author is very clear that if this "falling away" ever happens to a Christian, it's impossible for that person to find repentance again.

Now you have probably been confronted by people who believe you are not forever secure in your salvation. This is one verse they point to as evidence that it's possible for Christians to lose their salvation.

But that argument does not hold water here, because this verse says that if you lose it, you can't ever get it back again. Now I assure you, people who believe you can lose your salvation also fervently believe you can get it back. So they can't use this verse to bolster their argument.

This is a place where systematic theology can help us. When you look at the totality of the New Testament's teaching, the conclusion you have to draw is that it's impossible to lose your salvation in the same way it's impossible to stop being your parents' child. You can't be unborn.

Besides, the Bible says that you don't hold God. God holds you (John 10:28–29). There's a big difference between a child holding her parent's hand and a parent holding her child's hand. In the latter case, even when the child lets go, she's still being held. Romans 8:38–39 says nothing can separate us from the love of God. So anyone who is truly saved is saved forever.

The Real Problem

So if you can't lose your salvation, what is going on in Hebrews 6:6? I believe the author is saying it is possible for Christians to go so far backward in their spiritual lives that they come to a point where they "re-crucify" Christ.

Now, no one can put Christ on the cross again. The key to understanding this is the last phrase of verse 6: "put Him to open shame." Let me explain what this means.

When Jesus Christ hung on the cross, there were only two basic ways of viewing His crucifixion. Some saw Him hanging there and said, "He's a blasphemer and a criminal being justly crucified."

But others saw Him and concluded with the Roman centurion, "Truly this man was the Son of God!" (Mark 15:39).

Those were the options—and still are. Jesus Christ was either a criminal or the Son of God. When you received Him as your Savior, you said, "This is the Son of God." But when you leave your first love and start moving backward, you are in effect re-crucifying Jesus Christ.

Why? Because by your lifestyle you are saying to the world, "World, I now agree with you that Jesus is a criminal. I agree with you that He ought to have been crucified. I agree with you that He has nothing to offer you and you don't need to put your faith in Him. I am now going to live the way you live, which will make you think the way you're living is OK."

Sounds serious, doesn't it? It is. When you stagnate and move backward in your Christian life, it can come to the point where it's like nailing Jesus to the cross again and sticking a spear in His side.

You see, He died to bring people out of their sin into righteousness. But now you leave your righteousness to go back with them in their sin. The result is that Jesus is made an open spectacle again, held up to open ridicule again, just like He was on the cross.

It will start off slow. You decrease your Bible reading and your prayer. You slack off on going to church. You start doing things you shouldn't—a little bit at first, in secret, so no one knows you are doing it but you. You haven't re-crucified Jesus yet because it hasn't come to open shame.

But you get used to sin and you get bolder in it. And then all of a sudden, you don't care anymore. So you start walking like sinners walk, talking like sinners talk, acting like sinners act, and people begin to take note.

Hebrews 6:6 says when people get to that point, "it is impossible to renew them again to repentance." Repentance means to change your mind. It is impossible to change their minds.

Here's where it gets confusing. The author is not saying it's impossible for God to renew such a person to repentance, because nothing is impossible for God. Besides, we've already established that the issue is not the loss of salvation, which would require God's intervention to restore.

Instead, the author is saying it's impossible for other people to renew this person to repentance. Have you ever known people who just wouldn't listen? You try to renew them to repentance. You try to help them see what is right and change their mind, but they just won't listen.

All you can say is, "Well, someone else is going to have to get you right. I'm through!" There comes a point where no human effort makes a difference. It becomes impossible to deal with someone because the world has a stranglehold on the person.

Let me illustrate this from Scripture. When Israel left Egypt in the Exodus, that was an Old Testament parallel to salvation. As redeemed people, the Israelites were to go to the promised land of Canaan—that is, their inheritance. To get there, they had to cross a territory called the wilderness. The wilderness was very inconvenient: little water, no meat, just corn flakes from above called manna.

So the people grumbled. "We're tired of this. Back in Egypt, it wasn't this bad. Back in Egypt, we had garlic and leeks. We had the stuff. We're tired of this!"

They grumbled all the way across the wilderness. But finally, they came to the border of the promised land and sent twelve spies in to check it out. Two spies, Joshua and Caleb, said, "Let's go in. God has given it to us. We can take it."

But the people sided with the ten spies who said, "The giants are too big!" They voted not to go in and rebelled against Moses (Numbers 14:1–4). (By the way, that's why you don't vote on the will of God. The will of God might lose.)

God looked at the mess and said to Moses, "I'm through with this people!" (see vv. 11–12). They had crossed the line. The land God had prepared for them was no longer going to be their experience. They would not get to enjoy their inheritance.

Now notice, the Israelites didn't drop dead when they crossed the line. They lived for years. We know that because God said they would stay in the wilderness for forty years until the last member of that generation died (vv. 33–35). Most of them lived, but they never got the blessing they were supposed to get.

These people lived out their lives never being able to experience why they were taken out of Egypt in the first place. They wandered around in a little circle. Did God forgive them? Absolutely (vv. 19–20). If He hadn't forgiven them, He would have destroyed them, as we saw in verses 11–12.

When they saw they were in big trouble, the people asked for forgiveness. They came to Moses and said, "We are going to obey God. We'll do what you say" (vv. 39–40). But it was too late to regain their inheritance. God had already sworn to take it away from them (vv. 22–23). They could not be renewed to repentance to the point where they could recapture God's blessing.

Forfeiting Plan A

Don't miss the point. When you re-crucify Christ and put Him to open shame, when God says, "You have crossed the line," it means you forfeited His "Plan A" for your life. How long you live after that is irrelevant.

A pastor who had been living a wicked life and got caught once came to see me. He was telling me how every day of his life was miserable because he knew where he should have been. He knew that God had called him and saved him to minister. But because of his open shame, he had to live out the rest of his life never getting to Plan A.

Someone will say, "You're being too harsh. What about God's grace and forgiveness?" Oh yes, the Israelites still experienced the grace of God in the wilderness. The Bible says that neither their shoes nor their clothes wore out. God still took care of them, but they never got what they were saved to get.

The worst curse is to die never having really lived; to have been given all the privileges of salvation and yet go to heaven (remember, we're talking about saved people) with regrets because you left your first love and crossed the line.

The way to die is like Paul died:

> The time of my departure has come. I have fought the good fight, I have finished the course, I have kept the faith; in the future there is laid up for me the crown of righteousness. (2 Timothy 4:6–8)

All of us as Christians should be ready to go if God called us home today. We should be able to say, "Lord, if it's Your time, it's my time. I can't wait for You to come get me."

CHRISTIANS WHO UNDERGO DISCIPLINE

In light of the seriousness of "falling away," becoming spiritually stagnant, the next two verses of Hebrews 6 should not surprise us:

> For ground that drinks the rain which often falls upon it and brings forth vegetation useful to those for whose sake it is also tilled, receives a blessing from God; but if it yields thorns and thistles, it is worthless and close to being cursed, and it ends up being burned. (verses 7–8)

What's not surprising is that believers who persist in living like they never knew Christ risk the judgment of God (v. 8). This is a very clear and simple illustration that makes the point I've been trying to make for the last few pages. If you get this, you get the message.

Drinking the Rain

The ground here is the life of a believer. It drinks rain. What rain? The heavenly bestowal from God, salvation and all the blessings that go with it. People who say this is not talking about saved people don't know what to do with this because the ground absorbs the rain. The rain doesn't just stop close to the ground, it enters the ground.

But notice that the same ground may produce either vegetation or thorns and thistles. Since it's the same piece of ground, he must be talking about a Christian who has the potential either of being fruitful or being a wasteland. In the language of Hebrews 6, this would be the difference between a Christian who presses on and one who stagnates.

The results of these two ways of living are radically different. If your life produces fruit—that is, stuff that is usable and beneficial because it comes from the life of one who is growing in faith—you will receive a blessing from God. You are going to see God's hand on your life. That doesn't mean you won't have problems. There are always problems in the wilderness. But in spite of the problems, you are going to see the hand of God moving you along.

A Worthless Life

If, on the other hand, your Christian life produces only thorns and thistles, the text says it is worthless. Now I would never say that. That's strong. But the Bible says it.

What do worthless Christians look like? Please understand that the writer is not saying God no longer values these people, no longer loves them or cares about them. They are worthless in the sense that God can't use them for anything good in the same way that a farmer can't use a field full of thorns and thistles.

This goes back to the fact that it's impossible to renew someone to repentance when they cross the line and God says, "That's it." If a piece of ground insists on being a thorn field instead of a cornfield, it has no benefit. You might as well burn it. At least that way you'll kill the thorns.

Some people say, "You see, this can't be talking about a Christian, because it says a person like this is put in the fire. And Christians don't go to hell."

That's right. Christians don't go to hell. But hell isn't the only kind of fire the Bible talks about. The Bible talks about Christians being judged by fire: "If any man's work is burned up, he shall suffer loss; but he himself shall be saved, yet so as through fire" (1 Corinthians 3:15).

Paul is talking about Christians who get into heaven by the skin of their teeth. They made it, but nothing they did made it with them. All that their lives produced were thorns. They have nothing to show for their lives, for they produced no vegetation.

The writer of Hebrews is concerned that Christians be fruitful so they won't undergo judgment by fire, so they won't be cursed.

There are two curses: a curse in time, and a curse in eternity. Cursing in time is when God resists you and allows nothing to go right with you: no answered prayers, no blessings, nothing. Cursing in eternity is the loss of rewards. It's the idea we talked about earlier where you get into the kingdom, but you don't inherit the kingdom. You stand outside looking at the kingdom banquet, but you aren't invited to be a participant.

There are different levels of reward in heaven. Everyone is not equal. Everyone doesn't have the same privileges, the same joy. The Bible talks about tears at the judgment seat of Christ. We need to come to grips with this, because some Christians have the attitude, "Well, it doesn't matter just as long I make it."

Well, if you are a true Christian and you are living a stagnant, backsliding life, you may wind up in heaven sooner than you think, because God takes seriously this thing of salvation and sanctification. I'm not saying you don't struggle. I'm not saying you don't ever have times when you fall. We all do. My point is that if we just let things go on without pressing on, it's going to become harder to get out of the problem.

It's like the frog in the pot we hear so much about. He's sitting comfortably in the water, and if the water is brought to a boil slowly enough, he doesn't notice until it's too late.

CHRISTIANS WHO RECEIVE GREAT REWARD

Aren't you glad Hebrews 6 doesn't end with burning and a curse? Let's look at verses 9–12:

> But, beloved, we are convinced of better things concerning you, and things that accompany salvation, though we are speaking in this way. For God is not unjust so as to forget your work and the love which you have shown toward His name, in having ministered and in still ministering to the saints. And we desire that each one of you show the same diligence so as to realize the full assurance of hope until the end, that you may not be sluggish, but imitators of those who through faith and patience inherit the promises.

Who inherits the promises? Not just people who accept Christ, but people of "faith and patience," people who hang in there with Christ. None of us likes to see someone quit when the going gets tough. And sometimes the going gets tough for us as God's people. But He says to us, "Don't quit!"

By the way, that's why your involvement in the life of the church is critical. Remember I said earlier that because we are part of a larger body, there's more to this matter of being a Christian and serving Christ than just what we can get. According to verse 10, one of the things that determines whether you are an inheritor is whether you minister to other believers.

That's why the writer says over in 10:24–25 that we need to keep meeting together so we can keep each other from quitting. There have been times when I have wanted to quit my church. There have been times when I wanted to say "I just can't take this anymore" and turn in my resignation.

But I didn't, because people were there to encourage me. We all need encouragement, because there are times when we all feel like quitting, and quitters are not inheritors.

So if you want to press forward and get in on the good stuff, you can do it. God will permit you to press on. He won't press you forward. Love can't be forced. But He will permit you to grow if you want to grow.

By the same token, if you are stagnating and losing ground as a Christian, you need to turn around. God is not going to turn you around. But He will permit you to get it together if you will turn back to Him.

You may say, "I'm scared I may have already fallen away. I'm afraid it's too late for me to be anything but a thorn patch." Well, the very fact that you're worried is a sign you haven't done that. People who have crossed the line don't care.

We opened this chapter talking about the timeouts in sports. Most sports also have something called halftime— an extended break in the middle of the game so you can get yourself together. It's a period of grace. That's part of the beauty of halftime. The other beauty of halftime is that no matter how messed up you were in the first half, you have another half to play, another half to get it together.

For many of us, it's halftime. It's time to get it together.

RETURNING TO YOUR FIRST LOVE

I f the pump to a sparkling swimming pool gets turned off, the water stagnates. But you can bring it back by starting the flow again and introducing water-cleansing agents. Love is like that. Your love for Christ may be stagnating right now, but you can bring it back to its sparkling beauty. These ideas may help you to press on:

1. One way to stir up a love relationship that's become stagnant is to write your loved one a note expressing your love and appreciation, telling that person how much he or she means to you. If you've never done it before, try writing out a prayer of love and appreciation to Jesus Christ. Take some time with it; put some soul into it! Then read it back to Him as a sacrifice of love and praise.

2. A wonderful cleansing agent for a stagnant spiritual life is the blood of Christ. Ask the Holy Spirit to search your heart. Be ready to confess any sin He puts His finger on, claiming the promise of 1 John 1:9.

3. Try to get alone for a few hours and do a "fruit inspection." Recall times of special fruitfulness, joy, peace, or spiritual power. Then ask yourself two questions: (1) How far back did I have to go to recall such experiences; and (2) What has happened in the meantime to change things?

4. Read Hebrews 6:9–12 again. If the writer of Hebrews was pulling for his readers to come out on top, think how much more God is pulling for you to make it! He wants you to move out. Thank Him that you've got all the resources of heaven at your disposal every day to help you press on.

CHAPTER SEVEN

THE DANGER OF TOLERATING SIN

Any child can tell you hospitals are to help sick people get better. Therefore, the most important measure of a hospital is not its beauty, the friendliness of the staff, or its sophisticated equipment. The measure of a hospital is its ability to make hurting people better. If a hospital doesn't do that, everything else is a waste of time.

I don't know anyone who goes to a hospital for fun and games or to admire the architecture. Everyone I know who goes to a hospital has only one question: "Can you fix what's wrong?"

The church is God's spiritual hospital. It is called to open its doors to people who are sick with sin, addictions, burdens, and hurts. They are welcome to come into the church because it is God's hospital.

That means the pastors and other spiritual leaders God has appointed are physicians of the soul under the direction of the Great Physician. If a physician diagnoses disease in your body, if the tests show that you are suffering from a malignant tumor, don't get mad at the physician if he has to operate.

Some people who come to church don't want to be operated on. They want to hear the music come over the speakers. They want to hear the doctors talk about the situation, but they don't want to go into surgery.

In the first section of this book, I have tried to do some biblical diagnosis and surgery based on Jesus' diagnosis of the church at Ephesus in Revelation 2:4: "I have this against you, that you have left your first love."

Now I know that surgery is seldom pleasant. And, like any doctor, my goal is not to hurt, but to heal. So if the Holy Spirit has used my diagnosis to help you identify a problem area, I'm grateful for that, because my desire is to help God's people get better, not just feel better about their illness.

We must take seriously what Jesus says in Revelation 2. His warning in verse 5 about what would happen if the problem persisted, and His prescription of a remedy, mean that we as individual Christians and the church as a whole have a responsibility to deal with anything that causes us to leave our first love for the Lord. That's the simple thesis of this book.

Looking at the problem through our analogy of medicine, we can say that whatever eats away at our love for Christ is a malignancy that must be cut out. The worst thing you can do with patients who have a serious disease is tell them they're OK.

So in this chapter I want to diagnose and help cure another love-stealer, a malignancy that, left untreated, can damage not only individuals, but the life of a church. This is the malignancy of sin in the body of Christ that is tolerated, ignored, or excused by the church.

THE MALIGNANCY

Since we're talking about hospitals, doctors, and patients, let me show you the patient's chart, which reveals the disease he's suffering from and the prescribed cure:

It is actually reported that there is immorality among you, and immorality of such a kind as does not exist even among the Gentiles, that someone has his father's wife. (1 Corinthians 5:1)

The church at Corinth had a malignant tumor growing in its midst. Yet the people didn't recognize it because this church looked healthy on the outside. They had enjoyed some of the greatest preachers ever: Paul, Peter, and Apollos. The church was located in the great city of Corinth. But it was suffering from a deadly illness: a strain of immorality so virulent, so destructive, that even the pagans around them avoided it.

Worse yet, the church was ignoring what the spiritual X-rays showed. Its members weren't confronting and trying to eradicate the disease. The failure of the church to confront sin means it is failing to be the hospital God intended it to be.

The problem in the Corinthian church was truly shocking. A man was having an affair with a woman we assume was his stepmother, since Paul doesn't say she was the man's mother. Paul says, "Even the pagans don't approve of what you are allowing to go on in the name of Jesus Christ." The present tense shows that this affair was still ongoing when Paul wrote.

In other words, this man had developed a pattern of immoral living that scandalized the community. This reminds us of something we noted earlier: Christians have the capacity to act as bad as non-Christians, and sometimes worse. Though we name the name of Christ, because we still live in the flesh we have the same propensity toward sin as the unredeemed world.

How do I know this? Look ahead for a minute to verses 10–11 and you'll observe something interesting: The sins attributed to unbelievers in verse 10 are repeated in verse 11 where Paul refers to a "so-called brother."

In fact, Paul even tosses in two sins that aren't listed in verse 10: revilers and drunkards. The point is, being converted does not exempt us from sin, even the basest kind of sin.

If I am capable of falling into the same sins that a non-Christian commits, what's the difference between us? The difference is, I don't have to. The difference is, I have been given power within me to overcome the sin outside of me.

But we can't escape the fact that these two lists are basically the same. That's why Paul had to diagnose and remove the malignancy of immorality in the church at Corinth.

So spiritual malignancy can attack the family of God. That's not good news, but at least the church is equipped to deal with it because the church is a hospital.

With the diagnosis made, Paul is now going to don his surgical gloves and proceed to cut out the malignancy. This is where it gets painful, but as I said above, please don't get mad at me. Surgery is never very popular, but like Paul I'm not called to be popular. I'm called to be biblical.

THE CURE

In this chapter our focus is more directly on the church, because 1 Corinthians 5 gives us a very clear picture of the damaging effects that untreated, tolerated sin had on the whole church as well as on the violator.

A church as a body of people can lose its first love for Christ too. As a matter of fact, Jesus was addressing the church at Ephesus in Revelation 2, not just one person or a few people. The need for radical surgery in the Corinthian church is obvious from verse 2 of 1 Corinthians 5: "And you have become arrogant, and have not mourned instead, in order that the one who had done this deed might be removed from your midst."

Admitting the Problem

Paul says, "Instead of a weeping church, you are a proud church. You are going around bragging on your building, bragging on your preacher, bragging on your choir, bragging on your programs instead of mourning over your sins."

When you go to a hospital and find out you have cancer, anything else you can brag about doesn't matter. You don't want to brag about your bank account anymore. You don't want to brag about the neighborhood you live in anymore. You don't want to brag about the car you drive anymore. You don't want to brag about your looks anymore, because all of that is irrelevant now.

When you have cancer, there's only one issue on the floor, and that is, "Get this mess out of my body."

The fact that this scandal could go on as long as it had been going on shows that the Corinthian church was way off the mark. It wasn't a hospital. It was a country club.

Making the Diagnosis

That's what a lot of Christians want. They want country club Christianity. They want to be pampered and patted, but they don't want to undergo spiritual surgery. But if a church doesn't do spiritual surgery, it's not a church. So the first thing Paul says is, "Get rid of the tumor. Cut it out of your midst."

The Corinthians' pride had produced indifference to sin. Their desire for human recognition blinded them to sin. People may come through the church's doors with their sin. That much is fine. The church is a hospital.

But they should never come through our doors and be made to feel good about their sin. No doctor says to a patient who has a debilitating illness, "I want you to feel good about it. Don't let it get you down." Wait a minute. It's already got you down. That's why you are there.

One mark of a true church is that it does not cut corners with sin, especially with an ongoing problem. When you hear of a brother entrapped in a sin it ought to break your heart, not make you pick up the telephone. It ought to make you cry because part of the body has been contaminated. Paul continues:

> For I, on my part, though absent in body but present in spirit, have already judged him who has so committed this, as though I were present. In the name of our Lord Jesus, when

you are assembled, and I with you in spirit, with the power
of our Lord Jesus. . . . (1 Corinthians 5:3–4)

I want to stop here for now. Obviously, something
important is coming, and we'll get to that. What Paul is
saying is, "If you are a church, act like a church." Being a
church means acting on behalf of Christ, under His authority. That's what "in the name of our Lord Jesus"
means.

The church acts on behalf of Jesus Christ. We fulfill
God's demand. Because this man's sin had gone public,
his judgment needed to go public. Sin could not be overlooked.

This is where some people object. "Well, you know
we shouldn't judge." That's not what Paul said. He had
already judged the man (v. 3).

We need to get this straight because there is a lot of
misinformation floating around about Christians and
judging. Most people who throw out this objection are
thinking of Matthew 7:1–5 where Jesus said not to judge
so you won't be judged.

But Jesus wasn't forbidding Christians from ever
making a judgment about people. Most people never read
past verse 1 of Matthew 7. If you read on, Jesus clarifies
how and what we should judge. The problem is we usually judge the wrong stuff or we judge others while holding
on to our own sin.

For instance, you don't judge people's motives. Only
God can see the heart. You don't know what this man is
thinking. You don't know how that woman is feeling. But
we spend time talking about, "He thinks he's something!"

How do you know what he thinks? You have no knowledge of what a person is thinking or feeling. But there is
something you can judge. You can judge what a person
does.

Someone may be living an evil life and say, "Well,
my heart wasn't in it." Yes, but your feet were. Your eyes
were. Your hands were. I'm not judging what was in your
heart.

Someone may sin and say, "I didn't mean it." Yes, but you did it. Let's talk about what you did. I can judge that. Of course, I first have to take the "log" out of my eye before I can see the "splinter" in my brother's eye (Matthew 7:3–5). What that means is don't judge someone else for something you are doing, because the judgment you pass on them boomerangs on you.

Applying the Cure

So Christians cannot judge the intent of a person's heart. But we can judge actions. In fact, the church is commanded to deal with sin in its midst.

Here's another objection to the church undertaking spiritual surgery: "But what he does is his business."

We might as well get this one straight too. Ephesians 5:11 says we are to "expose" the works of darkness that would otherwise remain hidden. That means when a Christian sins, it's not just his business. It's *our* business.

Would you say to a loved one who has cancer, "Well, that's your business. It's up to you whether you want to go to the hospital or not"?

If someone is hit by a car, would you say to him while he's lying in the ditch, "This is your business. I don't want to interfere"?

That's not how families work. When one member of our family is in pain, all of us share the pain. That's how the church is supposed to work.

As I tell the people at my church in Dallas, if that's not what you want, then what you want is a club. You don't want a church, because when there is a malignancy in the family of God, it's the family's business to take care of it.

So it's crystal clear. The church is not just a building. The church is a family. And just as parents can't ignore children who are rebelling, so churches can't ignore members who are rebelling. That's as much a part of the church as the choir or the services or the programs or anything else.

So if we can brag on our church's programs and ministries, we ought to be able to brag also on the fact that we locate cancer quickly and deal with it. If we can't brag about our commitment to purity, then we have nothing to brag about.

If the church is not addressing the issue of sin, then we need to shut up about anything else we're doing because God has called us to be pure. No one in his right mind wants to go and be made well in a dirty hospital. The church is to be God's clean hospital in order to render surgery as needed.

THE RESULT OF A FAILURE TO TREAT

What happens when the church fails to render the treatment needed for open sin? Paul tells us in 1 Corinthians 5:5: "I have decided to deliver such a one to Satan for the destruction of his flesh, that his spirit may be saved in the day of the Lord Jesus."

If the offender at Corinth was a Christian, and Paul assumes he was, what does it mean to deliver him to Satan? It means he was excommunicated from the church, which is much more serious than simply pulling his membership card. It means that God was removing His protective custody from this man's life, which would open him up to destructive attacks from the enemy—even to the loss of his life if that's what it took.

The Necessity of Discipline

We don't take church discipline too seriously today. We say, "Well, if we put this person out, he'll just go to another church and join there." Well, he may go to another church, but he will go without God's protective custody. And you don't want to be sitting too near him because the roof may fall in!

I'll never forget the time my younger brother rebelled against my father. He didn't like my father's rules. He didn't like the instructions. Now, little brother was the Maryland state wrestling champion in the unlimited weight class. At 250 pounds, he was big and strong. But he brought that stuff home from school, talking about, "I'm the champ!"

My father said, "I'm the only champ in this house."

My father told my brother to do something. I don't remember what it was, but my brother didn't think he should have to do it. So he frowned, shook his head, and said, "No!"

Dad said, "Oh yes!"

Little brother said, "No!"

My father balled up his fist. Lord have mercy! He reached back and flattened brother, took him upstairs, and helped him pack his suitcase. My brother jumped bad and said, "Yeah, I'm leaving! I don't have to take this!"

And he walked out of the house. But he forgot a few things. He forgot he didn't have a job. He forgot it was snowing outside. He forgot he didn't have a car. He jumped bad, but he forgot that when you don't have anything, you don't jump bad.

So twenty minutes later . . . knock, knock! Brother was at the door wanting to come home. My father delivered him to the elements that he might be taught respect.

If I ever thought about jumping bad, it died that day! When he was put out, my brother was no longer under the protective custody of our home. He had to fend for himself.

Do you remember when Satan came after Job in chapter 1 of the book of Job? Satan said to God, "Let me have Job for a while and do this and that to him."

And God said, "You can do this and this to Job, but you can't do that." Because Job was under God's protection, Satan could only go so far with him.

If God removes His hedge of protection from around you, that means Satan can have his way with your life. Once God removes His hand from a Christian because the church has acted on His behalf by performing surgery, there is no more protection.

It's like a person being put out of a hospital because he won't submit to surgery. The cancer is going to metastasize now. There is nothing to stop it because he didn't allow the doctors to cut it out. I have been a witness to this discipline and judgment in the lives of willfully sinning Christians. I have watched people's lives deteriorate, and I have seen people die.

Yes, God will try to woo the sinning saint back. But if that fails, He will not stop Satan from having his way with him. And if the person keeps on sinning, he's headed for destruction.

This goes against our modern grain because our thing is, "Now, let's be patient and understanding. Why do we have to put him out? Why do we need to take action in her case?" Verse 6 explains why: "Your boasting is not good. Do you not know that a little leaven leavens the whole lump of dough?"

In other words, "One bad apple spoils the barrel." Paul is saying, "Cut the sinning part off, or it will rub off." Good apples don't make bad apples good. Bad apples make good apples bad. What happens when there's one rowdy kid in a class? He can so control the class that you can't teach. He gets the kids laughing or goofing around and he totally disrupts the class. If you want your class back, that kid must go.

If you have a rebellious teenager in your home who won't follow the rules; who is determined to stay out all night; who is going to take drugs; who is living in immorality; sooner or later, something's got to give. Because if this child keeps getting away with it, the other kids are going to get the idea, "Hey! This is really not that big a deal!"

The Effects of Sin

So it is with the family of God. "A little leaven leavens the whole lump." The effects of sin can damage others. Do you remember Achan? He rebelled against God's command, and Israel suffered defeat at Ai. Achan's sin cost other men their lives. Read about it in Joshua 7, and notice what happened to Achan (vv. 24–25). He didn't undergo counseling. He underwent stoning.

Since we're in the Old Testament, let me make another important point from the life of Jonah. Whenever you run from the will of God, you get to pick up the tab. Whenever you rebel against God and go the other way, you pay the freight.

Jonah, as you'll recall, was the rebellious prophet who took off toward Tarshish when God told him to go to Nineveh, which was in the opposite direction. Jonah "paid the fare" himself to go to Tarshish (Jonah 1:3). But the beautiful thing about going to Nineveh is that God would have paid the fare. The horrible thing about going to Tarshish is, you pick up the tab.

You know what? Many of us are paying a high price for our "Tarshish trip" when, if we had done things God's way, He would have picked up the tab. Many of us are paying high emotional, psychological, and physical tabs because we rebel against the will of God for our lives.

This is the part of church people don't want, but doctors are supposed to help you stay well. You have to follow their advice, however. If there's a problem, hospitals are designed to fix what's wrong. But you have to submit to the treatment.

That's why a part of every church service should be judging your sin. Paul tells us why later in 1 Corinthians: "If we judged ourselves rightly, we should not be judged" (11:31). That's the point. Come, gather with the Lord and judge yourself so that God, through the church, does not have to judge you.

If that's not what you want, then the church is not what you want. Why? Because this is the heart of what the church does. It maintains the purity of the people of God.

So when a brother puts his hand on my shoulder and says, "You ought not do that," I should be glad because it means someone loves me. You don't love me if you see me going in a ditch and you say, "Well, it's your business, but I'll pray for you." I don't want just your prayers. I want you to stop me if I'm going down the wrong road. That's family, that's church.

Early Detection

Just like in medicine, the key in spiritual diagnosis is early detection. That's why the Bible only gives so many steps before you deal with sin. You don't let it go month after month and year after year, because it spreads. So Paul goes on:

> Clean out the old leaven, that you may be a new lump, just
> as you are in fact unleavened. For Christ our Passover also
> has been sacrificed. Let us therefore celebrate the feast, not
> with old leaven, nor with the leaven of malice and wicked-
> ness, but with the unleavened bread of sincerity and truth.
> (1 Corinthians 5:7–8)

You probably know that leaven is yeast. Anyone who
bakes bread knows the importance of yeast. A little bit of
yeast can make a whole loaf rise. Here, leaven represents
sin.

When Israel was in Egypt, the Egyptians cooked with
leaven. God used that to teach Israel a very important
spiritual lesson. The Passover was when the death angel
passed over the houses of the Israelites who had put the
blood on their doorposts.

In preparation for Israel's departure from Egypt, God
told them to remove all leaven from their homes. Later,
they were instructed to follow the observance of Passover
with the Feast of Unleavened Bread. The leaven of Egypt
was no longer to be used by the children of Israel.

Why? They were leaving Egypt through the blood of
the Passover and moving to a new way of life. They were
not to bring that old mess with them. We are saved
through the blood of Christ, our Passover lamb, and we
should be living new lives too.

You know what the church is supposed to do? Confront a member who is using that old leaven again before
the leaven of sin gets mixed in with the new bread of his
Christian life.

Paul's command to "clean out the old leaven" reminds us that one person can stop God's blessing on the
whole congregation. When sin is known and goes unad-
dressed, it can stop God's blessing on everyone. No one
should have that much power. I don't want you stopping
my blessing, and I don't want to be stopping your blessing, so something's got to give.

We are unleavened people. When we received Christ,
the old life was removed from us. We became new creatures in Christ. What God wants us to do is live in light of

the new people we are rather than in light of the old people we used to be.

So if you know believers who are living in sinful rebellion, guess what? You are the doctor. Don't let that go without confronting them. If they don't want to hear it, that's not your fault. You can't do anything more, but you must not let another Christian get sick without confronting him about it.

The first thing a person with a malignancy wants to know after surgery is, "Did you get it all?" If the doctor didn't get it all, it's going to show up again. You can't half-step with sin. You've got to get it all.

If I see my child going down the tubes, I want to confront the whole mess, get it all out on the table, and deal with it all now. I don't want to get part of it, because what I leave will grow back. The job of the church is to call members to purity.

THE PLACE FOR SURGERY

So we have here a member of the church who needs to be put under severe discipline to correct blatant, ongoing sin. Now Paul makes an important distinction between the church as the place of discipline and the world outside the church:

> I wrote you in my letter not to associate with immoral people; I did not at all mean with the immoral people of this world, or with the covetous and swindlers, or with idolaters; for then you would have to go out of the world. But actually, I wrote to you not to associate with any so-called brother if he should be an immoral person, or covetous, or an idolater, or a reviler, or a drunkard, or a swindler—not even to eat with such a one. (1 Corinthians 5:9–11)

Please notice the difference. You can't help associating with sinners, Paul says, because the planet is covered with them. Besides, there's no issue of discipline here, because sinners do just what you'd expect sinners to do. They sin.

In other words, sinners aren't guilty of leaving Christ as their first love since they didn't ever love Him in the first place. So you aren't forbidden to associate with these people. You still have to work and live next to them. Sinners will be sinners.

No Fellowship

But it's a whole different ballgame if we're talking about a "so-called brother." The word *associate* means "to keep intimate company with." It doesn't mean you don't speak. It doesn't mean you become cruel and hard. But it means there is no intimate fellowship with this person.

This is a "so-called" brother, because a person living in sin may or may not be a Christian. You can't judge the heart, but you can say, "If you are a Christian, you are not supposed to be acting like this. And if you persist in acting like this, the rest of the church cannot have fellowship with you."

The Corinthian church had this backward. They were associating with the sinning member, even bragging about their openness, and not associating with the world. Now, lest someone think Paul was singling out the sin of immorality for excommunication, he lays that charge to rest in these verses.

Look at the list in verse 11. Paul's not picking on immorality. You also get judged if you are covetous, lusting for stuff that doesn't belong to you. You get judged if you are an idolater, worshiping another god. You get judged if you are a reviler, a violent person. You get judged if you are a drunkard. You get judged if you are a swindler, a cheat in business.

We had to remove a man from our church fellowship some years ago who was guilty of terrible business practices. We've already seen that excommunication is a very serious step. But according to the end of verse 11, it goes even further than putting the offender out of the church.

You can't have breakfast, lunch, or dinner with that person. In other words, no social intercourse or fellowship. There can be no intimacy when a man who is a "so-called brother" is living in rebellion toward your heavenly Father. Just like I didn't go to my brother when he was showing disrespect to our father, slap him on the back, and tell him I was on his side, that he was all right, and that Dad sure was being cruel to put him out.

The Goal of Discipline

Why is God being so radical? To call the sinning brother or sister to his or her senses. He's not doing it to be hard. He's doing it to be loving, and to protect the rest of the family.

You don't go to dinner with someone living in rebellion unless the purpose for the dinner is to help the person take steps toward repentance. Understand, this is not the person trying to get help. This is not the person who says, "I'm a drunkard, but I want to get over my drunkenness." Paul is talking about a believer who has adopted sin as an acceptable lifestyle.

You say, "That's hard."

No, that's God's house. See, if you come to my house there are some things you can't do. If you smoke, you'll have to put it out before you come into my house. If you drink, leave it outside. You can't use profanity. If you and your girlfriend spend the night, you will do so in separate rooms, because in my house, unmarried people don't sleep in the same bedroom.

Now you might argue, "I don't like your rules."

Then don't come to my house. I mean, it boils down to that. In my house I have my rules, just like in your house you have your rules.

The church is the Father's house, so when we come into His house He says, "Leave that leaven outside. Leave that worldliness outside. Don't bring that into My house. Don't corrupt my family with sin."

The church is God's house, and it is the job of the temporal head of the house, the pastor and the church leadership, to render judgment about the rules of God's house. If you have a problem, we will help you. If you are sick, we will give you medicine. We can do surgery, but only if you want help.

I have challenged my church people in Dallas to help us keep a clean hospital—not by keeping spiritually sick people out, but by refusing to let them stay sick when they come in. If we ignore sin in our midst, the entire church will eventually be led away from the purity of our first love for Christ.

I can't imagine anything worse than for Jesus Christ to say to Oak Cliff Bible Fellowship Church, "You have left your first love. I'm going to have to remove your lampstand." If that happened, if our church lost its testimony, a whole lot of good people would be hurt. We can't afford to let that happen.

Several years ago, my family and I had a scare. I had a growth on my body that my doctor thought was cancer. He told me and my wife, "We need to operate very quickly."

As I lay in bed the night before the operation, I can assure you I wasn't thinking, "I hate for them to cut on me. I'll have a scar. It will hurt. I'll be sore for a week." No! I thought I might have cancer. I couldn't wait for the doctor to perform surgery.

They cut out the lump. I opened my eyes in recovery and said, "What's the verdict, Doc?"

"I've got good news for you. Your lump was benign, but it's good we took it out when we did, because they have been known to become malignant."

Do you know what? That doctor did me a favor that day. If he had played around and said, "I got lumps. You got lumps. All God's children got lumps," I could be in trouble today. But even if a lump is malignant and has spread, chemotherapy and radiation can address it so that it regresses.

You may not be able to get rid of your alcoholic urging all at one time. But the church can help to "chemo" it back. You may not be able to cut out the malignancy of your temper all at once, but we can radiate it back. You may not be able to eradicate all your immoral passions with one treatment, but for your sake, the sake of the rest of the body of Christ, and for His sake, let us put the medication to it!

RETURNING TO YOUR FIRST LOVE

One growing trend in health care is home-based treatment. Hospitals have people who can care for you at home, or show you how to care for yourself, and keep you from having to go to the hospital for more serious treatment. Here are some "remedies" you can take at home to help you treat sin or keep yourself healthy:

1. No one said it would be easy to confront a brother or sister living in sin. But it is crucial. If you know someone who is making Jesus Christ look bad and risking God's judgment, pray for the courage and opportunity to confront the problem. If a third party is close enough to the offender to help, you might consider taking along a brother or sister.

2. Think of the people you associate with. Are they better off spiritually because of your influence on them, or are you worse off spiritually because of their influence on you?

3. Is there a habit, thought pattern, or attitude in your life that you would be touchy about if someone tried to bring it to your attention? This one will require some thought, but here's a clue that may help you know if you are harboring something that could turn malignant. Are you defensive or nonchalant about it when the Holy Spirit brings it to your mind?

4. If a doctor saved you from possible cancer by skillful surgery, you would express your thanks! When was the last time you wrote your pastor a note of thanks and encouragement for his ministry? Do it next chance you get. Here's one pastor who's always glad to get one!

CHAPTER EIGHT

THE HIGH COST OF LEAVING, 1

How serious is your love?

That may seem like an unusual question, but it really isn't. When you love people, you take what they do very seriously. And when someone you love is hurting himself, you, and the people around him, you don't look the other way if your love is serious.

You don't let the bad behavior of a family member continue unchecked month after month. And if it goes far enough, you may have to cut off that person's benefits and put him out of the house because he is misusing his privileges badly and bringing shame on the family.

Sometimes you hear people say, "Oh, I love my son (daughter, friend, etc.) far too much to do anything like that." There's a two-word phrase for that kind of love: phony baloney.

God is very serious about His love for us and our love for Him. Jesus had a list of commendations for the church at Ephesus in Revelation 2, but none of it mattered because their love for Him had grown cold. So Jesus said, "Since you're cold toward Me, I'm going to snuff out your lamp because you aren't using the warmth of the flame."

I hope I've made the point by now that if our "first love" for Christ isn't truly first in our lives, we need to do whatever it takes to return it to its proper place.

That isn't my idea. Jesus said to remember, repent, and redo (Revelation 2:5)—the steps of returning to your first love, which we'll deal with beginning in chapter 10.

But before we close this first section, I want to take this chapter and chapter 9 to consider both sides of a very important coin: the earthly and eternal consequences for Christians who leave their first love and don't turn around; who don't get off at the next exit, cross over the overpass, and head the other way on the freeway; who refuse to put God back in His rightful place.

We've touched on this several times so far, but I want to deal with the subject in depth, for three reasons. First, the Bible has a lot to say about judgment for Christians. Second, I wouldn't be fair to you if I didn't give you the whole story. Third, I want to help you turn around before you hit the wall.

My point in this and the next chapter is simply this: the Christian whose first love is cold, who persists in living a self-centered, carnal life rather than a Christ-centered life, risks severe loss both in time and in eternity.

Now let me say it once more just in case you've forgotten. We're not dealing with loss of salvation here. For Christians, that is a settled issue. Nothing can separate us from the love of God in Christ Jesus. We're dealing with loss of God's blessing on earth and loss of reward in heaven. This chapter deals with earth. In chapter 9 we'll talk about heaven. So let's look at the earthly consequences of persistent carnality.

DIVINE DISCIPLINE

We see this consequence or result very clearly in Hebrews 12:5–6:

You have forgotten the exhortation which is addressed to you as sons, "My son, do not regard lightly the discipline of the Lord, nor faint when you are reproved by Him; for those whom the Lord loves He disciplines, and He scourges every son whom He receives."

Notice that in order to qualify for discipline, you must first be a child of God. That just reinforces the point that salvation is not the issue. The writer of Hebrews, who has become a familiar friend to us by now, says in effect, "If God loves you, God will spank you."

Discipline Demonstrates Love

Just as when our children rebel, when we rebel against God we discover that His definition of love includes discipline. As we said above, love is concerned about correcting wrongs and turning them into rights. In fact, the writer says in verse 7: "It is for discipline that you endure; God deals with you as with sons; for what son is there whom his father does not discipline?"

Since fathers are responsible for discipline in the home, the writer compares the heavenly Father to an earthly father. He is asking, "What kind of father are you if you do not discipline your children? If you say you love them too much to spank them, you really hate them. If you say you love them too much to restrict them, you are derelict in your duty as a father."

Since this is true, what kind of Father would God be if He let you keep getting away with your rebellion? What kind of Dad would He be if He just stood by and watched you careen down the wrong road until you hit the wall? When I was growing up, my parents would say, "Keep on. Just keep on." They were letting me know that discipline was not far away. If you are living in carnality, in persistent rebellion against God, He wants you to know that discipline is not far away. He's going to spank you. But He's going to spank you because He loves you.

In fact, if God does not spank you, if you go year in and year out without being disciplined by Him, you've got an entirely different problem. Look at verse 8: "But if you are without discipline, of which all have become partakers, then you are illegitimate children and not sons."

In other words, your problem isn't that you need discipline. Your problem is you need to get saved. If God does not spank you, it's because you are not one of His kids. You belong to another family—the family of Satan—and He's going to discipline you in eternity. That's when you get your spanking.

When I see neighborhood kids doing bad things, I don't spank them because I'm not responsible for them. I may say something to them, but I don't spank them because they are not my children. But my kids are a different story.

If my kids were to say to me, "Hey, the neighborhood kids' parents don't spank them," my answer would be, "Well, when you start living with them, you won't get spanked either. But as long as you are here, the fact of your sonship or daughtership means that discipline is absolutely necessary."

Discipline Engenders Respect

According to verse 9, discipline engenders respect. There is a direct correlation between the two. If you don't discipline, you won't engender respect. People who are disrespectful are undisciplined. They weren't disciplined at home, and you see the result in society in the way young people talk to older people. These young people were never corrected.

Have you ever seen a wild kid and said to yourself, "That boy needs a good spanking"? What you are saying is this boy is not being corrected properly. Your deduction is probably correct, because there's a cause/effect link between discipline and living.

If your father disciplined you as a child at home, that may keep you from being disciplined later by the police. I have never been locked up. A lot of my friends have been locked up. But I never have been, because I learned early that I didn't like being spanked.

I had all the spankings I wanted growing up. My father wore me out. He had a barber's leather strap. When Dad spanked me, I was sure I could feel a razor blade still implanted somewhere in that strap! But because my father spanked me then, I've not had to be spanked by any police officer or judge.

Discipline Corrects Rebellion

Given our subject, I want to note the difference between the discipline all Christians undergo simply because we are in the family and the much more severe discipline required to correct rebellion—even to the loss of life if necessary, as we'll see.

Notice that all Christians get corrected. Remember, we've been saying all along that all believers sin. We all blow it. But our concern is a persistent pattern of rebellious living, a deliberate choice to abandon our first love to chase after someone or something else.

You might ask, "How can I tell the difference? How long will God have to spank me?" Well, the Bible doesn't say in precise terms, and I think I know why.

If God said, "Two licks for lying," some people would say, "Shoot, I can handle two licks," and they'd go ahead and lie. If He said, "Ten licks for adultery," there would be those who would figure it was worth the pain. So they'd lie or commit adultery, take their licks, and go on their way no better off.

I learned this lesson in discipline from my father. When it was time for a spanking I would always ask my dad, "How many licks am I going to get?"

He would always answer, "I don't know. We'll see."

My father was saying, "Son, I want you to get the message I'm trying to convey through this discipline. I want you to be an obedient son by the time we're through with this. So I'm going to spank you until I see you got the message." Depending on the hardness or softness of my heart at that particular time, it could be one lick or ten.

Every parent has seen this difference in their children. Most of us have two kinds of children when it comes to discipline. There's the kid who crumbles in contrition at the first word of rebuke and corrects the problem.

The other kid stands up after a spanking, looks you in the eye, and says, "That didn't even hurt." Obviously, Junior didn't get the message. So you have to try again to keep from disappointing your offspring!

The idea is that you spank until the person gets the message. You spank until it becomes absolutely clear to the recipient that he doesn't ever want to do this again. This is a pretty fine line, and since parenting is not a precise science, parents don't always get it right.

Hebrews 12:9–10 remind us of the fact that earthly parents don't always discipline perfectly. Your sister did it, but you got it because your dad didn't see who did it and your sister lied about who did it. So your dad did what "seemed best" to him (v. 10a).

You don't have this problem with God. He disciplines us perfectly. He doesn't make mistakes, because He doesn't mess up on who did it. God is never caught by surprise. He knows why you did it, when you did it, whether you thought about doing it first, and whether you are thinking about doing it again.

I remember one day our family went to the beach. I don't remember what it was, but we had brought some important household item with us. I broke it. I was just throwing it up in the air, and I threw it out too far and it cracked. A few minutes later, my father picked it up and asked a very simple question. "Did you crack this?"

Well, I had looked around before this and as far as I was concerned, no one saw me throw it. So I said, "Oh Daddy, I don't know who threw that. Oh, look at that! That's terrible!"

Dad wasn't buying it. Lord have mercy! He took me over to some bushes and wore me out. He said, "Boy, don't you ever lie to me again."

I may do a lot of things, but I am very sensitive about lying, because he disciplined me and I never forgot that. There must be consequences for sin if we are going to be holy and be what God wants us to be.

JOYFUL OR PAINFUL?

Verse 11 says, "All discipline for the moment seems not to be joyful, but sorrowful." God is honest. If you are living in carnality, He is going to discipline you and it will hurt. His discipline comes in an array of forms. It could be physical. The Bible says sometimes God sends sickness. It could be mental distress, a financial setback, or any number of things.

You say, "But don't these things also happen to Christians who are in God's will but undergoing testing of their faith?" Yes, but there's one very important difference. You can see it when you put verse 11 together with James 1:2.

The difference between a Christian in the will of God going through trials, and a Christian out of the will of God going through discipline, is this. If you are undergoing trials sent by God to strengthen your faith, James 1:2 says you can "consider it all joy." That is, even in the midst of the pain, God will give you His joy.

But if you are undergoing the severe discipline of one who is heading down the wrong road and is about to hit the wall, you will have no joy in the midst of your problems. You will have only sorrow. Is there joy or sorrow in the situation? That tells you whether it's a trial or a punishment.

Now, I realize there's a third category of trials, which is simply the stuff that comes our way regularly as a result of living as imperfect people in an imperfect world. But the test still holds. Is there joy in your situation or sorrow? That can tell you how healthy your relationship with God is.

But notice that even in the case of severe discipline, if we get the message, if we allow it to train us properly (Hebrews 12:11), afterward we can be at peace again because we are back on track with the Lord. It's like a father who puts his arm around his crying child after disciplining him and says, "I just want you to know I love you." The child can be at peace even in his tears because he has the assurance of his father's love.

The story is told of a little boy who was floating his boat on a pond when the boat floated away. A man came by, saw the boat out on the pond, and began throwing stones on the far side of the boat. The boy asked, "What are you doing?"

But then something very interesting happened. As the stones hit the water beyond the boat, they created ripples which pushed the boat back toward the boy. Even though the stones disturbed the smooth water, they achieved the desired result.

That's how God's discipline is. When we drift away from Him on the "Sea of Sin" or the "Pond of Unrighteousness," He throws the disturbing stones of His loving discipline out beyond us in order to push us back to the shore of our first love.

UNANSWERED PRAYER

Another earthly consequence of leaving our first love and chasing after something else is unanswered prayer. Let's look at James 1:5 to set the stage: "If any of you lacks wisdom, let him ask of God, who gives to all men generously and without reproach, and it will be given to him."

If you are going through a God-ordained trial, not only can you have joy despite the pain, you can also call on God for His wisdom in handling the situation.

This is one of the great promises of the Bible. God says He won't hold out on you, and He won't scold or belittle you for asking. But then James gives a corrective for those who are not approaching this thing right:

> But let him ask in faith without any doubting, for the one who doubts is like the surf of the sea driven and tossed by the wind. For let not that man expect that he will receive anything from the Lord. (James 1:6–7)

A Double Mind

If you come to God not in faith, but as one who is doubtful and "double-minded," you will go away empty. This is referring to a pattern of life because this person is "unstable in all his ways."

Have you ever known double-minded people? They say yes one minute and no the next. They don't know which way they're going to go.

Now here's what it means to pray in faith. It means to come to God knowing that whatever He reveals to you, you are going to do it. God will not answer the prayers of Christians who don't know if they are going to do what He says once He says it. That's why you must be willing to say to God, "Not my will, but Yours be done."

Here's why it's important. If God knows you are going to debate about doing His will, guess what? He's not even going to tell you what it is so you can debate it. The reason is, God's not into suggestions. He's only into commandments.

God is not going to give you a suggestion to think about. He's not going to give you a revelation for you to consider. He's going to tell you what to do because He knows you are going to obey. Otherwise, you receive nothing from Him.

So the result, the consequence, of living in carnality is that none of your prayers get answered. God is not going to compromise with our double-mindedness.

Imagine a couple who comes to me for counseling and the husband says, "Look, I'm not sure whether I want my wife or this other woman. I love them both. But until I decide, I want my wife to stick with me.

"I want her to keep cooking and cleaning for me. I want her to be understanding. I want her to serve me and be faithful to me while I decide whether I want her or this other woman. My wife has some good qualities and meets my needs. But so does this other woman. So I want my wife to keep being the wonderful wife she is while I decide whether I want her or the other one."

Now if that crazy man is in *my* office, I'm going to tell him, "You'd better make up your mind before you leave this room, lest when you get home tomorrow night all her clothes and the furniture be gone and you start paying up!"

Clear Your Mind

You cannot function in a relationship if you are double-minded. Sometimes people say, "I don't know what I want to do." That's the wrong answer. It may be a truthful answer. You may not know what you want to do, but it's still the wrong answer.

See, if all you can think about is what *you* want to do, you'll be confused forever. The question is, what does *God* want you to do? For this husband, there should be no debate, because God says, "You must be faithful to the one you committed yourself to." God isn't double-minded about stuff like this.

When you get into head games like, "Well, I think," "I wonder," "I'm considering," or "I'm not sure," you can solve all of that in a day. Clear your mind by clearing your feet. That is, get your feet to follow God and your mind will cease being double and start being single.

Obedience precedes emotion and desire. When you obey, then you get to feeling right about what God tells you to do. That's how it flows. If you don't get into this flow, God will not answer your prayers. Friendship with the world makes you an enemy of God, who resists the proud but gives grace to the humble. You need to submit yourself to God (see James 4:4–7). If you have left your first love, forget praying because God has no obligation to you at all.

LOSS OF ASSURANCE

A third consequence of failing to return to your first love is that you lose the assurance of your salvation.

This may be why some people believe you lose your salvation when you backslide. In 2 Peter 1:9, the apostle does say you can lose the *assurance* of your salvation, which would make you feel unsaved. But there's still a huge difference between those two positions.

Second Peter 1:4 makes clear that Peter is writing to Christians. In verses 5–7 Peter goes through a list of spiritual traits that must be developed in order for us to grow and experience God's work and power in our lives. Then he writes:

> For if these qualities are yours and are increasing, they render you neither useless nor unfruitful in the true knowledge of our Lord Jesus Christ. For he who lacks these qualities is

blind or short-sighted, having forgotten his purification from his former sins. (2 Peter 1:8–9)

SPIRITUAL AMNESIA

The Christian who is not growing and experiencing God's power has forgotten he's saved. Some Christians have been in the world so long they have forgotten they are born again. They have hung out with the unrighteous for so long they have taken on their lifestyle. So what happens?

They lose the certainty of their calling (v. 10). They aren't sure whether they belong to God. They are not sure of their election—that God has selected them. And they live in spiritual defeat.

Lacking the qualities Peter outlines, not growing and maturing, leaves a Christian vulnerable to all kinds of doubts. People in this condition are not confident because God isn't doing anything in their lives. They have lost the comfort, the joy, and the peace that go with certainty of the knowledge of salvation. The remedy is to get back on track: "Therefore, brethren, be all the more diligent to make certain about His calling and choosing you; for as long as you practice these things, you will never stumble" (v. 10).

PHYSICAL DEATH

This is the most serious consequence of all, at least from the perspective of earth. In 1 Corinthians 10:1b–5, Paul is drawing a parallel between disobedient Israel in the wilderness and disobedient believers in Corinth:

> Our fathers were all under the cloud, and all passed through the sea; and all were baptized into Moses in the cloud and in the sea; and all ate the same spiritual food; and all drank the same spiritual drink, for they were drinking from a spiritual rock which followed them; and the rock was Christ. Nevertheless, with most of them God was not well-pleased; for they were laid low in the wilderness.

Now, we know Israel was God's people. They had observed the Passover, which was an act of faith, and had come out of Egypt, a picture of salvation.

Paul says all the Israelites also enjoyed all the benefits of God's provision. They were under the cloud; they had God's guidance. They passed through the sea; they had God's deliverance. They were baptized into Moses; they had God's leader. They ate and drank spiritual food, a picture of Christ; they had God's provision.

Crossing the Line

But as we saw in an earlier chapter, every adult Israelite who came out of Egypt was "laid low in the wilderness." I mean, we are talking about six feet under. Now what laid them low?

The answer is their incredible lack of faith, gross sin, and unconscionable disobedience to God. These people crossed a terrible line, and they paid with their lives. If you have any doubt Paul is talking about death, check out verses 8–10.

How might this severe discipline be carried out with blatantly disobedient believers today? Let me answer it this way. If you are a Christian, you have a guardian angel, one of God's agents sent to carry out His program on earth. So that time you were driving down the highway and you were about to fall asleep and hit another car, that was your guardian angel who tapped you on the shoulder and said, "Wake up!"

One day I turned on the stove to heat some water for tea, then went to lie down while waiting for the water to boil. Of course, I fell asleep. But I remember very clearly that even though I was sound asleep, a message kept going through my head, "Get up! Get up! Get up!"

I tossed and turned and tried to ignore it, but it kept pounding. So I jumped up and ran into the kitchen just as the stove was about to catch on fire. I bowed my head and said, "Thank You, Lord, for Your provision."

That's what God does. You have someone who is with you. But if you are a Christian who is far off track, far from Christ, deep in the far country—whatever analogy you want to use—your guardian angel can become your destroyer (see 1 Corinthians 10:10) because God may say, "Don't wake him up this time."

A Serious Lesson

This is serious business. We are not talking about shucking and jiving with God. Death is serious stuff.

Why is God telling the Corinthian church—and us— what happened to Israel? That we may learn from their failure: "Now these things happened as examples for us, that we should not crave evil things, as they also craved" (v. 6).

Leaving your first love, or what Paul calls in 1 Corinthians 2–3 living the carnal Christian life, is craving for yourself what God doesn't want for you. It is going after the exact opposite of what God wants. In fact, this is so important Paul says it again (10:11).

You say, "Yeah, but it's awfully tempting out here. There's too much temptation for me to handle." Not so:

> No temptation has overtaken you but such as is common to man; and God is faithful, who will not allow you to be tempted beyond what you are able, but with the temptation will provide the way of escape also, that you may be able to endure it. (v. 13)

Paul acknowledges that temptation may have "overtaken" you. It may be beating you down. You can't help thinking about whatever it is you want. You can't help craving it. You connive to go after it.

But do you know what? You are not the first Christian who has gone through this. You are not the first man to see a pretty woman. You are not the first woman to see a handsome guy. You are not the first believer to have this or that temptation.

Sometimes you say, "Whew! Boy, I can't handle this!" Well, there are a lot of folks who have handled it before. The only reason you and I don't escape sometimes is that we are too much in love with the temptation. We want the temptation, so we don't want the escape.

So what do we do? We play with the temptation rather than hitting the exit. God builds immediate exit doors to get you out of a temptation if you want to get out. But if you don't want to escape, if you would rather crave evil things, God will discipline you.

As we have seen, you are hit with all kinds of setbacks. God doesn't answer your prayers. You lose the confidence that you are really saved. If all that doesn't do the job, He may have to take you home early.

Now this is very heavy stuff. This is the most severe discipline you can have on earth. The sins described in 1 Corinthians 10:6–10 are of the basest sort. They're even worse given what God had done for Israel.

But we know that it's possible for God's people to get this low. And when that happens, He may have to lay us low. Christians can die before their time. Those Israelites weren't supposed to die. They were supposed to get into the promised land. Big difference!

Turning It Around

But God has a provision to bring us back even when we're dancing with His ultimate earthly discipline:

> My brethren, if any among you strays from the truth, and one turns him back, let him know that he who turns a sinner from the error of his way will save his soul from death. (James 5:19–20a)

For you to ignore a brother's sin may be to contribute to his untimely death. You may be an accessory to his being destroyed by God because you kept saying, "It was his business."

I have given every member of Oak Cliff Bible Fellowship Church the right to come and grab me and turn me back if they see me heading down the wrong road. I want them to do this before God has to call His destroyer and say, "Bring Evans home."

In 1 John 5:16, John urges us to do the same thing that James urges us to do. But then John adds this very sobering note: "There is a sin leading to death; I do not say that he should make request for this."

The problem is, you don't know when you have arrived at that point. You may not get any advance notice. God may just call you home as He did Ananias and Sapphira (Acts 5).

How do we avoid the risk of God's severe discipline? Not by being perfect, because that won't happen. Not by ceasing to struggle, because we will struggle with sin as long as we are in the flesh.

We avoid God's judgment by getting off at the next exit, crossing the freeway, and getting back on going the other way.

RETURNING TO YOUR FIRST LOVE

Discipline on any level isn't pleasant, and probably never will be. But God's discipline can produce some very fruitful results if we will submit to it with the proper attitude. The goal of the application ideas below is to help you toward self-discipline in these areas so God doesn't have to come along later with heavier discipline:

1. All of us as God's children need discipline, but we don't need to go so far that we lose His blessing and benefits. Take a close look at your life and try to determine if that nagging problem, troublesome relationship, or persistent trial is a normal discipline from God designed to strengthen your faith or a product of disobedience. The presence or lack of God's joy and peace in the midst of the problem may be a good indicator.

2. If you already know you're dragging your feet on a specific step of obedience God has asked you to take, step in front of the nearest mirror and confront yourself! Determine that you'll be obedient now. Ask a friend to hold you accountable.

3. We're told that the number one question Christians ask is, "How can I know for sure I'm saved?" As we saw in this chapter, assurance of salvation is more than understanding theological truth. It's often tied to our obedience or lack of it. A great little Moody Press book you need to have in your library and loan to other Christians is *How to Know You're Saved,* by Moody radio pastor C. Donald Cole.

4. One of God's greatest gifts to us is His Book, which is loaded with timeless precepts and examples from history that will help you and me stay on the right road, learn from the triumphs and tragedies of others, avoid their pain, and enjoy God's best. Is there anything else out there offering you that kind of benefit? Then you need to make sure nothing keeps you from reading and heeding your Bible. You don't have any reason to wait. The Holy Spirit is eager to be your Teacher. Open your Bible, and ask God to open your spiritual eyes and ears.

CHAPTER NINE

THE HIGH COST OF LEAVING, 2

In the previous chapter, we learned that there are definite consequences, even severe ones, in this life for failing to turn around once we've left our first love for Christ.

I want you to know that staying on the wrong road—living the kind of Christian life we have called fleshly, carnal, regressive, immature, fruitless—also has a painful payday in eternity. I want you to know that now so you can make your decisions based on this fact.

Nobody wakes up one morning saying "I want to be a doctor" and starts practicing medicine that day. The only way you can be practicing medicine today is if you made the decision years ago to be a doctor. That desire would have had to guide you to the right school and the correct courses to take. It would have had to govern your financial choices, and maybe even your marital status and your choice of when to have children if married.

In other words, if you want to be a doctor today, today is way too late to get started on that goal. You should

have started working on that about ten or fifteen years
ago.

My point is that knowledge of the future controls activity in the present. Knowing where you want to wind up
will help you know what you should be doing right now.

There is a day coming when all Christians will stand
before God and account for how they lived as His children. On that day, it will be too late to make any needed
adjustments.

So let's learn more about that day and what it involves. We have touched on some of these points before,
but this chapter puts it together in a systematic way.

After we consider the high cost of leaving our first
love in light of eternity, in part two of the book we'll study
in depth how you can return to your first love and enjoy
God's very best both here on earth and in heaven.

THE PLACE OF JUDGMENT

This day of reckoning is called the judgment seat of
Christ. Look at 2 Corinthians 5, a very important passage:

> Therefore also we have as our ambition, whether at home or
> absent, to be pleasing to Him. For we must all appear before
> the judgment seat of Christ, that each one may be recom-
> pensed for his deeds in the body, according to what he has
> done, whether good or bad. Therefore knowing the fear of
> the Lord, we persuade men. (vv. 9–11a)

Paul says, "We must all appear." There will be no ex-
ceptions. Every Christian who has been given a new body
(v. 1) will one day be called to a meeting.

If Jesus Christ were to come back today, all who have
truly accepted Him as Savior would immediately disap-
pear. We would be transported into His presence. Immediately following the rapture, we would appear before
Christ at His judgment seat.

The Greek word *bema*, translated "judgment seat,"
was a familiar one to Paul because in his day the Corinthian
world held the Isthmian games. During these games, which
were much like our Olympics, a rostrum or podium called

the *bema* was built in the marketplace. The judges would sit on the *bema* to judge the events of the games and hand out penalties and rewards.

A Place of Reward

When an athlete won an event, he was escorted to the judgment seat in the same way that Olympic winners are escorted to the platform to be awarded their medals. This was the place of reward. The winner would receive a garland for his head and other rewards. He was also given prestige. For example, the winner of a major contest no longer had to pay taxes.

A Place of Evaluation

But the judgment seat was also the place of evaluation. Other athletes came who thought they had won. That is, it looked like they won the race. But they would find out at the judgment seat that they had broken some rule. Even though they thought they had won, they would be disqualified at the judgment seat.

Paul had the Isthmian Games and the judgment seat in mind when he wrote, "I buffet my body and make it my slave, lest possibly . . . I myself should be disqualified" (1 Corinthians 9:27). He was worried about standing before Christ one day thinking he was a winner only to learn he had been disqualified.

Every Christian will one day stand before the judgment seat. Christ will determine whether you won your race, whether you lived a Christian life that was pleasing to Him or got yourself disqualified. In that day, the Bible says, "The first shall be last, and the last shall be first."

Many people who think they are going to get applause at the judgment seat of Christ are going to get boos. Many people who thought they were winners are going to find out they were losers because the judgment seat is where the real story gets told.

People can fool you on earth. You know, they may have a spiritual smile and spiritual talk. But at the judgment seat of Christ, all that's going to be cleared up.

THE PROBLEM OF JUDGMENT

This poses a problem, one we touched on earlier. The Bible clearly says that anyone who is in Christ is no longer under condemnation or judgment (John 5:24; Romans 8:1). Yet the Bible also says, "The Lord will judge His people" (Hebrews 10:30).

No Contradiction

Is this a contradiction? No, this is an apparent contradiction. What's the difference? A contradiction is two things that cannot be true at the same time. An apparent contradiction looks like a contradiction only because we don't have all the facts yet. Don't let people tell you the Bible contradicts itself. They just don't have all the facts.

Here's why the Bible says you are not, and yet you are, going to be judged. Even before you accepted Jesus Christ, God judged all of your sins on the cross. The Bible says the death of Christ paid for all the sins of all people everywhere (1 John 2:2). Right here in 2 Corinthians 5 Paul writes, "God was in Christ reconciling the world to Himself" (v. 19).

Now if God has already paid for everyone's sins, how come people go to hell? All sin has already been paid for. But people go to hell because they reject the Savior, because they refuse the only payment God has provided for sin.

People who go to hell either reject Christ outright, or try to add something to what Christ has done on the cross. Christ paid for the sins of all people for all time. But their failure to accept the Savior does not allow them to benefit from His payment.

No Other Savior

You must trust Christ alone to save you—not the church, not baptism, not living a good life. It's not Christ plus. It's Christ plus *nothing* that saves us. Many people stumble over that nothing part. They want to add something to what Christ did.

When you trust Christ, you are born from above into God's family. You become His child. Once that happens, your status as a child of God will never be called into question. Once you are born from above, you cannot lose your salvation.

At His judgment seat Christ is not going to judge you to determine whether or not you are His legitimate child. You will be judged as a servant; that is, how you functioned as a Christian, how you lived your Christian life.

Let me illustrate. Suppose you are a schoolteacher and your daughter is one of your students. She is misbehaving in class, so you say, "Get up and leave the room. You're going to detention!"

You have just evaluated your daughter's behavior as a student and judged her on that basis. So she cannot say, "Hey, I'm your daughter. You can't send me to detention." Her relation to you is not the issue on the floor. Now when she comes home that afternoon from detention, she'll still be your daughter. But her status in the family does not relieve her of her responsibility to be a good student.

As Christians we are related to God both as children and as servants. You won't even be at the judgment seat unless you belong to Christ. But He's going to judge you by how you served Him as His servant. We must understand these two relationships.

THE BASIS OF JUDGMENT

So far, I haven't said anything about the consequences of self-centered Christian living because I wanted to establish first that every Christian appears at Christ's judgment seat.

We'll get to the consequences now as we look at the basis of Christ's judgment. Verse 10 of our text above, 2 Corinthians 5, spells it out plainly. We will be judged for the "deeds [done] in the body."

Back in 1 Corinthians 3, Paul gives us some very important detail on this:

According to the grace of God which was given to me, as a wise master builder I laid a foundation, and another is building upon it. But let each man be careful how he builds upon it. For no man can lay a foundation other than the one which is laid, which is Jesus Christ. Now if any man builds upon the foundation with gold, silver, precious stones, wood, hay, straw, each man's work will become evident; for the day will show it, because it is to be revealed with fire; and the fire itself will test the quality of each man's work. If any man's work which he has built upon it remains, he shall receive a reward. If any man's work is burned up, he shall suffer loss; but he himself shall be saved, yet so as through fire. (vv. 10–15)

The fire here is not hell. He is talking about Christians and how they build on the foundation. Fire in the Bible means judgment. When applied to the non-Christian it means hell, but when applied to the Christian, it means God's judgment or discipline in time and also in eternity.

These verses are so straightforward they need little comment. Christians who live faithful, not perfect, lives—who make the pursuit of God their focus—will receive a reward because they built with gold, silver, and precious stones.

These are things fire can't destroy. All fire does is purify them. But if you build with wood, hay, and straw and you light a fire, we are talking about quick smoke.

Since Paul uses the imagery of a builder, let's say you pay top dollar to have a new house built. But the builder comes with blue bricks, black bricks, white bricks, turquoise bricks, and purple bricks all mixed together.

You wouldn't appreciate that because that's not what you paid for. You will wear that builder out for putting in that mess when you paid top dollar. You want top-dollar material if you are building a top-dollar house.

On the cross, Jesus paid top dollar for our sins. God gave His only Son that you and I might have a relationship with God. No wonder Paul says, "Be careful what you build. Don't use cheap material when God paid top dollar."

What does it mean to build with wood, hay, and straw? It means you have nothing to show for being saved. The life work of some Christians will burn up at the judgment seat of Christ. God is going to pierce their work with His holiness and their lives will crumble before Him because they had nothing of any eternal value to transfer from earth to heaven.

They lived to please themselves. They lived for their dreams, their goals, their desires, their wants, and their drives. God is going to pierce them with His eyes and say, "What did you bring here for *Me?*" All of it will crash to the ground because "the day will show it" (1 Corinthians 3:13).

Our Deeds

Let me give you the three things God is going to look for when He judges us. First of all, He's going to check out our deeds. Look at Hebrews 4:12–13:

> The word of God is living and active and sharper than any two-edged sword, and piercing as far as the division of soul and spirit, of both joints and marrow, and able to judge the thoughts and intentions of the heart. And there is no creature hidden from His sight, but all things are open and laid bare to the eyes of Him with whom we have to do.

One day we will stand before God laid bare. There will be no facades, no hiding, no secret places. God is going to evaluate what we did based on two criteria. Did we do what He said to do? And did we do it for the right reasons?

Some of us are going to stand at the judgment seat of Christ and say, "But I thought. . . ."

And Christ is going to say, "No, I said." In other words, He is going to judge whether your actions coincided with His Word. That's why your ultimate allegiance must be to the Word. It's OK to follow a man as long as that man is following the Word.

But don't let the man lead you away from the Word, because God is not going to judge you on the man; He's going to judge you against the standard of His Word.

God is not only going to look at what you did, but why you did it. First Corinthians 4:5 says we shouldn't judge anything before the time, because the hidden things will be revealed. What you see now may not be what God sees later.

You and I can go through the motions of doing the right thing. But without a heart of love, without commitment to Christ, and without a desire to bring glory to God, we are just play-acting. That's why God is going to lay bare the intentions of the heart. He is going to turn that baby inside out to see what was working internally.

Our Dependability

The second thing God is going to judge you and me on is our dependability. First Corinthians 4:2 says a steward must be faithful. Revelation 2:10 says to be faithful unto death. Christ's commendation on that day is going to be, "Well done, good and faithful servant."

Some of us get happy when we do one big thing for God a year. We say, "I did a biggie for God on November 26. I know heaven was applauding." At His judgment seat, Christ is also going to evaluate what you did on November 1–25. Then He's going to talk about the other eleven months. He's going to go back and say, "Did you live a life of faithfulness to Me?"

Now, no one does it perfectly. But when Christ overviews your life, what pattern will He see? Is there a consistency about following and obeying, and, when you fail, about repenting and getting back up and moving on?

Our Declarations

The third category He's going to judge us on is our declarations, our words. Every "careless word" we speak will come under scrutiny (Matthew 12:36). That's convicting, isn't it? The bad language is in the computer. Someone says, "I didn't say that." Christ is going to call it up on the computer.

Some of us will say, "Lord, I don't remember gossiping." Ding! There it is. It's going to be plain. "Whatever

you have said in the dark shall be heard in the light"
(Luke 12:3).

THE RESULT OF JUDGMENT

Beginning in Matthew 25:14, Jesus told the story of a
man who went on a journey. He left varying sums of money
with his three servants to take care of his business while
he was gone. The first two invested wisely and doubled
the master's money.

But the guy who got one talent hid it. He did nothing
with what his master gave him. The problem was that his
master, who represents God, came back and said to all
three servants or slaves, "Show me what you've done with
what I gave you" (see v. 19).

The first two slaves had plenty to show, and each
won his master's commendation along with a handsome
reward (vv. 21, 23). But this one-talent guy had nothing to
show his master except what he started with.

This is what many Christians do. They take the gifts,
abilities, and money God gives them and hide their treasures. They never use them for God. Oh, they may use
these things to gain power, prestige, and profit for themselves. But they gain no profit for God's kingdom.

But this faithless slave's master wasn't buying his excuse, and the slave incurred his judgment (vv. 26–30).
Since I believe this story is a picture of believers at the
judgment seat of Christ, we need to grasp the seriousness
of what's going on here. We are talking about the loss of
reward for Christians who fail to give God His rightful
place. This is a tremendous loss that involves three parts.

The first is a stinging rebuke (vv. 26–27). When you
stand before Christ, when He shows you the price He paid
so you could enjoy heaven, and when you see what you
could have had, this will be a very uncomfortable time.

The second is kingdom disinheritance (vv. 28–29).
Christ will show you what you could have had and been
and what He could have done with you in His millennial
kingdom, His thousand-year reign that follows immediately after His judgment seat.

The third judgment is exclusion from Christ's kingdom wedding feast (v. 30). I believe some of His children will be excluded because of unfaithfulness.

What a tragedy to know what we could have had! Sometimes we can do something to fix our regrets. But at the judgment seat, there will be no fixing of anything.

THE DURATION OF JUDGMENT

Let me explain how I think this judgment works in terms of duration, using an analogy from ice hockey. In hockey, when you break a rule the referee sends you to the penalty box. You are still on the team. You can see everything happening on the ice, but you can't play because you broke the rules. Which rule you broke determines how many minutes you are in the box.

That's the best way to explain what I think happens to carnal Christians in the kingdom. God assesses your life and determines that you broke the rules. And He escorts you to the penalty box. You are still on the team. But since you lived for the flesh, you don't get full participation.

The Bible teaches that there are degrees of punishment in hell (Matthew 11:21–24). By the same principle, there are degrees of blessing in heaven. So when some Christians show up at Christ's judgment seat, all their stuff will burn up, and they will be sent to the penalty box. However you see the details of this unfolding, I can tell you it's something you don't want to experience as a child of God. And neither do I.

NOT WORTH THE HIGH COST

I hope that everything I've said in chapter 8 and so far in this chapter leads you to the same conclusion: Leaving your first love for Christ carries so high a price tag that it's not worth the cost. Whatever the momentary pleasures of living in spiritual disobedience may be, they are far too costly in the long haul—and sometimes in the short haul!

Living for Today

I want you to look at another verse of Scripture with me, Galatians 6:7. You may know it already. It's a familiar verse, but don't let familiarity breed contempt in this case: "Do not be deceived, God is not mocked; for whatever a man sows, this he will also reap."

Let those words sink in for a minute and you will realize this is a powerful principle. Paul is saying that whatever we do in the short term today has long-term consequences tomorrow. That's a heavy thought in light of Jesus' command to return to our first love.

One way to measure a person's maturity is the degree to which he is able to connect present reality with future consequences, and the degree to which he lives his life today with tomorrow in mind.

The essence of maturity is that you live now in light of the future consequences. That is, you weigh the cost of a proposed action and determine what you will do now based on the price tag you will pay later.

In the Galatian letter, Paul is writing to a church that is showing serious signs of carnality and spiritual immaturity. Look at passages like 3:1–5 and 5:1–4 and you see that Paul used some of the strongest language in any of his letters to warn these people of the consequences of allowing themselves to be put back under the Law.

So here are the Christians in Galatia being sweet-talked by the Judaizers, about ready to take a giant step backward in their spiritual walk. Paul wants to motivate them to take a fresh look at the grace of God and wake up to the reality of the decision they are about to make.

Built-in Consequences

Galatians 6:7 is an axiom, a universal truth, a statement so patently true it is a truism. When it comes to the issue of our first love for Jesus Christ, the truth of Galatians 6:7 kicks into operation whether we like it or not. Beyond that, the principle of sowing and reaping operates no matter how hard we try to ignore it or even reverse it.

Would Christians actually attempt to ignore or reverse God's principles? Christians who are out of step with Christ and heading down the wrong road would— and often do. If we're not careful, we can become cold and indifferent in our love for Christ and begin to think the rules that apply to other believers don't apply to us.

It's kind of like someone who says, "I'm not into gravity. I don't like gravity. I have never liked it. I don't think the law of gravity should even exist, and to prove it I'm going to rebel against it." So this person goes to the top of a tall building, waves his fist at the air, and says, "Gravity, I don't like you! I reject you. I'm going to defy you." So he jumps.

For the first few seconds, this guy will feel as free as a bird. If he can get his breath, he might even say on the way down, "See what I did, gravity! I showed you who was boss!"

But a few seconds later, as they sweep him off the pavement, a couple of realities will have demonstrated themselves. First, gravity doesn't care what you think. And second, you don't break gravity, gravity breaks you.

Mocking God

So Paul urges us, "Do not be deceived." That is, "Don't let anyone tell you anything different than what I'm telling you right now." Don't let your mama or daddy tell you anything different. Don't let your friends or coworkers tell you anything different than this. Don't let anyone convince you that it isn't very costly to leave your first love.

Notice the next phrase: "God is not mocked." Now this is a very interesting word. It means to thumb your nose at something, to sneer at it, to put it down.

Match that definition with God as the subject and Paul's meaning is very clear. God will not allow people to thumb their noses at Him or snub Him. God will never let anyone get the last laugh on Him. Don't let anyone deceive you into believing you can get one over on God.

We all know people who have been living lives of spiritual coldness and indifference for years. You might be tempted to say, "Well, nothing has happened to them yet."

Paul says, "Don't kid yourself."

Like counterfeit dollar bills, some Christians are living counterfeit lives. They look good to other people. We see their "printing" and say, "They must be good Christians. They've got a spiritual smile. They talk spiritual talk. They carry a Bible."

But one of these days, the falseness of their lives is going to be exposed at the judgment seat of Christ. And when that happens, the axiom of Galatians 6:7 will be shown to be true.

Sowing and Reaping

This isn't hard to understand. You don't have to be a theologian to get it. All you have to do is understand farming. "For whatever a man sows, this he will also reap" (v. 7b).

Any farmer will tell you that what you sow is what you harvest. If you plant corn, you don't get wheat. And if you plant potatoes, you don't get squash. Whatever you plant, that's what you get.

It's amazing how many people want to plant unrighteousness, but expect God's blessing. They want to plant bad, but they want to harvest good. They want to sow seeds of wrong, but gather a harvest of right.

But that's not how God's system works. There's something you need to know about sowing. Once you sow whatever you sow, it will grow naturally. The consequences of your sowing are set. You don't have to do anything extraordinary for growth to occur. What you have sown will push up through the ground someday. It's built into the process.

I hope you see the seriousness of this in relation to something as vital as our love for Christ. It's so important that we get this on track that the second half of the book is devoted to helping you return to your first love.

Before we get there, though, let me point out one more principle about sowing and reaping: According to 2 Corinthians 9:6, how much you sow determines how much you reap. Paul says, "He who sows sparingly shall also reap sparingly; and he who sows bountifully shall also reap bountifully."

If you invest only a little in spiritual things, you will reap a little from the Lord. If you invest a lot in spiritual things, then you will reap a lot. Notice that both here and in Galatians 6:7, what you sow is up to you.

Sometimes you hear Christians say, "Well, if God wants me to do it, He's going to have to move me to do it." Well, you may be waiting a long time, because the sowing is up to you. The issue is what you choose to do, the direction you choose to go in. "Whatever" you sow has consequences waiting for you at the end of the line.

You say, "But I've been going this way for a long time and I haven't hit the wall yet." That's because you are still accumulating your "harvest." It just hasn't come in yet. But when it finally does, you will see that leaving your first love is not worth the cost. So why not get things turned around now before that harvest arrives.

A FINAL QUESTION

We've been talking a lot about the judgment seat of Christ, the loss of rewards, and the pain that will accompany the revelation of what we could have had and the knowledge that we were not faithful to Christ.

Now that leads to a final question. If we're in heaven with perfect bodies and new minds, how is it going to be possible for us to feel pain?

First, we know it's possible because God is in heaven and He feels pain. When you sin, it hurts the heart of God. That's why Jesus wept over Jerusalem. It's also a major point in the story of the prodigal son. God feels the pain of our sin, even in heaven.

Second, it is precisely because you have a perfect body that you are going to feel pain like you've never felt it before. You see, here on earth we sin and feel bad about it the first time, kind of bad the second time, a little bad the third time. But by the fiftieth time, we get so used to sin we don't feel it at all.

Why is the pain of a sin so bad the first time we do it? Because it's new. We aren't used to the feeling. Well, in heaven you will have a brand-new body that will never get used to evil. You will have a sensitivity that you've never had before.

So if you suffer loss of rewards because of a carnal lifestyle, you will feel the pain of it. In Christ's kingdom, you will feel a sense of loss as you have never felt it before.

When I evaluate my church staff, I give one of two ratings. An unsatisfactory rating has profound ramifications, because it means a lower raise. It means the individual will not get the raise he or she hoped to get, wants to get, and maybe needs to get.

On the other hand, if the person gets a satisfactory rating, that means he or she gets the raise he or she had hoped to get. In fact, when staff members do a great job, we give them a year-end expression of appreciation.

At the 1988 Summer Olympics, Ben Johnson of Canada exploded from the starting blocks in the 100-meter race. I remember hearing the commentator say, "Did you see that start?"

As Johnson broke the tape, the clock on television showed that he had broken the Olympic 100-meter record like it had never been broken before. He was the world's fastest human.

The crowd went wild! The other runners congratulated him. Johnson ran a victory lap waving a Canadian flag. But when he came to the judgment seat, the truth was revealed. The judges found steroids in his blood. Word came back, "Ben Johnson, surrender your gold medal." The medal was snatched from Johnson and awarded to the American sprinter Carl Lewis, and Johnson went back to Canada in disgrace.

The crowd didn't know all this when Johnson was running. When he darted out of the blocks, people went wild. When he did his victory lap, he looked like a winner. But the judges went inside Ben Johnson's body and brought out what was there. The day revealed what sort of work Johnson's was.

At the judgment seat of Christ, some of us will be like Ben Johnson. We will see the gold medal we thought was ours given to another because we didn't run according to the rules.

On the other hand, many of us will take a victory lap and hear over the loudspeaker, "Ladies and gentlemen, the winner!"

Which will it be for you?

RETURNING TO YOUR FIRST LOVE

Will Jesus Christ announce you as a winner at His judgment seat, or will He strip you of your medal? If you want to be a winner on that day, make Him the object of your first love today. I hope these ideas will help you avoid loss of reward in heaven by running according to the rules here on earth:

1. If you want to have a very interesting family conversation at your next meal together, ask each member to try to identify his or her spiritual gift(s) (Romans 12, 1 Corinthians 12), and then talk about ways God can use each of you to put your gifts to work for Him. Read Jesus' parable in Matthew 25:14–30 and stress the importance of using what He entrusts to us.

2. Is there some gift or ability you know God has given you, yet you are hiding for whatever reason? Then get your shovel out! Dig up your "talent" (see Matthew 25:25) and ask God for an opportunity to serve Him with it. Then be alert for the answer.

3. We as Christians differ in gifts, abilities, and financial resources, but we can all be faithful. Look around you and take note of the people whose faithfulness to the Lord and to His people blesses your life. Make it a point to let at least three of these people know how much you appreciate them.

4. Take a piece of paper and write down three or four areas of your life (e.g., marriage, ministry, financial stewardship) where you especially want to hear Jesus' commendation, "Well done, good and faithful servant." Now opposite each item list the things you are doing *now* to reach your goal.

PART TWO

RETURNING TO YOUR FIRST LOVE

—— REMEMBER ——

CHAPTER TEN

REMEMBERING WHO JESUS IS

Now we get to the good stuff!

We've arrived at part two of the book, where we set out on the most important "journey" we as believers will ever take: returning to our first love.

To set the stage for this section, which itself is divided into three subsections (see the table of contents), I want to turn once again to our foundational text in Revelation 2:4–5. This time, let's look at the first half of verse 5, where the risen Lord Jesus commands: *"Remember* therefore from where you have fallen, and *repent* and *do* the deeds you did at first"* (italics added).

You can see from this where we get the three-part outline for this section: remember, repent, and redo. This is a powerful formula not only for personal spiritual renewal, but for revival in your family and in the church. As a pastor I'm convinced that if enough individual believers would take Jesus' exhortation seriously, we'd have revival! So let's get started on the journey.

When Jesus told the church at Ephesus to "remember therefore from where you have fallen," it's clear that what He wanted them to remember were the days when their first love was in first place where it was supposed to be. Since there is no question that He Himself is to be the object of our first love, reminding ourselves who Jesus is makes for a good place to start.

That's why in this chapter I want to review and reestablish in your mind some basic truths about Jesus Christ. Let me summarize them, then explore their implications in our lives.

Jesus Christ stands unique among all men. He claims unique authority over the lives of all those who call themselves children of God. Jesus Christ alone is Lord, above and beyond any other authority or name that can be named.

So when Jesus Christ demands our first love, our undivided loyalty, and our total commitment, He is demanding nothing more than what is His right and prerogative to demand.

Probably the clearest portrait of Jesus Christ in the New Testament is found in Philippians 2:5–11, which we will be looking at below, where Paul mentions everything that's important to remember about this One who commands our first love.

THE CRITERIA FOR OUR LOVE

Just so you know these verses are not merely a theological treatise hung in the middle of the book, let's go back and look at Philippians 2:1–4 for the context. Here we learn that our love for Christ is based not only on who He is, but on what He has done for us.

Paul is saying in verses 1–2 that if we can say, "The Lord has been good to me. He's encouraged me. He's come through for me," this reality ought to reflect itself in our relationship with other Christians. The "if" in verse 1 does not imply doubt. It could just as easily be translated "since," because that's the force of this construction.

In other words, when we remember what Jesus has done for us, we can't help but relate to our fellow believers in a spirit of self-giving love and unity of purpose and spirit. So even though Paul's focus is horizontal here, it begins when we look at Jesus Christ and say, "Yes, He's done all of this for me."

Verses 3–4 continue the apostle's emphasis on relationships between fellow Christians—but it's all anchored in our relationship with Christ. To the degree that you and I possess a dynamic relationship with Jesus Christ, to that degree we as individuals, families, and churches will exhibit the spirit of sharing and caring and oneness that Paul calls for in these verses.

THE MIND OF CHRIST

With this as the backdrop Paul comes to verse 5, the introductory statement in this tremendous affirmation of the deity and work of Jesus Christ. But notice that Paul didn't just start by saying, "Let Jesus Christ be your example."

Instead, Paul goes right to the point when he says in verse 5, "Have this attitude in yourselves which was also in Christ Jesus." To paraphrase, "Learn to think like Christ." In light of our emphasis on remembering Christ, thinking about Him, I find it fascinating that Paul is after our minds. He wants to teach us how to think.

As Christians, we should never get caught saying things like, "Well, everyone else says it's fine," "No one else seems to think there's anything wrong with it," or "This is what so-and-so says." As people under the Lordship of Jesus Christ we need to have another kind of mind —His mind.

Here's where I think a lot of us get started down the wrong road when it comes to keeping our focus on Christ. One of the big struggles we face is not allowing this world order to tell us how to think. The reason it's not easy is that we are constantly being bombarded by the world's messages, telling us how to think and what to think about.

If we're not careful, we wind up judging things using the world's criteria. And we know the world has no love for Christ—not as its first love, its second, or its third, for that matter. It's amazing how many times Christians say something the world says the way the world says it, indicating they have not had what Romans 12:2 calls a renewal of their minds (a subject we'll focus on in chapter 15).

THE DEITY OF JESUS CHRIST

If we are to remember where our first love lies, learn to focus on Christ and think like He thinks, then we must understand who He is. Here is the heart of what I want to share with you in this chapter. Beginning in Philippians 2:6, Paul identifies Jesus Christ through a series of unique statements about Him: "Although [Jesus Christ] existed in the form of God, [He] did not regard equality with God a thing to be grasped."

These words can be difficult to interpret, so let me sort of paraphrase: Although Jesus existed from eternity as God, He did not regard this as something He had to hold on to at all costs.

The Form of God

The word *form* Paul uses here referred to a Roman stamp. Official government documents were sealed with wax. While the wax was still hot, they would press a ring or stamp into it bearing the emperor's insignia. The impression made in the wax was thus an exact representation of the insignia on the ring.

We do something similar today when we wet a rubber stamp with ink and then stamp it on a piece of paper. The impression on the paper is the exact image of what is on the rubber stamp.

Paul says, "That's the relationship Jesus Christ bears to God the Father. Jesus is the exact representation of who and what God is."

So when you and I talk about Jesus Christ, we are not talking about someone less than God. We are talking about someone who is the "express image" of God—the eternal, preexistent God Himself.

The Son of God

This sometimes raises the question as to why Jesus is called the Son of God if He is the exact representation of who and what God is. Well, the Bible teaches that God is

Father, God is Son, and God is Holy Spirit. All three are equally God, but they do not bear the same relationship in the Godhead.

For example, God the Father sets the plan. God the Son implements the plan—which is what we see here in Philippians 2. God the Holy Spirit impacts the plan. Each member of the Godhead has a specific role within the Trinity, but each one is equally God. Jesus then is the Son of God in the sense that He bears the essence of deity, just as His being the Son of Man means He bears the essence of humanity.

In His preincarnate state—prior to His coming to earth—Jesus Christ had at His disposal all the conveniences of glory and none of the inconveniences of earth. He not only possessed deity, but He had the free use of His deity at His own choosing. That's what it meant for Jesus to exist in the form of God.

The Savior

But Paul's point in verse 6 is that Jesus willingly surrendered His divine prerogatives in order to redeem fallen creatures like us. To put it another way, Jesus did not think that being God, independent of earth, was something He had to clutch so tightly that when men needed salvation, He couldn't leave heaven and come to this earth to meet our need.

Now there's a thought that ought to rekindle any Christian's first love for Christ. When the plan of salvation was drawn up in the council chambers of heaven, it decreed that Someone had to come down to earth to provide salvation for men.

Jesus did not say, "I'm sorry. I'm not about to leave this comfortable spot in glory to go down to those miserable people on earth to provide them salvation."

Instead, He said, "I'm not so intent on being God up here that I can't become man down there. I am not so into glory up here that I don't care what happens to people down there."

If Jesus had thought for one moment that He had to protect His deity; if He had thought that leaving heaven might allow someone else to come in and take His place as Son; if He had therefore stayed in heaven to protect His deity from intrusion, there would have been no one to come down to earth.

There was no one on earth qualified to be our Savior. For everyone on earth had sinned. And since no one on earth was qualified to be our Savior, there would have been no Savior if Jesus had not willingly laid aside His heavenly glory.

Without a Savior, there would have been no salvation. And without salvation, there would have been no hope. And without hope, you and I would have nothing to look forward to for all eternity.

This is the Lord we are called to love above all other loves. How can we not love Him, seeing what He has done for us! No wonder Jesus said that if we stray from our love for Him, nothing else we do matters. So we're taking the first step in His three-part command (Revelation 2:5) by taking time to remember who He is.

The Implications

The power of this truth hits us right where we live. We Christians sometimes get the idea, just like the world, that we need to protect what we have. But having the mind of Christ means we release what we have for others. Jesus says to us by His example, "If I had protected what I had, you wouldn't have anything to protect because I would never have been your Savior."

Remember, Jesus didn't stop being God when He became man. Jesus was and is the eternal God. The difference was that He encased His divinity in humanity to meet humanity's need.

You see, when we leave our first love, when we get our eyes and our hearts off Christ, we start looking at ourselves differently. We look at ourselves as being big deals because of who we are.

But God doesn't look at us that way. He gets bored with that conversation. God says, "Who you are, you are only because I made you that way. And I only made you that way so you can help someone else experience My love demonstrated in Christ when He gave up heaven to come down and be your Savior."

Unless that mind-set pervades us, the mind "which was also in Christ Jesus," we have missed the whole point of Christianity.

THE HUMANITY OF JESUS CHRIST

We have already been reminded of some glorious truths about Christ in Philippians 2—and we have five more verses to go. Christ did more than simply lay aside the glory of heaven: He "emptied Himself, taking the form of a bond-servant, and being made in the likeness of men" (v. 7).

I love this verse because it means that what was thought out and decided in eternity, Christ acted on. So often our thoughts, beliefs, and statements never get translated into actions.

But unless there is a corresponding action to my statement, then my statement is suspect. If I tell you I love you, but there follows nothing identifiable that makes my statement concrete, then it's just mumbo jumbo. Christ could have stayed in heaven and said, "I love you down there!"

And the answer could have come back, "So what? I'm in trouble. I'm down here and You're up there. That doesn't help me. I need You to do something." But Christ didn't stay in heaven, and if we are thinking with His mind, our words will result in actions that demonstrate our love.

Christ's Self-Emptying

What does the self-emptying of Christ mean? The theological doctrine is called the *kenosis*, from the Greek verb meaning "to empty." Did He empty Himself of His deity and become merely a man? No, the focus of His self-emptying is not heaven, but earth; that is, what Christ emptied Himself *into*.

He didn't empty out God and pour in man. Rather, He emptied all of God into man. In other words, He didn't stop being God. He didn't say, "Deity, I'm going to leave You in heaven and go down to become humanity."

Perfect Man

What Jesus did was take all of His deity and pour it into humanity so that He became much more than mere man. He became the God-man, God poured into man. What you have now is a Man like man has never been before, because now you have perfect Man.

Let me tell you something important. When Jesus Christ did something about your sin and mine, He didn't give us the leftovers. He poured all that made Him God into man so that man would have all of God. There is nothing that belonged to God that man didn't have when Jesus emptied Himself into man.

Jesus was some kind of Man because God is some kind of God. When all of that some kind of God was poured into Christ's humanity, what you've got is some kind of Man.

That's why the life of Jesus Christ is extraordinary. He emptied Himself. He poured all of deity into humanity to save us. So when we look at the grace and blessings of God in our lives, we need to remember—and I do mean *remember*—who made it all possible.

Christian, remember who Jesus is and what He's done for you! I don't know of anything that will restore your first love faster than looking at what you have and saying, "This is what Christ has done for me." We should say it every day.

Christ's self-emptying love for us and our love for Him should also make a "so what" difference in our lives. You say God has blessed you with ability, intellect, or resources? So what? What are you doing with them? You say Christ is everything to you? So what? How is His love motivating you to serve others? Serving others is the mind-set of Christ.

THE HUMILIATION OF CHRIST

See, Christ did even more than lay aside the glories of heaven. He did even more than give up the free, independent use of His divine attributes to empty Himself into man. Verse 7 reminds us that He took the form of a bond-servant. Let me show you why that's so important.

How wealthy was Jesus Christ in heaven? Very, very wealthy. The Bible says that by Him all things were created (Colossians 1:16). So you figure He's got a little bit of change in the bank. He's fabulously wealthy.

Paul says Jesus gave up that wealth, His possession and enjoyment of glory, and became not just a human being, but a "bond-servant." The Holy Spirit who inspired Paul chose this word carefully. It's the word *doulos*, which means "slave." It was used of Roman slaves who were the most abused, misused, and ill-treated people of the day.

In Jesus' day, you couldn't get any lower than a bond-servant. If you were born as a *doulos*, a slave, you were at the bottom of life's barrel. That's why it bewildered everyone when Jesus Christ, the King of kings and the Lord of lords, was born in a dirty stable with the animals, laid in a trough, and wrapped in clothes used for dead people.

That's all they had to wrap Jesus in. He was born of poor parents and lived in poverty all His life. He owned creation, but He went to the bottom of life's barrel for us. Do you see why it's a serious thing to leave our first love for a Savior like this who spared no loss or degradation to redeem us?

As we remember who Jesus Christ is, we also need to remember that Paul wants us to have the same mind-set Jesus had in His self-humiliation. It's the mind-set that says no matter how elevated we may seem to be, we are not so high that we cannot go to the bottom of the barrel if necessary to meet someone's need because Jesus went to the bottom of the barrel for us.

That's why the most service-oriented people on earth ought to be Christians. We should be willing to take all our resources and all our blessings and wisely make them available to anyone because that's what Jesus did for us.

THE DEATH OF JESUS CHRIST

Someone reading and understanding these verses in Philippians 2 for the first time might say by now, "Jesus couldn't have gone any lower than this. He couldn't have suffered any greater humiliation than this to save us, right?"

Wrong. Verse 8 describes the final step of Jesus Christ's willing humiliation for us. He surrendered the splendor of heaven for the agony of the cross: "And being found in appearance as a man, He humbled Himself by becoming obedient to the point of death, even death on a cross."

We are talking about the incarnation, the "in-fleshness," of Jesus Christ. He became a man. As we saw above, He didn't arrive on earth like a king. He didn't live like a king. And now we learn from verse 8 that He didn't demand to be treated like a king. That is, Jesus Christ humbled Himself to do the will of another.

Jesus' Obedience

If you had walked with Jesus on earth, you would have heard and seen something phenomenal. Jesus would always say that He had come to do someone else's work. Wherever you went with Him, He would always tell you why He was here. If someone asked, "Jesus, why did You come here?"

"To do My Father's will."

"Jesus, where are You going?"

"To carry out My Father's business."

Someone might object, "Now Jesus, let's not overdo this humility thing. After all, You're human. You must have Your own agenda. There have got to be some things You do strictly for Jesus."

To which Jesus would have responded, "No, you don't understand. 'I have come (in the roll of the book it is written of Me), to do Thy will, O God'" (Hebrews 10:7). When He was on earth, Jesus was "God with us," God in the flesh, but He wasn't focused on His own program. He submitted Himself to the will of His Father.

Why did Jesus have to humble Himself? First, because no one could make Him do it; and second, because the need He came to meet, paying the price for our redemption, was more important than His privileges. So Jesus gladly humbled Himself. He gladly gave up His rights. The writer of Hebrews says He endured the cross because of "the joy set before Him" (12:2).

You remember that as Jesus hung on the cross, the people on the ground made fun of Him. "If You are the

Son of God, come down. Then we'll believe You. Come
down and show us!"

What they didn't realize was that "He could have
called ten thousand angels." Those people really didn't
want Jesus Christ to come down, because with one word
of His command, heaven would have been unleashed.

But Jesus didn't do that. He humbled Himself. He
said, "There is a need down there, and even though I am
God and don't have to go, the consequences of not meeting it are too high."

Jesus humbled Himself—and as His people we are
called to do the same. God has a lot of problems blessing
us because His blessings don't produce humility in us,
they produce pride.

God never meant for His blessings on your life and
mine to produce pride. The more we are blessed, the more
humble we should be. The more we have, the lower we
should go.

But we have this thing turned the wrong way in the
upside-down kingdom of earth. The more we have, the
higher our shoulders go, the higher our heads are raised.
That's why of the seven sins God hates, pride tops the list
(Proverbs 6:16–17) because pride says, "I pulled myself
up by my own bootstraps."

What God says is, "I gave you the boots! I put them
on you." So we are to think about our blessings with the
mind of Christ, which tells us we are blessed that we
might make a difference among men for the glory of God.

Death on a Cross

How far did Jesus humble Himself? He became "obedient to the point of death." That's a lot of humbling. I
mean, I'll humble myself to do some things. But humbling
myself to die, that's some serious humility.

Now if Jesus had humbled Himself to die peacefully
in His sleep of old age, or die quickly of something like a
heart attack, that would have been one thing.

But Jesus understood in the Garden of Gethsemane
what God was requiring of Him. God was asking His Son

to humble Himself to die the agonizing death of a criminal on a Roman cross.

See, Jesus didn't just die. He had to die the way no man wants to die. First He was carved up by a Roman scourge, a whip implanted with metal tips so that every time they hit Jesus on the back, they lifted out pieces of His flesh.

Then Jesus had to carry the beam of His own cross on His bloody, raw back. No wonder He collapsed. It wasn't the weight of the cross beam that Jesus couldn't bear, it was the unbelievable pain of a rough-hewn chunk of wood rubbing against the bloody holes that used to be His back.

They beat Jesus and bruised Him. They insulted Him and spat on Him. They forced a crown of needle-like thorns down on His head. They made fun of the King of kings and Lord of lords. Psalm 22:14 predicted that every bone in His body would be put out of joint. Have you ever had one bone out of joint?

All of this, and the Bible says Jesus was God. He created the tree from which the wood of His cross was made, and then He had to carry it. Is anyone else worthy of our first love?

Remember, Jesus suffered all of this to the full because He was fully man. This was no pretend suffering. His humanity was evident in the Garden of Gethsemane when He prayed, "My Father, if it is possible, let this cup pass from Me" (Matthew 26:39).

That says Jesus would have preferred another way. But He concluded His prayer with words that show us His heart and His mind-set: "Yet not as I will, but as Thou wilt" (v. 39b).

THE EXALTATION OF JESUS CHRIST

How could Jesus humble Himself all the way to an excruciating, humiliating death on a cross? Because He knew it was His Father's will. And He knew His Father would raise Him up. Which is exactly what God did:

> Therefore also God highly exalted Him, and bestowed on Him the name which is above every name, that at the name

of Jesus every knee should bow, of those who are in heaven, and on earth, and under the earth, and that every tongue should confess that Jesus Christ is Lord, to the glory of God the Father. (Philippians 2:9–11)

The world may not bow to Jesus today, but it's going to bow later. There's coming a day when every knee will bow. It won't matter on that day what anyone thinks, because every person is going to recognize that God sent Jesus to die for him. Lost people will spend eternity wishing they had bowed on earth.

Those of us who name the name of Jesus Christ ought to be saying, "I'm going to bow here and now willingly. I'm going to bow to Jesus as Lord and be willing to take all that He has made me to be and use it for His purposes."

Now please don't let me give you the wrong impression. When you get your love for Christ in first place where it belongs, you will find a cross waiting for you too. Jesus said, "If anyone wishes to come after Me, let him deny himself, and take up his cross, and follow Me" (Mark 8:34).

I am here to serve you notice that if you are going to be real with Jesus Christ, you're going to experience some inconvenience in your life. I want to deal straight with you. Some people would have you believe that if you commit your life to Jesus Christ, all your problems are going to be solved.

Well, a lot of your problems are going to be solved, but you will get a bunch of new ones. Because when you bow to the lordship of Jesus Christ, you go against the way this world operates. It may affect the profit margin of your business. It will definitely affect your family life, your moral life, and your mental life.

But I am also here to serve you notice that living under the lordship of Jesus Christ is the only way to truly live!

RETURNING TO YOUR FIRST LOVE

How can you lose by humbling yourself before the One who loved you so much He humbled Himself to die for you? Answer: You can't! The first step in restoring your first love is, remember who Jesus is and what He has done for you. These action steps will help you as you remember and bow before Him:

1. Philippians 2:5–11 is such an awesome passage of Scripture that it makes a powerful prayer. Pray these verses back to the Lord, prefacing each statement about who Jesus is and what He did with the phrase, "Thank you, Lord, that You. . . ."

   Close by asking the Lord to help you think like He thinks, and thank Him that you have the privilege of bowing before Him now rather than later.

2. If you're like me, you can't think about who Jesus is for very long without singing a song of praise. If you have a favorite hymn that causes you to praise, worship, and adore Jesus Christ, sing it to Him now. If a good hymnal is not part of your family's home library, hurry to your nearest Christian bookstore and get one.

3. You often hear people refer to an illness, a family difficulty, or some other problem or setback as their "cross" to bear. But that's not what Jesus meant by our cross. He said we had to deny *ourselves*. That's much more comprehensive. It means saying no to what we want, think, need, think we need, etc., so we can say yes to what Jesus wants, thinks, plans for us.

   Is there something you've said yes to in your life that Jesus wants you to say no to? The Holy Spirit will show you what it is. I urge you, change your answer to Jesus' answer!

4. I hope your prayer list includes people you want to see bow to Jesus as Lord now rather than being forced to bow before Him later on their way to hell. If you can't name lost friends and loved ones you're faithfully praying for and reaching out to, don't get off your knees until God puts them on your heart.

───────────────
CHAPTER ELEVEN
───────────────
REMEMBERING WHO YOU ARE

Now that we have reminded ourselves who Jesus Christ is, we're ready to understand who we are. In fact, you can't know for sure who you are as a Christian until you understand who Jesus is.

That's because who you are only makes sense in relation to who Jesus is. Your identity is found totally in Him. You can't know yourself until you know Jesus the way you should. And you for sure can't love Jesus the way you should until you know Him the way you should.

But a lot of Christians are confused about who they are. A lot of Christians are having an identity crisis. So we're going to turn to Romans 6 and unfold this classic passage that explains what we need to know and understand about our relationship with Christ in order to put our first love back in first place and live in spiritual victory.

In this chapter I want to bring out four critical truths we find in Romans 6, each of which can be summarized by a key word.

WE MUST KNOW SOMETHING

If you don't know who you are, you won't know how to act, which road to take, whom to get your cues from. So in Romans 6:1–4, Paul wants to clarify the identity question. The key word here is *know*.

Paul is going to use a couple of different words for knowledge in Romans 6. One has to do with experiential knowledge, and one refers to intuitive knowledge. Combine them and we see that Paul not only wants you to understand this truth academically or intuitively, he wants you to experience this truth as well.

Paul writes so that what is true might become part of our experience. He wants doctrine to become part of our duty. His desire is that the instruction of God's Word become real to us.

Understanding Grace

So he begins with a question: "Are we to continue in sin that grace might increase?" (v. 1). Paul is anticipating a misunderstanding here. He is anticipating that when people hear about the grace of God, they might mistake that to mean they are now free to do what they want to do, when they want to do it, and how they want to get it done.

Because Christians are secure in Christ and can't lose their salvation, Paul is worried that these believers in Rome will misinterpret grace as a license to sin. So he answers his question in very strong language. "May it never be!" (v. 2a). Or, "Heaven forbid that you would think the grace of God frees you up to sin."

The reason for such a strong denial is found in the rest of verse 2, which is Paul's next step in teaching us who we are in Christ. "How shall we who died to sin still live in it?" Anyone who says, "Now that I'm saved, I'm free to sin" has totally misunderstood his new identity in Christ.

Now the mere fact that Paul raises this issue suggests that some Christians could get trapped into thinking this way. It's a horrible thought, but it could happen if we don't get our identity straight.

Our Identity with Christ

So in effect Paul says, "Sit back, class, and pay attention. We are going to discuss our co-identity with Christ. We were co-crucified with Christ, we were co-buried with Christ, and we were co-resurrected with Christ":

> Do you not know that all of us who have been baptized into Christ Jesus have been baptized into His death? Therefore we have been buried with Him through baptism into death, in order that as Christ was raised from the dead through the glory of the Father, so we too might walk in newness of life. (vv. 3–4)

To put it another way, what happened to Christ two thousand years ago happened to you in the mind of God. When Jesus died, you died. When Jesus was buried, you were buried. And when Jesus rose from the dead, you rose from the dead.

God took what happened to Christ two thousand years ago, brought it forward, and applied it to your experience when you got saved. He made it happen to you.

What happened physically to Christ two thousand years ago happens to us spiritually today. This is the principle of identification, a principle summed up in the interesting word *baptism*.

The word means "to plunge" or "to dip." It was used of a person in the Roman world who dyed cloth. If the dyer wanted purple cloth, he would dip it into the purple dye. The cloth now reflected the color of the dye because it had been baptized, dipped, or plunged into the dye.

The Bible says in 1 Corinthians 12:13 that the moment you accepted Christ, you were baptized or dipped into His body. Just as the dyer dipped the cloth in the dye, you've been dipped in the blood of Christ, making you a part of Christ and of His body. This is identification. You are now identified with Christ.

Identification is not a concept we meet for the first time in Romans 6. All through the Bible, God sees us as identified with something. For example, Romans 5:12 says that everyone outside of Christ is identified with Adam.

Because Adam rebelled and we are the fruit of Adam, we rebelled too.

Some people say, "It's not fair that I should be identified with Adam. I didn't ask Adam to represent me." Well, even if we represented ourselves, we would show we are in Adam because in Adam all sinned, and we sin. We sin because we were identified with Adam.

As Christians, though, we are now identified with Jesus Christ. But unless we recognize who we are, we will not live out the life we were meant to live. Satan is a master magician. He can put thoughts in your mind and make you think they are your thoughts. So what Satan gets you to think is, "I can't get rid of this sin. I can't overcome this temptation. I can't."

That's a lie. "[You] can do all things through Him who strengthens [you]" (Philippians 4:13). So stop believing the lie. You are not in Adam anymore. You are in Christ.

So it is critical that we learn to think in terms of our new identity. Your brain is like a bank. It has a lot of deposits of memories from the old you. The old you will continue to try and identify you with who you used to be. The old you will try to identify you with what you were in Adam.

That's why your mind must be renewed to who you are in Christ. A good place to start is with a Bible verse you ought to memorize and quote every day when you get up:

> I have been crucified with Christ; and it is no longer I who live, but Christ lives in me; and the life which I now live in the flesh I live by faith in the Son of God, who loved me, and delivered Himself up for me. (Galatians 2:20)

This is the verse of our new identity. I'm dead to the old Tony Evans. You are dead to the old you. Anything that tells you that you are alive to it is Satan's lie.

A New Power Source

Sometimes Christians look at other Christians and say, "Boy, I wish I could be as spiritual as they are."

Paul's response would be, "Don't you know? You can be. You have the same identity they do." So if other Christians are progressing and you are regressing, it is because they are living in light of who they are and you are not.

In my house I have a toaster, a can opener, a microwave oven, and a refrigerator. They are all different, but they all draw from the same power source. So when I plug them in the refrigerator refrigerates, the microwave microwaves, the toaster toasts, and the can opener opens cans.

Each appliance, though different, lives up to its manufacturer's specifications because it has the same power source. Even though I am different than you, and you are different than me, all of us have the potential of living up to God's specifications for us because His power is available to all who belong to Christ. There are no special kids in the kingdom.

A New Owner

Your new identity in Christ is like moving into a house whose previous owners were filthy and unkempt. The house reflected who they were, but now you've purchased the home and you are a clean person. You wash off the dirt and clean the carpets and paint the walls. Because of who you are, that house takes on a whole different appearance.

Before you met Christ, a previous owner was living in the house called your body. But now Jesus has moved in. You've got a new Resident who is holy, clean, pure, and righteous.

So even though He's living in that old house, He can make it look good. He can paint, clean those carpets, and hang new drapes. You're new not because your body is changed, but because Somebody new has moved in.

WE MUST RECKON SOMETHING

Paul goes on in verses 5–11 to discuss the fact that we've been united with Christ. The key word in this section is *reckon*, which we'll come to in verse 11. Let's put this together:

> For if we have become united with Him in the likeness of His death, certainly we shall be also in the likeness of His resurrection, knowing this, that our old self was crucified with Him. (Romans 6:5–6a)

In other words, you died with Christ so that God is no longer holding you accountable for your sin. Therefore, you should be living a new kind of life with Christ that reflects the fact that you died with Him. This new kind of life is resurrection life, since you have been raised with Christ.

The Old You

Who you were before you got saved was nailed to the cross. Now this raises a question. If your old you was nailed to the cross, how come your old you is still kicking?

The reason is that the old you is so contaminated by the principle of sin that still pervades your body that the old you reacts almost like a reflex. Even though it's been crucified, your old self still reacts to sin as though it's alive.

Any mortician will tell you that cadavers can do very interesting things. For example, a dead person's hair and nails continue to grow for a period of time. One mortician friend told me that the cadaver sometimes quivers on the table, which explains why I will never be a mortician.

Another mortician told me that on one occasion, the cadaver had a muscular nerve reaction and actually catapulted itself off the table—which means that if I were there, there would have been two dead people in the room.

But it never bothers my mortician friend, because he says, "Even though there may be the quivering, jumping, nail- and hair-growing actions of life, I know and act on something the average person doesn't understand, and that is that dead is dead even when it acts alive."

So it is with you and me who are crucified with Christ. Even though sin still rears its ugly head because the sin principle is still around, you've got to know that it's your old cadaver wanting to act like it's alive. But you must recognize that it's dead because it was crucified.

Why did God crucify us? Romans 6:6b–7 says: "That our body of sin might be done away with, that we should no longer be slaves to sin; for he who has died is freed from sin."

The "body of sin" is this body that has been contaminated by the principle of sin. It's not that the body is sinful. It's that the sin principle is sinful, and the sin principle expresses itself through the body. The outcome of co-crucifixion with Christ is that our body of sin might be rendered ineffective, inoperative, or powerless.

Sure, you are going to sin. But you don't have to be a slave to sin. Before you were saved, you were like a radio with only one station—the old you. Everything you heard came from that station.

But when you come to Christ, you get a new station. Unless you tune in, though, you will never hear the music. Too many Christians are still listening to the old station and so are living the old way when God has given them a brand-new channel.

The reason you don't hang around believers who are only playing the old music is that you will soon be singing the same old song. God has given you a new channel. He wants you to understand that you've been united with Christ. Your "body of sin" that wants to do things against God has been rendered inoperative.

You can now say to your hand, "You don't have to touch that anymore." You can now say to your feet, "You don't have to go there anymore." You can now say to your tongue, "You don't have to say that anymore." You can now say to your mind, "You don't have to think that anymore."

That is, you now dictate to this body contaminated by sin the new direction it will walk in, the new thoughts it will think, and the new words it will use because of who you are in Christ. That's so because of the power of crucifixion.

The New You

Your new life in Christ should sustain you so that when you want to fall, no matter how hard you try you don't go anywhere because Christ sustains and supports you. So Paul says:

> Now if we have died with Christ, we believe that we shall also live with Him, knowing that Christ, having been raised from the dead, is never to die again; death no longer is master over Him. For the death that He died, He died to sin, once for all; but the life that He lives, He lives to God. (Romans 6:8–10)

You say, "Well, how come I'm not experiencing that?" Because you must do something. Look at verse 11 and our key word: "Even so consider [reckon] yourselves to be dead to sin, but alive to God in Christ Jesus." Paul says, "You must reckon it to be so. Count it as true. Buy into your new identity in Christ."

He is saying that if you know you've got a million-dollar spiritual bank account, start writing checks on it. It's no good to have a million dollars and never reckon it to be so. You act on a million dollars by writing a check. Otherwise, you could live like you're broke.

During the Civil War, it was legal for a man who wanted to stay out of the Union Army to pay someone to fulfill his draft obligations. Well, a man named Pratt paid a man named White to go to war in his place.

White was killed. Pratt was re-drafted. But Pratt took the agreement between himself and White to the draft board and told them the second draft was invalid because he died "in White." The draft board had to agree Pratt was legally dead.

When Satan comes to re-draft you into your old life —when he tries to recall you to your old way of thinking, talking, and acting—you've got to show him the agreement.

You've got to say, "Jesus Christ has already died in my place. You can't draft me to that old life anymore. You can't take me back to that old way of thinking anymore. The payment has been made. You can't call me back into your service."

Satan has no more claim over you, because when Jesus died, He died once (v. 10). No more payments are necessary for you to have victory in your spiritual life. You've already died. Satan is like a deposed dictator who wants to keep running the show of your life. You must tell him that he has been kicked off the throne once and for all.

WE MUST YIELD TO SOMETHING

What the grace of God has accomplished is that sin is no longer in control of your life. Jesus Christ now sits on the throne of your life.

But for that to become your experience, you must first *know* you are united with Christ. Then you must *reckon* or count it to be so. Third, you must *yield* to your new identity in Christ. This is our next key word (it's translated "present" in the New American Standard Version). Let's begin with verse 12: "Therefore do not let sin reign in your mortal body that you should obey its lusts."

Now it doesn't say you won't have lusts. The Holy Spirit will stop you from fulfilling the desires of the flesh, but He won't necessarily stop you from having the desires of the flesh.

Instead, God's provision is that you don't have to let your desires "act like the boss" in your life. You don't have to obey what your fleshly desires are telling you to do:

And do not go on presenting the members of your body to sin as instruments of unrighteousness; but present yourselves to God as those alive from the dead, and your members as instruments of righteousness to God. For sin shall not be master over you, for you are not under law, but under grace. (vv. 13–14)

One of my ministerial responsibilities is performing weddings. In every wedding I get to the place in the ceremony where I ask, "Who gives this woman to be married to this man?"

Generally, it's the father or some surrogate for the father who says, "I do." When that happens, an exchange takes place.

Now I have bad news for the father. Once he says, "I do," he can go sit down. I'm through with him. I will have no other conversation with him in the whole ceremony. Why? Because he's irrelevant now.

The bridegroom steps up to replace the father. He and the bride come before me, I go through the wedding vows, they exchange rings, and then I close the ceremony by saying, "I now pronounce you husband and wife." Then the audience will stand and receive the new Mr. & Mrs. So-and-So.

That young lady has been transformed, not because she's not the same person, but because she has a new identity now. Once she has been presented by her father, she comes under a new authority. She enters into a new relationship.

The result is that her father, who could have said to her twenty minutes earlier, "I want you to do this," has been superseded by another, younger man who can turn to that woman and say, "I don't think so."

The first man is overruled by a newer man for one reason alone. This woman has transferred identities. The Bible says you have transferred your identity to Christ. So when that old man called the flesh starts telling you what to do, you are supposed to respond, "I have a new Husband now. See, I'm wearing a new ring. I have a new name."

That's what water baptism signifies. Water baptism says, "I'm married now. So world, I can't do what you want me to do. I'm married now. I can't go where you want me to go. I'm married. I can't think, talk, and act like you want me to think, talk, and act. I'm married now. I've yielded to a new Husband."

You must yield yourself to God on a daily basis. You begin your day by saying, "Lord, I am married to You, so please enable me today to be crucified with You." You must yield, or present, the members of your body to Christ. You bear His name now.

WE MUST END OUR SLAVERY

The fourth section of Romans 6 we want to deal with focuses on our fourth key word: *slavery*. In verse 15 we read: "What then? Shall we sin because we are not under law but under grace? May it never be!"

Notice how similar this verse is to verses 1–2. Paul has come full circle back to his original thought, which is that grace is not a license to sin.

Grace and the Law

Here he adds another element by bringing in the principle of law. He says if you are living under grace, you will keep the law. That is, you will obey God's standards. But the motivation isn't the standard itself and its threat of punishment. The motivation is the grace of God.

If you truly understand grace, you will not go out and sin just because you know you will be forgiven. You will want to please God out of gratitude for all He has done for you.

The law shows you the standard. Like a mirror, it shows you what you really are. It can reveal your problem. It can show you your sin. But the law can't fix your problem. Because when you hear, "Thou shalt not lie," you are condemned because now you know that lying is wrong and you know you've done it.

But what the law could not do, Christ did. He fixed the mess—and our gratitude for His love and grace should motivate us to gladly comb our hair, wash our faces, and brush our teeth—in other words, clean up our lives.

Serving the Right Master

So who you are should control who you serve. That's what Paul says in verse 16:

> Do you not know that when you present yourselves to someone as slaves for obedience, you are slaves of the one whom you obey, either of sin resulting in death, or of obedience resulting in righteousness?

Did you know it's possible for a Christian to become enslaved to the wrong master? Even though you belong to Christ, you might wind up slaving for the wrong person.

According to Paul, serving sin leads to death. Serving God leads to life. He continues:

> But thanks be to God that though you were slaves of sin, you became obedient from the heart to that form of teaching to which you were committed, and having been freed from sin, you became slaves of righteousness. . . . For when you were slaves of sin, you were free in regard to righteousness. Therefore what benefit were you then deriving from the things of which you are now ashamed? For the outcome of those things is death. (Romans 6:17–18, 20–21)

In other words, what was the benefit or fruit of your old life? Where did that old life get you? Yeah, you had fun sinning. But where did it get you? There was no benefit—unless you consider death a benefit!

As Christians, we have something far better to commit ourselves to: "But now having been freed from sin and enslaved to God, you derive your benefit, resulting in sanctification, and the outcome, eternal life" (v. 22).

Because of who you are, watch out who you present yourself to. Don't enslave yourself to the old you, because you are already a slave to the new you in Christ.

Be clear on who you are. Present yourself as a slave of righteousness, not a slave of sin. You owe sin absolutely nothing. You are going to sin, but don't be a slave to sin. Don't let sin control you.

There are many illustrations in the Bible of what it means to be a slave to sin. Samson (Judges 13–16) was a great man of God, but he became a slave to lust. Samson was controlled by women most of his adult life. His sexual passions ran amok year after year, and as a result he wound up in chains with his eyes plucked out (Judges 16:21).

Jesus said in John 17:3 that eternal life is knowing the Father and knowing the Son. So if you are a slave to sin, you lose out on the enjoyment of God. You lose out on your full participation in the will of God.

It's like the earthly consequences of leaving your first love, which we talked about back in chapter 8. We saw there that believers can lose their joy. They can become weak and sick and lose purpose and meaning.

Slavery and Freedom

During Paul's day, the Roman law said that no Roman citizen could be enslaved. So unscrupulous men began using the law to work a clever scam. A man would agree to sell himself into slavery to someone for a large sum of money, without revealing that he was a Roman citizen.

The man would collect the money, then bring a friend and say, "Would you please confirm that I'm a Roman citizen?" The friend would confirm it, and the man would have to be released because the law said a citizen couldn't be enslaved.

Well, this was wreaking havoc in Rome because a person could pull this scam many times, and the Roman economy was built on slavery. So the Romans got smart and enacted a new law that said any man who sold himself into slavery could no longer claim free status. He would have to remain a slave.

That's what Paul is referring to in verse 16 when he says, "When you become the slave of someone, that person owns you. You became the slave of Jesus Christ, and He owns you. So stop letting your old master, the old you, own you."

It reminds me of the story of the prodigal son in Luke 15. When the prodigal went his own way, he found slavery. But when he came home and became a slave to his father, he found freedom.

Do you know how you find freedom? By becoming a slave to Christ. Do you know how you become a slave? By becoming free to the world. Ask any slave to drugs how great it is to be free to take drugs. The world will enslave you by offering you freedom. C. S. Lewis captured the idea here when he said that hell was having your own way for all eternity.

But God makes you free by offering you slavery. It's another of the great paradoxes of our faith. God says, "If you will become a slave to Me, then you will be free indeed."

In January 1863, the Emancipation Proclamation was declared. All slaves were set free. But in Texas, it was kept a secret. They didn't tell the ancestors of my people that they were free.

So for a couple of years after the Emancipation Proclamation was declared, black people in Texas continued to live as slaves. They were not acting like the free people they were because no one told them.

When someone finally told them slavery was over, they were so glad they had a celebration. And we are so glad today that we still hold this celebration every year. It's called Juneteenth.

Two thousand years ago on Calvary, Jesus Christ signed your Emancipation Proclamation. He declared you free, but Satan is trying to keep your freedom a secret from you. He's trying to keep you from coming to the realization that you don't have to say "Yes Massa" to his control any longer.

You can put down that plow. You can act on the freedom that has been offered to you. You can collect your forty acres and a mule and start plowing your own land now. You can start living in the freedom you have because you have been made free in Christ. That's who you are, but you must live like it.

British aviation pioneer Frederick Handley Page was once flying across Arabia when he heard the sickening sound of gnawing in his small plane. Unknown to him, a huge rat had been attracted by the smell of the food put in the cargo hold of the airplane and had managed to get aboard.

Page's heart began to pound when he realized the damage this rodent could do to the plane's control mechanisms. If the rat gnawed through certain critical lines, it would cause a great problem.

Page didn't know what to do. He was flying solo, and there was no such thing as an automatic pilot on those early planes. But then he remembered something he learned in school: Rats can't survive at high altitudes.

So Page began to climb higher, so high that it became difficult even for him to breathe. But he listened intently, and after a while the gnawing stopped. When he arrived at his destination, he found the rat lying dead behind the cockpit.

Too many of us have the rat of sin gnawing at our lives. We have the rat of immorality nipping at us, the rat of improper language biting us, the rat of marital destruction chewing on us. Our spiritual planes are about to crash.

But there is something you can do. You can climb higher. Increase your altitude! It may get a little tough to breathe up there, because you haven't been used to climbing that high before. But just keep climbing. The Holy Spirit will keep you alert and awake. Keep climbing until you don't hear the rats gnawing anymore. Keep climbing until God brings victory where you didn't think there could be any.

Climb to an altitude you never thought your spiritual airplane could reach, and you'll discover a freedom you never thought possible. Know, reckon, yield, be free!

RETURNING TO YOUR FIRST LOVE

As we've just seen, it's pretty hard to know what you're supposed to be doing or where you're supposed to be going if you don't know who you are. These application ideas should help you sharpen up the reflection you see in your spiritual mirror:

1. Early in this chapter I gave you Galatians 2:20, a verse I think every Christian should memorize and quote every day. Say it to yourself until the truth of it becomes part of your permanent memory bank.

2. Give your inner Resident, Jesus Christ, a paintbrush, mop, bucket, and whatever else He needs to scrub you clean and make you look good on the inside. Yield any known area of disobedience to Him. Give Him the key and the permission to enter any room of your heart that may be locked now.

3. Do you know where Satan is most likely to trip you up and get you acting like the old you? Review your spiritual defenses in this area, and fortify where needed: e.g., avoiding certain places or turning off certain TV shows you know are going to be especially tempting to you.

4. It's possible that those old handcuffs and leg irons you used to wear when you were in slavery to the world have left scars that are bothering you today. If Satan is using the memory of old, forgiven sins to cause you guilt and keep you down, apply the healing salve of God's promises. Remind the enemy you aren't who you used to be, so he can't charge you with anything, condemn you for anything, or separate you from Christ (Romans 8:33–35)!

CHAPTER TWELVE

REMEMBERING WHAT AWAITS YOU

We've seen several times already that the Lord's remedy for the loveless Ephesian church included this exhortation: "Remember therefore from where you have fallen" (Revelation 2:5).

The church at Ephesus had fallen out of love with Jesus Christ, which led to several other "falls." It's clear from the New Testament that one of the falls a church or an individual believer takes when falling out of love with Christ is a fall from the place of reward and blessing. We looked at the loss of temporal and eternal rewards in chapters 8 and 9.

Our assignment in this chapter is a happier one. We want to consider the blessing of falling back in love with Christ and putting Him first. The point I want to make is simply this: When we return to our first love, when we place Jesus Christ at the center of our lives and unreservedly give ourselves to Him, He has blessings without number waiting for us.

Since we studied both the earthly and heavenly consequences of failing to love Christ the way we should, we're going to consider the subject of rewards under the same two headings.

Let's begin with the earthly blessings Jesus Christ has for those who love Him supremely. We could do several chapters here, but I want to limit the discussion to two things in particular. Too many Christians today seem to lack these rewards, or at least fail to understand them properly. Both of the blessings I'm talking about are in the same powerful passage of Scripture, Philippians 4:10–19. In order to understand this discussion, we need to remember where Paul was when he wrote this letter. He was imprisoned in Rome, awaiting a possible verdict of death, evidently all alone.

According to verse 10, though, Paul is happy in the Lord: "But I rejoiced in the Lord greatly, that now at last you have revived your concern for me; indeed, you were concerned before, but you lacked opportunity."

When was the last time you could say that in hard times? Generally, when we're having a hard time of it, not only do we not rejoice, but everyone who comes in contact with us knows we are not rejoicing.

But Paul was rejoicing because of the care shown him by the Philippian church. These believers loved Paul. They were deeply committed to him. At a time of great need in his life, they had sent Epaphroditus with financial relief for Paul. Their gifts were especially welcome because no one else responded.

It's important to set the scene here because of what Paul says next: "Not that I speak from want" (v. 11a). He's not writing to tell the Philippians thank you when he really means, "Send more money."

What Paul is saying is, "I'm not hinting around for more money, because I have learned something very important." We need to ask what he learned because we need to learn it too:

I have learned to be content in whatever circumstances I am. I know how to get along with humble means, and I also know how to live in prosperity; in any and every circumstance I have learned the secret of being filled and going hungry, both of having abundance and suffering need. (vv. 11b–12)

Like a guest on that old television quiz show from the 1960s, Paul says, "I've got a secret."

THE REWARD OF CONTENTMENT

You and I live in a world grasping for contentment. People want it, but they don't know where it's located. They are striving to find this thing called contentment, this gift that brings satisfaction on the inside regardless of circumstances on the outside.

But most people don't find true contentment because they are looking for it in all the wrong places. Contentment is a by-product of faithfulness to Christ. Instead of frantically seeking contentment we need to pursue our love relationship with Christ, for it is this that brings the reward of contentment.

Counterfeit Contentment

What the world calls contentment is a counterfeit of the real thing. When the money is rolling in and the car and house are new and bigger, people feel content. When the bills are paid, when they have friends, they are content. But take away the money and the friends and the new toys and, all of a sudden, people plunge into depression and lose their contentment.

This is because the world doesn't have a clue how or where to find true and lasting contentment. In fact, a number of high-dollar industries depend for their livelihood on two things: making sure you and I are discontent with what we have, and making sure we will always crave more and better.

The advertising world, the boys on Madison Avenue, are very smart. They are making big bucks for themselves and their clients because they know how to create discontentment. They understand that all they have to do is keep something new on the market.

That way, we are never satisfied. After all, who wants the old and unimproved product when the "new and improved" version is sitting next to it on the shelf? In the 1960s a car company came out with a "Super Sport" model. Now how could a young man settle for being a sport when he could be a "Super Sport"?

With the whole world built to run like this, we can understand why when he was asked, "How much money is enough?", the late John D. Rockefeller reportedly answered, "Just a little bit more."

The Secret of Contentment

The story is told of a king who was sick with unhappiness and was looking for contentment. One of his astrologers told him that if his assistants could find a contented man, they should bring the man's shirt back to the king and he would be cured of his sickness.

So the king sent his men out, and they searched the kingdom for a contented man whose shirt they could bring back to the king. Well, they searched far and wide, only to discover that the only contented man in the kingdom didn't own a shirt.

We know that contentment is not found in how much we have. For most of us, that's actually good news. What that means is we are just as much live candidates for true contentment as the people who have it all.

See, the rich and famous don't have anything on us ordinary people because the secret of contentment is that it's a by-product, a reward given by Christ to those who love Him and are faithful to Him. If we have Christ, we have all the power and resources necessary to do that.

The Test of Contentment

How do you know if you're truly content? How do you know if you're enjoying this reward, this blessing from Christ? The test of contentment is how much you have of it not just in the good times, but in the bad times too. Most people who are trying to find contentment are looking in the wrong places and talking to the wrong people.

The fact is, contentment is not available to everyone. It's not even possessed by every Christian. Paul says, "The secret I have learned is that whether I'm in prison waiting to die, or alive and in prosperity (the money's rolling in), it really doesn't matter, because I have Christ."

Paul's perspective not only gave him joy, it kept him from being intimidated. When threatened with death, Paul's response was, "To die is gain." When challenged with the day-to-day issues of life, he responded, "To live is Christ." And when he faced suffering, he could confidently say, "I consider that the sufferings of this present time are not worthy to be compared with the glory that is to be revealed to us" (Romans 8:18).

It didn't matter what unbelievers did to Paul, because Jesus Christ was the sum total of his life.

Have you reached the point where things and circumstances don't really matter all that much? I'm not talking about being unconcerned about life. I'm talking about letting the things around you control your level of contentment.

Someone may say, "Well, that was Paul, and I'm me. He was the great apostle. I'm just an ordinary believer." Ah, but Paul's secret to contentment had nothing to do with him. It had everything to do with Christ. Paul says, "I can do all things through Him who strengthens me" (Philippians 4:13). That's the secret.

Now I hear another objection. "Is that it? I thought you were going to give me some juicy new truth I could grab hold of and devour. I memorized that verse years ago."

But the question is not whether you can recite this familiar verse. The question is whether it's been indelibly inscribed upon your heart. Paul says, "I can." Now if you want the power of positive thinking, here it is.

The Focus of Contentment

Notice, however, that Paul didn't say, "I can do anything and everything." He's much more focused than that. He's saying, "I can do those things that Christ has called me to do. I can be the person Christ wants me to be. I can do and be all those things because He enables me. Therefore, there is nothing Christ expects of me that I can't do, because He takes it upon Himself to give me the power to pull it off."

The reason most Christians aren't content is that they don't have this power. To put it another way, the secret of contentment is to have such a dynamic love relationship with Jesus Christ, to be so preoccupied with Him, that He takes personal responsibility to enable you to do and be all He has called you to do and be.

So the focus of contentment is Christ, not contentment itself. As I said earlier, one reason most people aren't content is because they are trying too hard to be. If we will preoccupy ourselves with Christ, our hunger for contentment—and a whole lot of other things—will be met. So we come back to the primacy of our first love.

Paul is not dumping on you if you have things, because remember he said he had times of relative prosperity too (Philippians 4:12). His point is that none of life's things will give you contentment. Preoccupation with Christ will.

Paul could speak from personal experience, both on the issue of having and losing things (see 3:7–8), and on the issue of being content and at peace (see 4:6–7). Do you see what the man was thinking about all day long? He was consumed with Christ, and therefore he was content.

Are you consumed with Christ? If you are, you don't have to worry about finding contentment. It's His reward to you.

THE REWARD OF NEEDS SUPPLIED

Here's another familiar verse in Philippians 4 you may have memorized years ago: "My God shall supply all your needs according to His riches in glory in Christ Jesus" (v. 19).

Now that's an amazing verse. There is no need you and I have that our God does not have the ability to supply. Whether our needs are financial, physical, emotional, or whatever, God can take care of them. This is another earthly reward He offers to those who love Christ as their first and only love.

God's Idea of a Need

But we have to clarify a few things. First, it depends on who is defining the need. Let me explain what I mean. Sometimes God supplies our need by delivering us out of problems. But at other times, He supplies our need by giving us the right kind of problems.

You say, "What kind of a need does that supply?" Our need to develop into the kind of people He would have us to be. In both cases God is still meeting a need, whether it's deliverance from or provision of difficult circumstances when He wants to take us to the next level of spiritual growth.

God's Supply of a Need

How does God meet our needs? "According to His riches in glory in Christ Jesus." That's a glorious statement because of that little prepositional phrase "according to." God doesn't meet our needs "out of" His riches in Christ, but "according to" those riches.

That's a big difference. A millionaire could give you one dollar out of his riches. But that would not be according to his riches. It would not be reflective of what he's capable of doing. God's giving reflects what He's capable of.

Another aspect of this is illustrated by a situation where you come to me and say, "I need ten dollars." So I give you ten dollars from my resources. But now I'm down ten dollars because my resources are limited. In fact, if you come to me too often asking for ten dollars, we are going to have a problem.

But you don't have that problem with God, because God does not run out of resources. You can never deplete His funds. So when God comes alongside you and your need comes alongside Him, He evaluates what you need and provides all the supply necessary to cover the totality of the need. And He is no poorer for having done so. That's why you can go to Him again tomorrow.

But notice something very important. God's resources are "in Christ Jesus." Christ is the focus, not what He can give us. Paul's motive in loving and serving Christ was not to get all his bills paid (see Philippians 4:17). In fact, that brings up another very important point about this issue of getting our needs supplied.

No Blank Check

Inevitably, when you start talking about this someone says, "Wait a minute. If God has promised to supply all my needs, how come I'm not having my needs met? I've got this need and I've prayed about it. I've got that need and I've asked the Lord to supply. But nothing's happening. The guys on TV make it sound like it's automatic, like God has to come through for me."

There's a lot of confusion about this promise, because most people don't understand that it's a conditional promise, not an unconditional one. An unconditional promise is one that God fulfills regardless.

But a conditional promise means there are conditions you must meet before God will act. Look at verse 16: "For even in Thessalonica you sent a gift more than once for my needs." Now put that together with the promise we're considering in verse 19.

When you do that, you discover that God's promise of needs supplied is embedded in the context of faithful, generous—even sacrificial—giving.

Paul is saying, "You've been doing what God told you to do. You've been sacrificing for the cause of Christ. You've been giving for the building of God's kingdom. You've been living for His glory. You've put God in His rightful place, first place. You are making Jesus Christ your first love."

That sheds a different light on things. God doesn't simply hand us a "blank check" we can take to the bank of heaven any time we feel like it without any thought as to how we're using the resources He's entrusted to us. His supply is tied to our obedience.

Just as a bank will inspect your account to see if you have sufficient funds accumulated before cashing your check, so God calls up your spiritual account to see if you've laid up any heavenly treasure. Or, as Matthew 6:33

says, "Seek first His kingdom and His righteousness; and all these things shall be added to you."

If you're involved in the ongoing of the gospel message, building up people's lives, bringing people to Christ, supporting His work—in other words, demonstrating your love for Christ—God says, "I've got good news for you."

Now even if you're not meeting the condition, God may still come through for you in a time of need. But that's because He's gracious and He loves you, not because He's obligated to come through for you. But if you've met the condition of verses 15–16, God says He will obligate Himself to the promise in verse 19.

You may not think you need this reward right now, but just keep living. You are going to need God's supply. It may not be financially. It may be emotionally, physically, or spiritually, but you are going to need it. When that time comes, the question will be, What does your account look like?

REWARDS IN THE KINGDOM

Now we come to the other side of our study, the rewards in eternity awaiting those of us who hold fast to our first love for Christ.

For this survey I want to turn to Revelation 2–3, another incredible passage of Scripture that's worth a book all by itself. In his messages to the seven churches, Jesus Christ describes a group of believers called overcomers. All Christians are overcomers in one sense, because "greater is He who is in you than he who is in the world" (1 John 4:4).

However, not all believers who are overcomers actually overcome. That is, we must live out day by day the victory God has given us. So even though all believers are overcomers in Christ, not all believers are living out the victory that is theirs in Christ.

But here in Revelation 2–3, the overcomers are clearly those who achieve victory, who keep their love for Christ burning brightly. To these faithful ones, the risen Lord makes some incredible promises. Let's look at them one by one, beginning with our old friends in Ephesus (Revelation 2:1–7).

A Special Intimacy

I won't spend too much time reviewing the first five verses of this chapter. Let me just say again that God never meant for our duty to Him to replace our love for Him. Duty and devotion must always go side by side.

As we've noted, Jesus admonishes this church to go back to how things used to be, to remember when there was dynamic love and caring and all the things that made their relationship with Him tick. That's exactly what we've been trying to do in these last three chapters.

When I'm in marriage counseling I tell a couple, "Turn back the hands of time. Do the things you used to do." People want the relationship they used to have, but they aren't willing to do the things they used to do.

Let's move on to verse 7: "To him who overcomes, I will grant to eat of the tree of life, which is in the Paradise of God."

An overcomer is a Christian who does not lose devotion to the Savior while carrying out duty for the Savior —a Christian who doesn't just do the right things, but does the right things with the right heart. Christ is saying, "If you overcome your lack of devotion, I will allow you to eat from the tree of life."

The tree of life was in the Garden of Eden, the original paradise. It was where Adam was supposed to enjoy intimacy with God. God is going to provide the overcomers with intimate fellowship with Christ in a place called the "Paradise of God." That is, Christ is going to have His own private garden, so to speak, where those who were devoted to Him in this life can have special intimacy with Him in His kingdom.

A Special Crown

The church at Smyrna is next (2:8–11). This is a suffering church. Smyrna must have been an interesting-looking place: History tells us that many of the buildings were shaped like crowns due to the influence of the emperor on the city.

Jesus picks up this crown emphasis and says to them concerning their suffering, "Be faithful until death, and I will give you the crown of life" (v. 10). This is His reward to those who have been faithful under trials (see James 1:12).

Many of us don't know what suffering is. But the believers at Smyrna were undergoing real suffering. Some of them were being thrown into prison for their faith. They were facing intense persecution, but Jesus tells them: "He who overcomes shall not be hurt by the second death" (Revelation 2:11).

What is the second death? Hell, the lake of fire. You say, "But wait a minute. I thought no Christian was going to the lake of fire." That's right. I believe what Jesus is saying is, "Don't let sinners, who are on their way to the second death, be responsible for causing you to lose your reward."

In other words, don't let people going to hell keep you from enjoying maximum blessing in heaven. If you can endure everything sinners throw at you and remain faithful to Christ, your reward is great. You are storing up crowns. When I find out people hate me because I'm committed to Jesus Christ, I say, "Praise God. Give me another crown."

When you suffer because you are living right and are glorifying God (1 Peter 4:12–16), it registers in heaven. You have a reward waiting for you if you don't quit, but are "faithful unto death."

A Special Honor

The church at Pergamum (Revelation 2:12–17) had also experienced persecution, including the death of a saint named Antipas. But this church had some things to overcome as well:

> You have there some who hold the teaching of Balaam, who kept teaching Balak to put a stumbling block before the

sons of Israel, to eat things sacrificed to idols, and to commit acts of immorality. (v. 14)

What Balaam and Balak were working together to do was to get God's people to compromise (see Numbers 22–24). Jude 11 refers to the "error of Balaam," which was a problem for the early church. Compromise has always been a temptation for Christians, but God says if His church takes a stand and refuses to compromise, He will reward us:

> To him who overcomes, to him I will give some of the hidden manna, and I will give him a white stone, and a new name written on the stone which no one knows but he who receives it. (Revelation 2:17)

Since manna and white stones don't sound like a reward to most of us, we need to talk about this. In the Old Testament, Israel took some of the manna God provided, put it in a jar, and put it in the ark of the Covenant in the Holy of Holies to remind the people that God had supplied for them.

The idea here in Revelation 2 is that God still has a special supply tucked away. Not everyone can get to it, but He's going to make it available to His overcomers. Keep reading and you'll see how I think this ties together with the white stone.

In Jesus' day, a white stone was like a ticket. It would gain a person entry to a sporting event, like their early version of the Olympics, or to the theater. The person would drop his white stone in the box or whatever as he went into the event.

That is, he would do that unless he was a season ticket holder, because they had season ticket holders back then too. In that case, they would write the person's name or some insignia on the stone and he could use it again and again, showing that he had ongoing entry into any event.

Jesus Christ is saying that if you are an overcomer on earth, in His kingdom He will give you your personalized stone as your ticket to His special supply, sort of a private dining experience that the "general public"—the non-overcoming believers, if you will—won't have access to.

In other words, you'll have a "season ticket" that you can use any old time a meal is being served. It's always available to you; Christ will give you special, ongoing access to private dining with Him, entrance into His very presence that is not available to the general group.

That's a special honor. Though there will be many people in heaven, not everyone will get season tickets. Not everyone gets the same level of access to Jesus Christ. If you remain faithful to Him, you get the benefit of special fellowship with Christ.

A Special Position

Now we come to the church at Thyatira (Revelation 2:18–29), an unholy church. This is the longest message given to the smallest city. Jesus says in verse 20, "I have this against you, that you tolerate the woman Jezebel."

I don't know if this was her real name or just symbolic. It's kind of hard to imagine a mother naming her daughter Jezebel (see 1 Kings 16:29–31). But either way, this woman was running the church, doing what she wanted, and leading the people into sin. And no one was saying anything.

They tolerated her and her sin. But if you are going to be an overcomer, you can't tolerate sin. Not only do you not participate in it, you condemn it when it shows up. Jezebel was publicly flaunting her immorality with no sign of repentance. So God says, "Since you won't judge it, I will" (see v. 22).

So what's the reward to the overcomer in this setting? It's in verses 26–28:

> And he who overcomes, and he who keeps My deeds until the end, to him I will give authority over the nations; and he shall rule them with a rod of iron, as the vessels of the potter are broken to pieces, as I also have received authority from My Father; and I will give him the morning star.

Jesus says, "I'm going to let you rule with Me." Now, this is something special because this description of the overcomer's authority is the same description used of Christ's millennial rule (see Psalm 2:9; Revelation 12:5).

And then Jesus says, "While you are ruling with Me, I will also give you the morning star." According to Revelation 22:16, the morning star is Jesus Himself. The promise is that if you are an overcomer, you will rule with Christ in a position that will make it evident to all that you are closely associated with Him. I don't know how it will all happen, but it will be glorious.

A Special Invitation

The Sardis church (Revelation 3:1–6) needed to "wake up, and strengthen the things that remain, which were about to die" (v. 2).

Here is a church that liked to live in the past. Do you know people like that? They can tell you all about yesterday: what they used to do, what they used to be. But they never move forward. This was Sardis, although they had a few faithful ones:

> But you have a few people in Sardis who have not soiled their garments; and they will walk with Me in white; for they are worthy. He who overcomes shall thus be clothed in white garments; and I will not erase his name from the book of life, and I will confess his name before My Father, and before His angels. (vv. 4–5)

Jesus mentions garments because Sardis produced woolen garments. He has a promise of reward for the overcomers. White garments are the clothes of people going to a party, a special event. This means it's show time. The overcomers will be on Jesus' guest list whenever a special event is held in the kingdom. And there will be a lot of them. If you're an overcomer, you'll be a special guest of the King.

Not every Christian will attend every function in the kingdom, because Christians are not equal when it comes to rewards. But once you make Jesus' guest list, your name will not be erased. That is, Jesus says, "I will continue to send you invitations to My special kingdom parties."

A Special Recognition

Philadelphia, the city of "brotherly love," was the home of the faithful church (Revelation 3:7–13). Jesus has nothing bad to say about this church. But it still needs overcomers:

> He who overcomes, I will make him a pillar in the temple of My God, and he will not go out from it anymore; and I will write upon him the name of My God, and the name of the city of My God, the new Jerusalem, which comes down out of heaven from My God, and My new name. (v. 12)

We know what pillars do for buildings. Pillars hold the building up and at the same time beautify it. Jesus says He will make faithful overcomers like pillars in God's temple. And He will write a special name on them as well.

In other words, if you are faithful to Christ, if you keep your love for Him in its rightful place, you will gain special recognition so that wherever any of the rest of us go throughout the kingdom, we'll keep running into your name. People will ask, "Who is this person?"

Answer: "Oh, she's that faithful saint who kept herself pure, who wouldn't compromise her moral principles. He's that believer who stood firm for Christ on his job, who led his family in following the Lord. They are the ones who were faithful to the Lord no matter what, no excuses."

A Special Authority

The church at Laodicea (Revelation 3:14–22) was the worst of them all. You can see the problem in verses 15–16:

> I know your deeds, that you are neither cold nor hot; I would that you were cold or hot. So because you are lukewarm, and neither hot nor cold, I will spit you out of My mouth.

There are many churches that Jesus wants to throw up over because they are shucking and jiving. They are not hot, not on fire for Him. They aren't even cold. They are trying to play both ends against the middle.

Laodicea was a rich community. It produced wool and a special salve for the eyes, and Jesus used those things to tell the church how deep its spiritual need was (Revelation 3:18). Then comes the reward to the overcomers: "He who overcomes, I will grant to him to sit down with Me on My throne, as I also overcame and sat down with My Father on His throne" (v. 21).

If you are an overcomer, in the kingdom Jesus Christ is going to call you forward publicly and give you a special seat of authority. That way, the glory that comes to Christ He will share with you in some special way.

Look at all God has for us if we will just stay true to our first love. If you want to be an overcomer and share in these rewards, you're going to have to go all the way with Jesus Christ. You say, "But it's so hard, and I'm not getting any credit right now."

Let me tell you about Henry Morrison, a missionary to Africa. He was coming home from Africa on a ship which was also carrying Theodore Roosevelt. When the ship docked in New York, thousands of people were there to greet Roosevelt. But no one was cheering for Morrison.

Henry Morrison had served the Lord for forty years in Africa. As he watched the crowds greet Theodore Roosevelt, he became dejected to think he had served the Lord all those years and yet no one was there to greet him.

Morrison said that as he walked down the gangplank in a depressed mood, a voice whispered to him, "Henry, don't worry. You are not home yet." Then he said he saw a vision of multiplied thousands of Africans standing at the gates of heaven, those who he had reached for Christ, applauding him as he entered the pearly gates.

So if people are not recognizing you down here, if you are not getting any applause right now, don't worry. You are not home yet. Remember what Christ has waiting for you.

RETURNING TO YOUR FIRST LOVE

We all need to be reminded that this world is not our final home, that we're laboring for something far better. As you seek to love and serve Jesus Christ faithfully, let these ideas help you keep your first love burning brightly:

1. One way you can tell whether you are consumed with Christ or just seeking His benefits is what happens to the flame of your love for Him after He tells you no to something you've been praying for. Does the flame in your heart flicker and grow weaker because you're either upset or disappointed, or does your love stay strong because you know that He said no in love?

2. Here's a question worth thinking about, and doing something about, if the Holy Spirit shows you it's a problem. If God gave you the necessities of life—food, clothing, shelter —"according to" your giving to His work, would you have plenty . . . or would you be hungry, naked, and homeless?

3. Of the seven spiritual problems that needed to be overcome by the churches in Revelation 2–3, choose the one that's your greatest need to overcome at this time and make it the focus of your prayers.

4. Since the Bible tells us repeatedly that the last shall be first and the first last when God opens the books, ask Him to help you not be overly influenced by the world's standards for measuring greatness and reward. It may help you to write the words "Not Home Yet" on a card and set it on your table as a reminder that you're operating on a different system.

CHAPTER THIRTEEN

THE IMPORTANCE OF REPENTANCE

We're now ready to consider the second element of Jesus' three-part command in Revelation 2:5, which He gave to call us back to our first love. His first command was to *remember*. Then He called us to *repent*. I want to spend this chapter and chapter 14 dealing with repentance.

As you know by now, I'm married. In 1970 Lois and I stood before a pastor in a church and entered into a lifetime commitment of love and faithfulness to one another.

Any married person can tell you that when you first get married, you are starry-eyed. You are beside yourself. The whole world looks wonderful. Every time you look at your mate, you see a lifetime of joy and excitement, vitality and vigor. I mean, it's going to be nothing but bliss.

Later, however, you wake up and say, "What in the world have I done?" Because what you found out is that being married is not necessarily all you thought it would be. You discover there's a little bit more to it than you anticipated. You're still committed, but, as the song says, "The thrill is gone."

Many of us have found this to be true in our Christian lives. We got saved and thought it was all going to be bliss. With God in our lives, there'd be no blisters. Just victory after victory and showers of blessings. No more difficulties, catastrophes, or trials. That simply isn't true, is it? Getting saved fixed a lot of our problems, but it also surfaced a whole new set of problems and left some of the old ones around for us to deal with.

We discover that sin is as sinful as it ever was. Temptation is as tempting as it ever was. That temper is still there. The stark reality hits that being a Christian does not exempt us from the impulses of the flesh.

Therefore, just as a married couple can have their fellowship interrupted, their intimacy negated, and their closeness canceled because of problems, so you and I as Christians can have our fellowship, our intimacy, our closeness with God interrupted by sin.

That doesn't cancel the relationship. You are still married to Christ. But sin has come between you and Him, and the intimacy is lost. The only cure is repentance.

Now the whole concept of repentance has fallen on bad days. What we want to do is excuse ourselves, get people to understand that we're only human, get them to skip over our sin.

But God doesn't do that. He always calls on people who are in a relationship with Him, or who desire a relationship with Him, to change their minds about sin. That's the basic meaning of the word *repent*. It means changing your way of thinking from the previous way to the proper way.

There must be a changing of the mind that brings about a change of direction. Repentance is crucial if we are going to restore harmony where there is chaos, if we are going to return to our first love for Christ. It's possible to be saved, but not be in fellowship with the Savior. Let's see how to restore fellowship and put a new bloom on our love.

WE CAN REPENT OURSELVES

The four points I want to discuss have to do with what it takes to bring a Christian to the point of repentance when sin has disrupted his walk with God. You'll see that these points are in descending order; that is, we begin with the easiest step and go to the hardest.

When you aren't feeling well, someone might say, "Get some rest and take aspirin." Well, you don't need a doctor for that. You can do that on your own.

In the same way, God says in 1 John 1:9 that if you will come clean with Him on your own, you don't have to take the harder medicine. The consequences of your sin don't have to get any worse if you will take care of it yourself.

The Fact of Sin

John, the one who lay on Jesus' breast at the Last Supper, was very concerned about intimacy. His favorite word was abide, which means "stay close to, remain in close fellowship with." But John also knew that intimacy with God must be based on the standard of His holiness (1 John 1:5).

God is utterly apart from us while we are sinful, or full of sin. In fact, "If we say that we have no sin" (v. 8) we are lying. Notice the singular here. Verse 8 is referring to our sin capacity, the principle of sin that's still within us even as Christians. But then John says in verse 9: "If we confess our sins, He is faithful and righteous to forgive us our sins and to cleanse us from all unrighteousness."

To confess, as you probably know, means to agree with. It means to count it as God counts it. One of the reasons we don't get our love relationship with Christ restored, which is the fruit of repentance, is that we don't fully understand what repentance is.

When God calls something sin, it's not a bad habit. It's not a mistake. It's not a weakness. It's a sin. And sin is an affront to the character of God. One reason some Christians remain in a state of carnality is they never come to grips with how sinful sin really is. We categorize sin by size and by consequences. But "in [God] there is no darkness at all" (v. 5).

Different sins do have different consequences. But when it comes to the *category* of sin, there is no difference with God. Sin is exceedingly sinful whether it's a little lie or first-degree murder. This is important because what people want to do is skip over the sinfulness of sin by saying things like, "I just got mad. I could have killed him."

But God does not say, "The self-righteous anger is less sinful because nobody died." He says, "Sin is an affront to My character."

The Need for Confession

So John tells us to confess our "sins." He uses the plural here as opposed to the singular in verse 8 because now he's talking about specific sins. He wants us to identify the sin—the lie we told at 10:00 A.M., the lust we committed at noon—and call it by its real name. This is especially important today because we have a lot of errant theology messing Christians up. People try to put such a positive spin on the Christian life that they end up spinning right on by sin.

That's not how I read my Bible. When Noah was preaching and building his ark, he wasn't saying, "Something good is going to happen to you."

When Jeremiah was put into the pit for preaching, he didn't say, "I'm OK, you're OK."

When Daniel was thrown in the lions' den, he didn't say, "Possibility thinking will move mountains."

When John the Baptist saw King Herod taking his brother's wife, John didn't say, "Smile, God loves you!"

That's not what people need to hear when they've sinned. Sinning saints, and sinners who don't know Christ, need to hear "What you did was sinful; it violated the character of God. You must repent."

The Time for Confession

When do you confess your sins? According to 1 John 1:9, you confess when you sin. But what do we generally do? We keep on moving through our day, then we get on our knees at bedtime and say, "Now Lord, if I have committed any sins today. . . ."

Say what? There are at least two problems with that statement. *If* means you are calling into question whether you sinned.

The second problem is that you have collectivized sin. You put it all into one basket. God is holy. So if you tell a lie at, say, 8:30 in the morning, and that sin is not dealt with until you get on your knees at 11:00 P.M., from 8:30 in the morning until 11:00 at night you were out of fellowship with God.

If the only confessing you do is sort of a generalized "Don't remember the details, sorry about that" prayer at bedtime, no wonder your love relationship with Christ isn't what it should be. No wonder you don't have peace or victory. You have to deal with the issue of sin when the issue needs to be dealt with.

We all know married people who say, "My mate doesn't ever want to deal with anything." Intimacy is damaged when a wrong is committed and the guilty party blows it off or pretends like it never happened instead of confessing and seeking forgiveness.

God is saying, "When you sin, confess it as sin. Call it what it is, and confess it as it occurs."

The Price God Paid

The reason God wants you to agree with Him about your sin is that He wants to remind you of the price He had to pay for it. He doesn't want you excusing it as a mistake or a bad habit, or ignoring it, because sin is a high price-tag deal for God.

Our sin cost God the life of His Son, and He wants us to remember that. John says in verse 7 that it takes the blood of Jesus Christ to keep on cleansing us from sin.

When David sinned with Bathsheba, he said, "Purify me with hyssop" (Psalm 51:7). Hyssop is a plant which priests in the Old Testament used during a sacrifice. The priest took a hyssop branch, dipped the leaves in the blood of the sacrifice, and sprinkled the blood on the altar.

So when David prayed, "Purify me with hyssop," he was saying to God, "Sprinkle the blood of the sacrifice on the altar of Your mercy."

When you confess your sins, you are saying, "Lord, sprinkle the ever-present blood of Jesus Christ on my unrighteousness, and exact from that blood the payment necessary to pay in full for the sins I've committed."

Someone will ask, "Didn't Jesus' blood pay for all my sins when I accepted Him?" Yes, it did. But in order to maintain fellowship with Him, you must come clean with Him and change your mind about your sin. You must call sin what God calls it so that He, knowing you view your sin as He views it, can apply to it the cleansing blood of Christ. In this way, fellowship is restored.

The Sin Detector

The importance of maintaining intimacy with God helps to explain why Paul says, "Pray without ceasing" (1 Thessalonians 5:17). Faithful confession of sin results in continual cleansing.

You say, "But man, I forget things. I know I miss stuff." Well, God has a solution for that. At the end of verse 9 John says God will cleanse us from "all unrighteousness."

In other words, if you take care of the sins you know about, God will take care of the ones you forgot. If you come clean about the sins you know, He will cleanse you of the ones you don't know. God wants to know that you are taking Him seriously and taking sin seriously.

You say, "How do I know when I've sinned?" First, you know because you've been exposed to the Word and you have a standard. God hasn't left us in the dark on this issue. Second, you know when you've sinned because, as a Christian, you have a built-in sin detector.

When I go to the airport, I usually have my keys in my pocket. I walk through the detector. *Beep!* The man calls me back. I lay my keys in the little bucket and he says, "Walk through again."

I go through again. *Beep!* The second time the man says, "Empty your pockets." So I reach in my pockets and pull out everything in them, and I take off my watch because the detector has found hidden metal on me and has sounded the alarm.

You have within you a sin detector called the Holy Spirit. So whenever you introduce sin into your life, you are going to hear an internal beep. That's the Spirit of God setting off your conscience. That's why when your conscience tells you something, don't skip it, because if you are seeking to love Christ with all your heart, your conscience is going to be very sensitive to sin.

God deals with His kids differently. It's like when one of your children comes to you and says, "Mom, I just did something wrong." You are going to deal with that child differently than with the one who is doing things wrong and never admitting it. Both are wrong, but one is confessing it. The other one is ignoring it.

OTHERS CAN BRING US TO REPENTANCE

By the time Paul wrote the letter we know as 2 Corinthians, the Corinthian church was doing a better job of dealing with the sin in its midst. Before, the church was overlooking the sin of one of its members and even bragging about it, as we saw back in chapter 7.

No Regrets

In 1 Corinthians 5:1–13 Paul had told them, "Look, you are messing up. You are an embarrassment." But after Paul confronted them with the mess, they dealt with it. So here in 2 Corinthians he says, "Though I caused you sorrow by my letter, I do not regret it" (7:8). Why? Because Paul was dealing with them based on God's Word, and because it did the job.

I know some people leave my church on Sunday mad at me. I once had a brother tell me, "When I came to this church and I heard you preaching the Bible, I said to myself, 'Who does he think he is?'"

But he went on to say, "After I kept listening to the Word, it was clear to me that what you were saying was what God was saying and, therefore, that's what I needed to hear."

If someone gets mad at what I say or write, if it's based on the Word then I have to say like Paul, "I don't regret causing you sorrow or anger if you are being confronted with truth, because only truth sets you free."

So Paul says, "I don't regret it, even though I know I caused distress when I told you to put the man out of the church." When we have to exercise church discipline and remove someone from our fellowship because he or she refuses to repent and continues in rebellion, many Christians don't understand.

But when the action is necessary and done according to biblical guidelines, the sorrow or anger is only for a little while. It passes. People get over it. That's what Paul tells the Corinthians at the end of verse 8. Then he says in verse 9: "I now rejoice, not that you were made sorrowful, but that you were made sorrowful to the point of repentance; for you were made sorrowful according to the will of God."

Worldly Sorrow

Sorrow is fine if it leads you to do something about what made you sorry. I know a lot of us have people in our lives who are constantly saying, "I'm sorry." The first time you accept it at face value, but when they keep doing the same thing over and over again and saying, "I'm sorry," you know they are not sorry "to the point of repentance," or they would stop the offense.

There are several kinds of sorrow, as Paul now explains in verse 10: "For the sorrow that is according to the will of God produces a repentance without regret, leading to salvation; but the sorrow of the world produces death." The kind of sorrow I described above may include a lot of boo-hooing and a big show. But unless it produces a change of mind, leading to a change of action, it is what the Bible calls worldly sorrow. The difference is in that phrase found in verse 9 and repeated in verse 10: "according to the will of God."

Worldly sorrow means you feel bad about what you did, but you don't have a change of mind about it. Worldly sorrow says, "I shouldn't have done that." "That was so bad for me to do."

Godly Sorrow

But godly sorrow says, "I feel sorry about what I did. That was bad for me to do. I'm going to change my mind about that sin and come up with a plan of action to turn it to righteousness."

That's sorrow "according to the will of God." It gets you somewhere. It produces a change of mind, repentance. And remember, whatever your mind thinks, your feet act out. Your mind controls your feet. So you ought to be formulating an action plan to carry out your repentance.

Husband, if you are sorry for the way you have been talking to your wife, you can't replace something with nothing. You can't just say, "I'm sorry I chewed you out yesterday. I'm sorry I showed you disrespect the day before. And I'm sorry for what I said a few minutes ago."

Godly sorrow says, "I am pained over what I did. I change my mind. This is wrong, so I'm going to replace that data with compliments and statements of love, support, and encouragement. I am going to turn my mouth around." That kind of sorrow produces no regrets.

Restoring the Guilty

Galatians 6 is also important here. We'll study this chapter in greater detail in chapter 17, so I want to save most of my comments for that chapter. Let me just note a few things here to round out this portion of the discussion. Paul writes: "Brethren, even if a man is caught in any trespass, you who are spiritual, restore such a one in a spirit of gentleness" (v. 1).

The word *caught* here is "overtaken." In other words, the offender is stuck. You know, some people begin committing a sin and get stuck there. They want to get out and they try to get out, but they are in quicksand.

The word "restore" used in "restore such a one" means to mend a broken leg or a torn net, to put it back together. It does *not* mean seeing someone caught in a sin and calling up your friend to say, "Girl-l-l, um! Let me tell you what I just found out."

If you do that, you don't fit the classification of "you who are spiritual." You are just as guilty as the person you are talking about. Because if you are spiritual, you are going to be setting the bone, mending the net, helping that person toward repentance and restoration.

The Bible says that spiritual Christians, when they see other Christians on the ground, don't come over to them and say, "What are you doing down there? Get up!" They say, "Let me help you up." Your job and my job is to restore a sinning brother or sister. The apostle James tells us:

> My brethren, if any among you strays from the truth, and one turns him back, let him know that he who turns a sinner from the error of his way will save his soul from death, and will cover a multitude of sins. (5:19–20)

I tell my church family that if they see me going astray, don't call my family and neighbors and the other church members and say, "I see the pastor going down the wrong road." Tell *me*, and help turn me around.

The failure of the church to do this is one of the great disasters in Christianity today. We shoot our wounded rather than restoring them. I'm not talking about the rebellious person who doesn't care. I'm talking about the person who has been overtaken, trapped in a sin, and wants to get out. The Bible says go get that person and bring him back.

When I was growing up one of the things I liked to do was tell on my brother, especially when I had just had a spanking. My attitude was, "I'm not going through this alone."

So the next thing I saw my brother do, I would tell my father, "Oooh Daddy, guess what I saw!"

But my father got wise to what I was doing. So one time after I had just got a spanking and tried my little trick he said, "Go back downstairs."

I said, "Go back downstairs for what?"

"I'm going to spank you again."

"But, Dad, I'm talking about my brother, not me."

My dad said, "Yeah, I know, but I'm going to spank you for intentionally trying to get your brother in trouble."

God is saying that when you see a brother sin, go correct him and help him repent instead of telling on him to someone else. Otherwise you might wind up sharing his spanking!

GOD'S DISCIPLINE BRINGS REPENTANCE

To those Christians who fail to repent on their own, and reject the efforts of brothers or sisters to restore them, God says, "I have tried to heal you twice. Now I am going to have to use heavier medication."

Look at 1 Corinthians 11:29–32, where the setting is the communion table:

> He who eats and drinks, eats and drinks judgment to himself, if he does not judge the body rightly. For this reason many among you are weak and sick, and a number sleep. But if we judged ourselves rightly, we should not be judged. But when we are judged, we are disciplined by the Lord.

Direct Intervention

Here's a case where the Lord steps in and takes this thing on Himself. Some of the Corinthian believers were getting drunk at the Lord's table; others were stuffing themselves (v. 21). Apparently nothing was being done about it.

So God says in effect, "You won't obey My Word and judge your own sin. You won't listen to your brothers and sisters. So I'm going to step in here." The seriousness of this is evident from verse 30, where Paul says that some Corinthian believers were weakened, and others had actually died, because of their sin.

How does God set out to weaken a sinning and unrepentant Christian? He may do it in any number of ways, using life's circumstances to so unravel a person's life that he can't seem to get his emotions, family, marriage, or finances together.

I think we've all experienced this at one time or another. As soon as you pay off one bill, something else breaks down. About the time you head off one family crisis, another one erupts. That's Holy Spirit timing.

Now I'm not saying every problem you have is God's judgment. I'm talking about a severe pattern of weakness where you just never get it all together. If He has to, God can so arrange life that it collapses around you.

Some people say, "If God doesn't want me doing this, why doesn't He just hit me with lightning?" He may be doing just that—only the "lightning" may be coming in the mail with words like "Past Due" or "Final Notice" on it. It may come as sickness, or some other dire circumstance.

Drastic Steps

We know what this is like because as parents we sometimes have to take severe steps with our children. A man came to me one time and said, "My son won't listen to me. The police picked him up and he's in jail. Should I bail him out?"

I said, "No. You've tried. Since he's not listening to a dad who loves him, maybe he will listen to the police." It's painful, but remember that the goal of God's judgment is to restore us in love, not to send us to an early grave. Sometimes our kids need catastrophic experiences to teach them a lesson.

That's what happened to King Uzziah, who became leprous by rebelling against God's authority (2 Chronicles 26). That's what happened to Ananias and Sapphira (Acts 5). That's what happened to David when he went a year without confessing his sin with Bathsheba and God had to intervene and judge him (2 Samuel 12).

Many people in church say, "I don't want to hear this judgment stuff. That doesn't make me feel good." But 1 Peter 4:17 says, "It is time for judgment to begin with the household of God." There should be one place where you hear the truth: the house of God. Sometimes, the truth includes judgment. And you are not supposed to feel right about what's wrong.

SATAN'S JUDGMENT BRINGS REPENTANCE

If nothing else works, then the Lord hands you over to the Devil. Let's consider 1 Timothy 1:18–20:

> This command I entrust to you, Timothy, my son, in accordance with the prophecies previously made concerning you, that by them you may fight the good fight, keeping faith and a good conscience, which some have rejected and suffered shipwreck in regard to their faith. Among these are Hymenaeus and Alexander, whom I have delivered over to Satan, so that they may be taught not to blaspheme.

You know what a shipwreck is. What causes it? Sometimes it's not having your oars in place. There are two oars you use to keep your spiritual ship on course: faith and a good conscience.

The Two Oars

Here's how this works. When you live in obedience to the revelation of God's Word, trusting God to honor His Word as you obey it, that's a life of faith.

Of course, your conscience is that part of you that lets you know right from wrong. Even non-Christians have consciences. But they have the wrong database, so they may feel right about what's wrong and wrong about what's right.

But when you get saved, your conscience is renewed along with your mind, because now you are operating according to a new database, the Bible. When you are living a life of faith, based on the Word of God, the Holy Spirit can guide your conscience, saying yes here and no there. The result is a good conscience.

Heading for Trouble

But what many of us try to do is fit the square peg of our conscience into the round hole of the world's system, to change the metaphor. If we keep twisting and turning that thing long enough and hard enough, we will cut grooves into the square peg and it will become like the round hole.

What happens is that the Holy Spirit pricks our conscience, but we give it a turn. Another prick comes and we turn it again, until we get so used to turning it that we become comfortable with our sin. Once that happens, we're headed for a shipwreck.

Some time back I wrote a letter to the friends who support our national ministry, The Urban Alternative, after I found out that three of my good friends in the ministry had fallen into immoral conduct. They had shipwrecked on the rocks. They were losing their families, the respect of their children, their ministries, and their reputations.

So in this letter I asked our constituency to pray that the Lord would keep me honest with my conscience and with His Word, and to deal with sin quickly, so that no one would have to read about me in the newspaper someday.

When I see this happening to men I respect and who love the Lord, I know it can happen to me. I am not beyond the power of Satan. And neither are you. You can be forgiven after a shipwreck, but it may destroy your ability to be used by God.

This had happened to Hymenaeus and Alexander. We know from 2 Timothy 2:17–18 that Hymanaeus's sin was teaching that the resurrection (the rapture) had already passed, causing some Christians to chuck their faith.

Handed Over

So Paul handed these men over to Satan, which means he put them out of the church. We saw earlier that excommunication removed a person from God's protective custody and gave Satan direct access to his life.

A lot of people don't understand the power God has invested in the church. If the church's judgment is based on legitimate criteria, when the church turns someone over to Satan, that's it. That's about as severe as it gets— although let me remind you once again, the goal is repentance and restoration as we saw in the case at Corinth (1 Corinthians 5; cf. 2 Corinthians 2).

When you don't repent yourself; when you don't listen to your fellow Christians; when you don't respond to God's direct discipline; then you must be handed over to Satan, a severe judge who wants to take you under. God will let you get to the place of going under if that's the only way you will repent.

How much less painful and more joyful it is when we change our minds and come back to the Lord on our own. You can tell by now that I like the story of the prodigal son. He's living in sin and degradation, eating with the pigs, when he comes to his senses one day and says, "Wait a minute! Back home at my daddy's house, the servants live better than this."

So this young man gets up and starts home. His father is looking for him. The prodigal comes to his father and says, "Father, I have sinned!"

This son doesn't try to excuse himself by saying, "I blew it." "I did something stupid." "Everyone makes mistakes." He says, "I have sinned. I have violated your standard." You know the rest of the story. The father forgives and restores his son, then throws him a party.

One man told me, "Whenever my wife and I argue, she gets historical."

I said, "You mean hysterical?"

"No, historical. She brings up everything I've ever done!"

The beautiful thing about God's forgiveness is that He remembers your sin no more. He acts as though it never happened because when you truly repent, He restores you to fellowship. Your first love is put back in first place where it belongs.

RETURNING TO YOUR FIRST LOVE

Isn't it like our Lord to give us the opportunity to repent and come back to Him of our own accord? Even Jesus Christ doesn't coerce love. My prayer is that whatever your need may be concerning repentance, you'll deal with it now:

1. Psalm 32 expresses David's joy at God's forgiveness after David had repented of his sin. Read this wonderful psalm. If you cannot honestly say this is your experience right now, go before the Lord and stay there until you have dealt with anything that might be blocking your fellowship with Him.

2. Based on what we learned about the way God uses our fellow Christians to draw us back, this is a good time for an attitude check. Answer this question in your heart: If another believer came to you, with the right motive, to confront you in love about a sin in your life, would your first response be anger and defensiveness, or openness and gratitude that someone cared?

3. Since your relationship with Christ is first and foremost one of love, ask Him to keep your heart tender toward Him. If your focus is on loving the Lord, you won't have to worry about being sensitive to sin. You'll feel it right away!

4. If you're like most Christians, one person in your life has done more than anyone else to keep you on track. Why not call or write that person and express your appreciation? Be specific in telling your friend what he or she means to you. If that person is already with the Lord, tell Him how grateful you are—and ask Him to relay the message!

CHAPTER FOURTEEN

NO MORE TWO-TIMING

A song popularized a few years ago contained this line: "Trying to love two ain't easy to do."

That's a good way to summarize the point of this chapter. An important part of repentance and returning to our first love is putting away any other love that could be a rival to Christ.

We all know what a "two-timer" is: someone who tries to juggle two loves simultaneously. He attempts to maintain a home and family and give the appearance that all is well, while at the same time carrying on an illicit affair.

Two-timing, otherwise known as adultery, causes a number of problems, among which is that after a while, one or both of the parties being two-timed gets tired of the juggling act.

THE PROBLEM OF TWO LOVERS

As the legitimate partner, the adulterer's mate has the right to claim exclusive affection and faithfulness. The "other woman" (or man) gets tired of being the other and insists that the adulterer make a choice. As every two-timer discovers, one cannot maintain two loves simultaneously.

The Other Lover

The Bible uses the analogy of adultery to describe spiritual unfaithfulness to Christ. Jesus not only has the right to claim our first love, but He demands to be our *only* love. Let's look at what the Lord has to say to Christians who "two-time" Him:

> You adulteresses, do you not know that friendship with the world is hostility toward God? Therefore whoever wishes to be a friend of the world makes himself an enemy of God. (James 4:4)

The Lord says, "You are trying to fake Me out by your Sunday morning attendance. You come to church on Sunday like everything is fine, like you just came home from work. But I know you are two-timing Me Monday through Saturday, although everything is 'Amen, praise the Lord' on Sunday morning. We have a serious problem we've got to discuss."

The Lord is talking to Christians who say, "I love You with all my heart. I'm thankful You saved me. I'm thankful I'm on my way to heaven. I want to live my life for You." But come Monday morning, they run back to their other lover called the world. Now let's talk about the world so we can make sure we are talking about the same thing.

Is it two-timing the Lord to go out where the sinners are? In other words, are you flirting with the world because you work with sinners, bank with sinners, or live in a neighborhood where you are surrounded on all sides by sinners? Is that what constitutes "friendship with the world"?

No, of course not. When the Bible talks about believers having an affair with the world, God's Word is using the term *world* to describe an evil system headed by Satan that opposes God and leaves Him out.

Leaving God Out

You see, the problem is not that we work every day where sinners work. The problem is when we leave God out as we go to work. It's not that we live in neighborhoods where sinners live; it's that we leave God out of our neighborhoods. It's not that we have friends who are sinners. The problem is that in our friendships we leave God out.

But at the same time, we go to church on Sunday saying to our main love, Jesus Christ, "Everything is fine. Brought my whole paycheck home. It's cool."

But the Lord is saying, "You tell Me one thing on Sunday, but then you leave Me sitting in the pew while you go do your thing the rest of the week. But what you forgot is I can sit in the pew and still see where you are going and what you are doing. I can sit right here and know that you have left Me out.

"You are doing things I can't do, going places I can't go, and saying things I can't talk about. But you come back home on Sunday telling Me we're doing all right."

This is like the guy who says, "Me and my lady at home are doing fine." Now he hasn't been home much all week to see her or give her any attention, but everything's great. He shows up Saturday night saying, "What's happening?"

She says, "Not you."

This is God's complaint. "You have a friendship and an intimacy with the world, and that's hostility toward Me. I am no fool. I know better than to be satisfied with hearing the words 'I love You' when there's no reality behind them.

"I know you've got this other lover called the world you are seeing all week. I know you are embarrassed to have Me as your main squeeze, to identify with Me. So don't try to fool Me by showing up next Sunday morning talking about, 'Me and Jesus are OK.' I'm angry because you are doing a number on Me, your first and only love."

Just like any loving spouse whose faithful and exclusive love is being met by unfaithfulness, Jesus Christ reacts to being two-timed. He's not satisfied with Sunday morning commitment.

One of the tragedies in our Christian community today is two-timing Christians who have a lover on the side; who say they love the Lord with all their heart and soul and mind and strength, but leave Him out of their thoughts, out of their activities, and out of their relationships.

He can't tell them how to live. He can't go with them where they go. They leave Him seated on the pew at church and say, "Stay here like a nice little boy. I'll come back and pick You up next week."

THE IMPOSSIBILITY OF LOVING TWO

What we've got today are too many Christians who sit on the fence with one leg in the world and the other leg in the kingdom. They politely shift at the right time. When it's time to be in the kingdom, they shift to the kingdom. Then when they are with their friends, they shift back to the world.

So they are constantly rocking back and forth, shifting from side to side because they want to have their cake and eat it too.

The Conflict

How do you know whether you have another lover besides Jesus Christ—and what do you do about it if you do? That's the question we want to answer from James 4:1–10. The apostle cuts right to the chase in verse 1: "What is the source of quarrels and conflicts among you? Is not the source your pleasures that wage war in your members?"

One of the ways you know you are two-timing Jesus Christ is when there is a lot of confusion, conflict, and friction in your life. When you start trying to live the good life, seeking "your pleasures," you find out that you've got to become like the world to get what you want.

Just look in the home. I can assure you that wherever you find a husband and wife in constant conflict, it's because both of them want their pleasure. In a case like this, the pleasure is usually that of winning. They are arguing, and both want to win. Both want to be right. Both want to have their own way.

Having to win, to out-argue the other, is a sure-fire recipe for conflict, because the goal of life is pleasing self. But if you can get both parties to agree that neither one has to win, there is no argument in a home that can't be solved. There is no argument in the church that can't be solved. But as long as everyone has to win, there's conflict. That's the world's way.

That's the way a person climbs the corporate ladder. Many people who climb that ladder do so in conflict. They climb over other people. They pull people ahead of them back down. They guard their rung so no one can pass them. It's dog-eat-dog because that's the way of the world.

The Solution

God says, "Don't transport that junk to My kingdom, because we don't operate that way. In My kingdom, there is only one love, and that's Me. And if I'm the only love in the kingdom, there should be no conflict, because everything is being done for one Person: Me."

Let me tell you a couple of ways to solve conflicts fast. One is to start with what's wrong with you. If you start there, you won't have so much time to talk about what's wrong with the other person.

The next time you and your mate or someone else start to argue, say, "You know, before I talk about what's wrong with you, let me talk about how I've failed in this area." You just killed the argument.

Another way is to say, "I can't remember who won our last argument, but I'll tell you what. It's probably your turn to win, so I'll just concede this one to you. Let me see what I can do to fix your complaint."

THE PROBLEM OF OUR PLEASURES

How bad do people, even Christians, want to fulfill their pleasures? Real bad, according to James: "You lust and do not have; so you commit murder. And you are envious and cannot obtain; so you fight and quarrel" (James 4:2a). That's wanting it bad. Sometimes people want something so bad they'll lust for it and do almost anything to get it.

Spiritual Murder

I don't think James is saying that Christians were carrying their daggers to church. The idea here is that you destroy someone else because you can't get what you want. You harm another person because of your own misery. You kill someone else's character because you are jealous. You murder your marriage because you can't live with yourself.

Jesus referred to an attitude of hatred that is as bad as the act of murder and often leads to it (Matthew 5:21–22). No one ever killed anyone until there was a wrong attitude first. The action presupposes the attitude.

The World's Way

James is saying that when you try to get what you want by the world's way and get blocked, you get mad and start tearing people down. I hear husbands and wives use their tongues to tear one another apart. They will get on each other and just tear each other down.

The Bible says the problem there is divided loyalty. If that man's wife were the "apple of his eye," the reason for his existence, instead of tearing her down he would be finding ways to make her happy and resolve the conflict. If this wife honored her husband, she would be trying to build him up rather than leveling him.

James says, "If you want something and you go about getting it the world's way, you are never going to be satisfied, because the world doesn't let you have anything easy. And even if you get it, the world is going to try to maneuver you out of it so that you have to keep playing the game to keep it."

Someone may say, "What do you expect? It's a rough world out here. I can't take that Bible stuff from Sunday and use it on Monday. I mean, that stuff is too salty. I know the Bible and all that, but that was another time and another era for another people."

Just Ask

To which James answers, "You do not have because you do not ask" (4:2b). You've been breaking your neck and getting into conflicts when all you had to do was spend some time with your main love, Jesus Christ, and ask Him. He would gladly give it to you. It takes the pressure off. It takes the frustration off.

The Lord says to us, "I'm in the business of dispensing to you those things that really matter in life. But you don't have them because you'd rather fight for them than ask Me. If you had only asked, you wouldn't have had to fight."

But we say, "I'd rather fight than ask."

Imagine what would happen if, the next time a husband and wife started fighting over money, he said, "Honey, before we fight each other, let's get on our knees and ask. Maybe God wants to write a check out. Maybe He wants to take care of our need without us fighting over it and being no further ahead after the fight than when we started."

See, Jesus Christ says, "I want to be your only love. But as long as you keep going to that other lover called the world to fix you up, then I'll let that other lover try to take care of you when you're down."

I know a man who left his wife and went to another lover who had it all. She was beautiful, young, vivacious, and going somewhere. He "outgrew" his wife. He had a middle-class job, two cars, a decent house, and a few dollars in the bank, and he says he outgrew his wife.

But there's one thing he and guys like him forget when they plunge into adultery. They take the risk that someone else a little further down the line will come along and take their new lover from them, and they will lose all the way around.

God is saying, "Instead of investing all that extra time and energy in the world, invest it with your main love. I want us to have such a love relationship that all you have to do is ask instead of fighting and quarreling, because that's the world's way of getting it."

Just listen to the stories of many of those who made it. They say, "I scratched and clawed my way to the top. I climbed over them before they could climb over me because that's the only way you get to the top." But the Bible says that the way a Christian gets to the top is crawl to the bottom.

Unanswered Prayer

Whenever we talk about asking for what we need, someone always objects. "Wait a minute. I pray. I've been praying and praying and praying. But God hasn't honored my asking. I ask and nothing happens." Ah, let's check out verse 3: "You ask and do not receive, because you ask with wrong motives, so that you may spend it on your pleasures."

This is like a guy who comes to his wife and says, "Honey, write me a check for $100."

She says, "What do you need it for?"

"You don't need to know that. Just write me a check." Now she already knows he's been two-timing her. And she knows that if she gives him the money he asks for, it's only going to help fund his adultery.

So she says no, because she's not about to be a party to helping her husband run around on her and leave her out. This is exactly why God doesn't answer a lot of our prayers. He knows that to give us what we ask for is to give us something more that He will be left out of.

We say, "Lord, give me that house You can't live in. Give me that car You can't ride in. Give me that money You can't use. Give it to me so I can use it for me."

Christ doesn't answer many of our prayers because He knows, and we know if we're honest, that our other lover is going to get the benefit. It's going to be used for the world and invested in the world, so why should the Lord help anyone two-time Him? He's not going to help feed any other lover.

When Christians enter the waters of baptism, they are supposed to be saying, "I have committed my life to Jesus Christ as My Savior. When I come up out of this water, I am going to be raised to walk with Him in a totally dedicated new life."

But what happens? Now we give Him a nod or two one day a week. That's why we don't get a lot of the things we want. Or if we do get them, we get them the world's way, which means we get the world's problems with them.

See, you can leave God out and become a millionaire. You can leave God out and have a big business. But let me tell you something. If you do this, there will come a time when God does not make Himself available to you.

THE REALITY OF GOD'S DISCIPLINE

What God does is change the locks on the door so that when you come back home talking about, "I've seen the light," the locks are different and God won't let you in.

Now why? Is He just being mean? Is He not a forgiving God? Yes, He will forgive you for your spiritual adultery if you are serious about your repentance. But He wants to let you know what it feels like to be out in the cold so that, if you ever do get in, you never want to two-time Him again.

God has no problem keeping you out in the cold for a while after you have been out playing around with the world. What God gets at His door is a lot of casualties who have had this affair with the world and have been beaten up by their other lover. So they come saying, "Take me back." But God knows they just want to get rested up and fixed up so they can step out on Him again.

So He says, "Stay outside for a while. Feel the blizzard. Stand in the snow. Then you'll learn that you just don't come and go as you please and play with My love like that. I love you and I want a relationship."

As Chuck Swindoll says, "You can't flirt with a holy God." You'd better get serious, because He's a jealous lover.

THE REALITY OF GOD'S JEALOUSY

This is where we come back to our theme verse, James 4:4, which I dealt with at the beginning of this chapter. I won't quote the verse again here, so I encourage you to turn back and read it again. It's serious stuff when God calls His people "adulteresses."

You say, "Wait a minute. Why is God getting after this thing so strongly?" Verse 5 helps answer that: "Do you think that the Scripture speaks to no purpose: 'He jealously desires the Spirit which He has made to dwell in us?'"

Like any good spouse, God is jealous. He doesn't want to share you with the world. Spiritual adultery is trying to love two when you've committed yourself to one. You can't sleep in another's bed, then come home and expect all to be well. You can't love this world and Jesus Christ too. You can't have two first loves. He's jealous.

Two Become One

I have a big question when someone invites me somewhere and says I can't bring my wife. I have to have a good reason why I can't bring Lois. If it's an all-men's meeting, that's fine. If it's something that would not be appropriate for her, fine.

I travel about eight weeks a year holding Bible conferences across the country. I let the people know that a certain number of those weeks, I bring Lois. That's just how it is. There is no negotiation. I say, "If you want me for those weeks, I bring my wife because she is part of me."

Then if you tell me you don't want my wife, you've just excluded me too. Because when people get married they become one.

Taking Christ with You

God says, "I married you and now you want to leave Me sitting here. Where are you going that I can't go with you?"

A lot of Christians want to know, "Now that I'm a Christian, what can I do and not do? Is it wrong to do this and that?" There is a very simple solution to that question. Ask yourself, "Can I take Jesus Christ along with me?" Or must you say, "Jesus, You stay in the car and I will be right back"?

See, if you cannot take Christ, if Christ can't look at it and you can't talk about it with Him, then you need to question what you're doing. If you have to leave your love at home all the time, something's wrong. Jesus is jealous. He wants you for Himself.

James isn't saying, "Don't be in the world." He's saying, "Don't be conformed to the world" (see Romans 12:1–2). In other words, don't go and have a relationship with the world that Christ can't participate in.

THE BENEFITS OF TRUE LOVE

Do you know what having a love affair with Jesus Christ alone will do? It will get you more grace, that's what it will do. Look at verse 6 of James 4: "But He gives a greater grace. Therefore it says, 'God is opposed to the proud, but gives grace to the humble.'"

Greater Grace

Grace is God doing for you what you can't do for yourself. And I guarantee you, all you have to do is keep living and you are going to run into situations where you will need God to do for you what you can't do for yourself.

Right now you may be able to pay cash. Right now everything may be going well, and loving two, two-timing Jesus Christ, may be looking fine. But we've all seen those television shows where a guy is trying to juggle two lovers.

What always happens? He comes to that time when the two lovers are in the same place at the same time, and he's going crazy trying to hide one and get the other one out of there. Why? Because he knows if they ever find out about each other, he's a dead man. Both of them will get mad and dump him. Instead of being a two-timer, he'll be a two-time loser!

What I'm saying is there comes a time when you get in a mess that only the grace of God can deliver you out of. I'm not implying that God will help you in a situation like the one I've just described. That's your mess. However, we often need "greater grace." And if your relationship with Christ isn't tight, that greater grace may be missing. You are going to want Christ to be there, but He will say, "I'm not going to be there for you when you have been cheating on Me with someone else."

Verse 6 says if you're proud, God's going to work against you. What does it mean to be proud? Some guys think they are "all-world cool breeze." They have that attitude of arrogance because they feel like the world wants them.

Well, God says, "Fine, since the world wants you, I am going to work against you. Then we'll see how the world and you make out when I decide I'm not on your side, when I back away from you and oppose you. Then we'll see what the world can do."

No matter who you are, you will come to a time when you need "greater grace." You are going to need God to do for you what you can't do for yourself. Whether He does that or not will be determined by how faithful you've been in your love affair with Jesus Christ.

Submission to God

So the question is, how do we make sure we're in a position where God can bestow His grace on us? Verse 7 answers that: "Submit therefore to God. Resist the devil and he will flee from you."

Notice there are two sides to the coin: submission toward God and resistance toward the Devil. Submission is a military term that means get in your proper rank. Privates don't tell generals what to do. Get in your rank. Place yourself under God's command. He is saying, "I'm in charge here. Fall in!"

Submission to God means I place myself under divine authority. It means I say, "Lord, whatever You want me to do, I will do it. No matter what anyone else tells me to do, I'll find out what You want me to do, and do it."

Resisting the Devil simply means saying no to him. Now, we know that the Devil is not going to just sit back and let you submit to God. The Devil's not going to say, "Oh, pardon me. You've submitted to God. I guess I'd better leave you alone." No. The more submitted you are, the more the Devil's going to try and break you down.

But James says there comes a point when even the Devil will run. A lot of people say, "I'm trying to get the Devil off my back. He won't leave me alone!"

Well, if the Devil's bothering you that much, you may have a spiritual problem, because Jesus says, "If you are submitted to Me and the Devil is riding your back, there comes a point where I slap him off. I will let the Devil test you. I will let the Devil tempt you.

"But when you submit to Me and hold on to Me, then I show up and say, 'Devil, let's move it!'" So if the Devil is riding you, slapping you around, beating you to death, and you don't ever seem to get any rest from his harassment, you may have a spiritual problem.

No Christian wants to be in resistance to God. It's a hard thing when God is against us, because no one can stop Him. He resists us. He pushes us back. He holds us off. We declare war with God when we live to please ourselves.

Drawing Near

Well, we don't want that, so how do we submit? "Draw near to God and He will draw near to you" (v. 8a). James is talking about a relationship. A lot of men complain about what their wives are not. A guy will say, "My wife's not this. She's not that. She can't do this. She won't do that. She won't do anything."

So he goes out and has an affair. He lavishes all this special attention on the other woman. He's alert to her every whim. Every time he sees her, he takes her to a special place. He wines and dines her. They go here and there together. And she responds, telling him he's wonderful.

But go home and check with his wife. When was the last time he treated her the way he's treating this other woman? What this foolish man needs to understand is that his wife might respond that way if he would draw near to her that way. He can't be drawing away from her and then complaining, because the further away he gets, the worse she looks. He's got to draw near.

But the nearer he draws, the nearer she will draw, because most women have response mechanisms within them that respond to the right kind of stimuli. So he doesn't need to draw away from her. He needs to draw near to her.

That's what Jesus Christ says. "I'm not the one having the affair. Draw near to Me and I will respond. Draw near to Me and I will draw near to you."

THE SECRET OF INTIMACY

How do you draw near? The rest of verse 8 tells you: "Cleanse your hands, you sinners; and purify your hearts, you double-minded."

That is, get your life together. You can't be doing any old kind of thing any old kind of way and expect God's blessing. There's no one more double-minded than a two-timer. He's on that fence, with one foot in the kingdom and the other one in the world. He's trying to keep two lovers happy, and it isn't working.

Cleanse Your Hands

What a double-minded two-timer needs to do is say to the Lord, "I'm wiping my hands of this affair with the world and moving on with You alone." That's what He wants.

Some Christians are happy because things are going well for them right now. They are just tickled to death. There's money in the bank. They have a nice house and a nice car. It's such a great thing being a Christian. They say, "God is so good." But they two-time Him all week long.

Some men don't complain about their wives. They loudly proclaim how wonderful their wives are, yet they're still stepping out. That's how a lot of Christians are. They're laughing and saying, "My God is great." But they're fooling with this other lover.

Purify Your Heart

To people like that God says, "You'd better stop laughing and start crying": "Be miserable and mourn and weep; let your laughter be turned into mourning, and your joy to gloom" (v. 9).

You say, "I don't feel like crying." Make yourself cry, if that's what you need to do. If you are two-timing Jesus Christ, you don't have anything to be happy about even though you are laughing. Men have affairs and think they're having so much fun; they're laughing and having a good time while their wives are crying.

But God says, "You'd better start crying now, because if you don't cry now, you will be crying later."

So what's the bottom line of it all? You'll find it in verse 10: "Humble yourselves in the presence of the Lord, and He will exalt you."

You've got to try this thing to believe it. You've got to try bowing down to the authority of the Lord. You've got to go all the way with this thing. You've got to try loving Jesus Christ as your first and only love. When you can say to Him, "Lord, I need You and I need Your grace. I'm going to love You and You alone. There is no room in my heart for anyone else," then, like a faithful spouse, He will care for you. He will exalt you in His time and in His way—and it will be glorious!

RETURNING TO YOUR FIRST LOVE

You don't need a song to tell you that "trying to love two ain't easy to do." Jesus Christ deserves to be your one-and-only, and these ideas are designed to help:

1. Here's a way to test your spiritual "faithfulness quotient." Since love is spelled t-i-m-e, figure out how much time you've spent in the past week fellowshiping with Christ through prayer, worship, and study of His Word. How does that match the time you've spent on other activities in the same period? If the ratio doesn't look very healthy for a love relationship, it may be time for some schedule changes.

2. Is your heart divided between the Lord and the world? Only you can answer that. Sometime soon, get alone with the Lord and read through James 4:1–10 prayerfully. Ask the Spirit to show you how your love life with the Lord is doing.

3. Since marriage is designed to be a picture of our relationship with Christ, I urge you to recommit yourself to be a faithful and *loving* spouse.

   Think about all the good reasons you had for marrying your mate—and then tell him or her what you come up with! If your mate is still standing after the shock, pray together that God will draw you near to each other and deepen your love.

4. Here's an encouraging thought to end with: Jesus Christ wanted to have a love relationship with you so much He pursued you for it! Pause, put this book down, and lift up praise to the Lord.

CHAPTER FIFTEEN

THINKING WITH A NEW MIND

We've come to the final section of the book. Time to kick it into high gear, because we're at another exciting point in our study. After remembering and repenting, we're ready to do the "first works" (Revelation 2:5 KJV). Jesus commanded us to *do* if we are to return to our first love. So let's get at it.

I want to start by talking about the importance of our minds, because as Christians we are supposed to think with Christian—that is, with brand new—minds. So what is a Christian mind? Let me start with a definition.

A Christian mind is that mind ordered by the Word and will of God so that the dictates of heaven penetrate the mind and the mind instructs the feet. The result is a walk on earth that reflects the new mind received from heaven. You often hear the adage that someone is "so heavenly minded he's no earthly good."

Well, if you are a Christian who has become so heavenly minded you are no earthly good, you have missed it.

The whole point of being heavenly minded is so that you can be of some earthly good. The point of thinking with a divinely directed mind is so that earth can see the divine option lived out by God's people.

So it is critical that you learn to think with your new mind. You must determine to "set your mind on the things above" (Colossians 3:2), because that's where Christ is. When you make the things of Christ your focus, they become the stimuli the Holy Spirit uses to inform you of God's will and purpose from above so that you might live successfully here below.

YOUR MIND AND YOUR WALK

If we are going to think with Christ-centered minds, it must become a way of life every day. We cannot be sacred on Sunday and secular on Monday. We are sacred all day every day, because we are all ministers under God no matter what our particular professions happen to be.

One of the great passages on what it means to think with a new mind and translate that into everyday life is Ephesians 4:17–24. The apostle Paul begins by saying: "This I say therefore, and affirm together with the Lord, that you walk no longer just as the Gentiles also walk, in the futility of their mind" (v. 17). Notice how Paul links the mind with a person's walk, which is a key word in this text.

The Walk

In the Bible, of course, the word *walk* is used for one's course of living, his lifestyle, his orientation in living. The imagery of walking is used because of the way a person's course is set.

When you walk, you put one foot in front of the other in order to make progress toward a particular destination or goal. Walking is the methodology whereby you move from point A to point B, and it's a process. You don't get where you're going in one giant step, but you walk step by step toward your goal.

Therefore, walking was used in Paul's theology to explain the step-by-step process of moving from where you are to where you ought to be going. The Christian life is not an airplane ride, it's a walk. You don't "jet" to spiritual maturity. You walk to maturity, one step at a time.

Believers at Christian gatherings often ask each other, "How is your walk?" By this they do not mean, "Do you cover twelve inches or twenty-four inches between steps?"

They are asking, "What's your lifestyle like? Are you living commensurate with your calling in Jesus Christ? Is the direction of your life moving in line with who you are?"

The Gentiles' Walk

Right here in verse 17 Paul gives us a negative comparison to measure our walk against. The people in question are "the Gentiles." Whichever way these people are walking, we need to head in the opposite direction because they are walking in "the futility of their mind."

Who are the Gentiles of Ephesians 4? They were the non-Jewish people living in Paul's day who had not come to faith in Christ and knew nothing about a new mind. Paul lived and wrote in the Greco-Roman world.

The Romans were the dominant military force, but the culture was embedded in Greek thought: the teachings of Plato, Socrates, and Aristotle. It was a culture of rhetoricians and debaters, a culture of eloquence at the top and slavery at the bottom.

If you are familiar with world history you know that in its heyday the Roman Empire was a sight to behold, a glorious empire from the human standpoint. But Paul comes to the Christians at Ephesus and tells them that no matter how glorious the empire they are a part of, they should not walk like the Gentiles.

The Ephesians themselves were Gentiles in their ethnic makeup. So they would have been tempted to walk exactly like the Gentiles around them walked, because the Gentiles were walking uptown. They were walking in strength. They were walking in knowledge. They were walking in education and degrees.

Yes, there was slavery and poverty at the bottom of that society, but the Greco-Roman world was still the place to be. And Ephesus was a key city in this world. But

Paul looks at the culture and says to the Ephesian believers, "Don't walk like these people walk."

Walk Like Who You Are

So how does God want His people to walk? Paul answers that back in 4:1, which the "therefore" of Ephesians 4:17 points us back to: "I, therefore, the prisoner of the Lord, entreat you to walk in a manner worthy of the calling with which you have been called."

In other words, walk in accordance with who you are. You've got a great calling. Make sure you walk a great walk. Don't walk like a pauper if you are living in the king's palace.

The story is told that when Queen Elizabeth was a girl, she used to sit in a very slouched position. She used to sort of hang out, lay back, cool out. But one day her mother said to her, "Sit up! You are going to be the Queen."

What the future queen's mother did was relate her posture to her person. She was saying, "When you understand, Liz, that you are going to sit on the royal throne, you have to make sure that everyone who sees you sit knows you belong to the royal family."

See, you ought not to have a sloppy walk if you are the King's kid. If you are the King's kid, your walk should reflect your new identity. You should "walk worthy" of your calling.

Do you know who called you? One day, God in heaven said, "Come here, boy! Come here, girl!" He tugged at your heart and called you. He drew you by the power of the Holy Spirit. He called you unto Himself. Now you are a child of the King. Walk like it.

Futility of Mind

Back in verse 17 we find out why Paul says we shouldn't imitate the Gentiles: that is, unbelievers. They have a mind problem. They walk "in the futility of their mind." Notice a couple of things here.

It's not that unbelievers don't walk. The problem is that when they walk, they have no place to go. The idea of futility is emptiness, vanity, something without purpose.

Unbelievers are constantly moving, but they aren't going anywhere. They are constantly on the road, but they arrive at nothing. Now their activities may produce money, power, and prestige, but when it is all said and done, it is all empty of purpose.

Why? Because it was produced by a futile mind. The problem with the unbeliever is a mind problem, because his mind has not been informed by the Life-Giver. Therefore, unless he turns to Christ he can never arrive at the meaning of life although he searches long and hard. He's trying hard to find his reason for being, to come up with various ways to satisfy his longing for purpose and significance, but he never seems to make it.

I recently came across an interesting bit of information about television, the most popular mindless entity available to us today. The major networks target their prime-time programs at twelve-year-olds. They figure if they can get the kids, they'll get the adults too, because when people sit in front of a television, they shut down their minds.

How many times have you turned on the television because you wanted to turn off your mind? That's one reason television is so influential. It has access to empty heads. So what television advertisers do is fill those non-thinking heads with all kinds of ideas, which is exactly why your MasterCard and Visa are filled! They caught you when your mind was empty.

Suppose you are at the airport having a bite to eat while you wait for your flight. Suddenly you hear over the loudspeaker, "Last call for Flight 74 to Atlanta." You are on Flight 74 to Atlanta, so you push your meal aside because the purpose of being at the airport is not to eat a meal.

Eating is a bonus of being at the airport, but the *purpose* of being at the airport is to catch your plane. So you don't debate when you hear the final boarding call for your flight. You don't argue over the fact that half of your hamburger is still left. Why? Because you understand your purpose.

Paul is saying that in the mind of unbelievers, the purpose of going to the airport is just to see the airport. So they wander around and visit different places.

They get a soft drink over here and visit the gift shop over there. They hang around trying to get turned on by the airport because they have not come to understand that the purpose of going to the airport is the plane ride. That's futility.

You and I understand that the reason we have the mind of Christ is that we might live the life of Christ under the dictates of Christ. So we readily push aside the meal to catch our flight. The unbeliever is satisfied with his hamburger because he doesn't have any purpose for being at the airport.

What God is calling you and me to do is to rid ourselves of a Gentile—that is, an unbelieving—mind. The first reason is that people who have this mind are characterized by futility and emptiness.

Darkened Understanding

There are still more reasons we shouldn't think like people with Gentile minds. Paul gives them to us in Ephesians 4:18–19a:

> [They are] darkened in their understanding, excluded from the life of God, because of the ignorance that is in them, because of the hardness of their heart; and they, having become callous, have given themselves over to sensuality.

We are still dealing with the mind, the way we think. Unbelievers cannot understand because they have "blinders" on. The Bible is clear as to where these blinders come from: "The god of this world has blinded the minds of the unbelieving, that they might not see the light of the gospel" (2 Corinthians 4:4). That's why it takes the Holy Spirit to bring a person to Christ. People are wearing "spiritual sunglasses" that block the light. It is interesting that one of the reasons people wear shades is to look good. Blocking the light is often a secondary motive.

You know that because some people wear sunglasses indoors. The motivation is not to see clearly, but to be seen, to be in style. So what does Satan do? Satan so stylizes the "spiritual sunglasses" that the non-Christian gets excited about the style and forgets he can't see.

That's how sin is. Sin has become stylized: Adultery is now an affair, abortion is now a choice, homosexuality is now an alternative lifestyle, and so on. Sin gets so stylized that it becomes acceptable. The unbeliever's mind gets so messed up that he's walking around in the dark thinking he's in the sunshine.

On top of that, he can do nothing about it because he has been "excluded from the life of God." He does not have God's life in him to provide him an alternative to the darkness that he does not even know he has.

So the picture is not good for the mind of the unbeliever. But why isn't the life of God in him, and why doesn't he remove his sunglasses so he can see? Because of two problems Paul mentions in the verses above. He says, "The reason you should not pattern your thinking after those who don't know God is because of their inbred ignorance and their hard hearts."

Inbred Ignorance

The inbred ignorance of unbelievers means that they were born separated from the life of God and without the capacity to re-create the life of God within themselves. They come into the world with the Adamic nature that automatically removes them from the life of God.

Because of this, spiritual ignorance is natural to unbelievers. They are born in sin and shaped in iniquity, but that's only half of the story. The other half is that they have hard hearts.

Hard Hearts

The word *hard* means calloused. It means that a hard covering has formed over the soft skin. That's why you try to win kids to Christ early in life before sin hardens them and you have to cut through all that callous to reach them.

So the Bible makes clear that the problem with unbelievers isn't just that they were born that way. They also choose to become hard-hearted.

Do you have any hard-headed children? What is hardness? It's the refusal to do what one knows is right. Comedian Bill Cosby says, "I think kids have brain damage, because when you tell them to do something, they don't do it. Then when you ask them why they didn't do it, they say, 'I don't know.' That sounds like insanity to me."

That's exactly what people have become spiritually. The classic biblical case of a hard heart is Pharaoh when he refused to let the Israelites leave Egypt even after all the miracles Moses performed. A lot of people have problems with this because Paul says in Romans 9:17–18 that God hardened Pharaoh's heart.

Well, if you read the account in Exodus chapters 4–14 you will find something very interesting. Ten times you will read that God hardened Pharaoh's heart, and ten times you will read that Pharaoh hardened his own heart.

In the first reference to hardening (Exodus 4:21), we do indeed find God saying that He would harden Pharaoh's heart. This deals with the sovereign will of God, which is Paul's subject in Romans 9.

But don't miss the point that Pharaoh hardened his own heart, and he was held accountable for it. In fact, on about seven of those occasions Pharaoh did the initial hardening before God finished it.

God told Pharaoh in effect, "Since you are determined to have a hard heart, I'll tell you what I am going to do. I am going to finish what you started. Since you want a hard heart, I am going to make it like granite. I am going to make it as hard as possible so you will know who is God in Egypt."

So even though people may be born in ignorance, a hard heart is something they choose to develop. They decide they don't want God in their lives, and they become calloused to Him.

So when you and I emulate the thinking of non-Christians, we are not just emulating their lifestyle. We are emulating their decision to tell God, "Leave me alone!"

That's why hell is the answer to the sinner's desires. The sinner says, "God, leave me alone. I do not want Your life. I do not want Your Son. I do not want Your heaven. I will make my own future. I will run my own existence. I will be captain of my own ship. I will be master of my own fate."

And so what God does for all eternity is give sinners exactly what they want. He leaves them alone forever.

So unbelievers have developed a way of walking where "they, having become callous, have given themselves over to sensuality" (Ephesians 4:19a). That is, they are committed to the satisfaction of the flesh rather than to the glory of God. One of the ways you know you are walking like the Gentiles is when it becomes more important to gratify your flesh than to glorify God.

LEARNING CHRIST

After painting that dismal picture of the unbelieving world, Paul is ready to make the contrast: "But you did not learn Christ in this way" (Ephesians 4:20). He has talked about the Gentiles. They walk a course independent of God. "But you"—the believers at Ephesus, and you and I—have learned a different way.

Where does learning take place? In the mind. So Paul is talking about your mind again. He's saying that if you seek to please the flesh rather than to please the Lord, you are living a life in antithesis to what you have learned about Christ.

The Mind of Christ

When Paul reminds the Ephesians that they have learned the truth about Christ, he's referring to two things: first, the fact that they were given the mind of Christ at conversion; and second, the fact that Paul had taught them for two years. None of what they had learned included walking like the Gentiles.

So any believer who tries to live like an unbeliever becomes a spiritual schizophrenic. He's trying to make the mind of Christ operate in the context of the world, and the result is a split personality, because the mind of Christ teaches us that now we walk to please Him.

One day, I was given directions to a certain destination, but I got lost and was traveling down the wrong road. I wound up in "never-never land" somewhere, way off course. When I finally called the guy who gave me the directions and told him where I was, he said, "Well, give me back the directions you have," and I gave him the directions.

He got a little ticked off. "You did not listen to what I told you. You ask me to tell you how to get there, and then you take my directions and do your own thing!" Have you ever done that? Someone gives you directions and you say, "Oh, I can cut some time off this." So you try to figure it out.

It's like when I was assembling a bicycle and didn't want to fool with the directions. I figured I could do in two hours what the directions were going to take me six hours to do. Ten hours later, I'm still getting the wheels out of the box!

Paul is saying, "When you walk like the Gentiles walk, you wind up where the Gentiles wind up. You wind up lost and purposeless if you don't follow what you learned of Christ."

The Truth of Christ

Paul continues in verse 21 of Ephesians 4: "If indeed you have heard Him and have been taught in Him, just as truth is in Jesus." In John 14:6, Jesus said He *is* the truth. Now, that's important because it is a statement of essence, not just of action. See, you and I may tell the truth right now, but if we aren't walking in the Spirit, what we say an hour from now may not be the truth.

Why? Because we are in the flesh and we are not *the* truth. Not so of Jesus. He not only speaks the truth, He is truth, so that anything He says must be the truth. The reason the Bible we're studying is the truth of God is because of who God is. Therefore, what we learn about Jesus from His Word can be called "the truth."

Jesus is saying in John 14:6 that you can stake your walk on what you learn of Him. Paul echoes this same thing here in Ephesians 4:21: "You can stake your walk on what you learn of Christ so you don't walk like the Gentiles walk and wind up getting nowhere like they do."

Take off, Put on

How do we do this? The next few verses answer that question:

> In reference to your former manner of life [your walk], you lay aside the old self, which is being corrupted in accordance with the lusts of deceit, and that you be renewed in the spirit of your mind, and put on the new self, which in the likeness of God has been created in righteousness and holiness of the truth. (Ephesians 4:22–24)

We talked about the "old you" and the "new you" in chapter 11, so I just want to review here. When you get saved, Jesus comes along and cuts the rope of the "old man" and says, "Drop him. Let him go. You're free!" That's what happens at salvation.

But many of us have gotten so used to the old life we are not totally convinced that putting on the new us is going to be better than getting rid of the old us. The imagery Paul is using in Ephesians 4:22–24 is that of putting on and taking off clothes. That meant a lot more back then than it does today, because we change clothes all the time.

But in Paul's world, getting new clothes was a very big deal. The average Roman citizen was only able to afford a couple of changes of clothes. If you were a slave, you might get two changes of clothes in your entire lifetime.

So when a person in the first century got a new set of clothes, he gladly tore off his old clothes and put on the new. Why? Because the old clothes were worn bare from being worn every day and being washed. They were stained, torn, and tattered. But the new clothes were clean and pure.

You see, old clothes were a reminder of the hard, torn-up years those people had lived. The new clothes were like a fresh start, a new beginning. When Jesus met you, He gave you a fresh start and a new beginning. He dressed you in fine new clothes, the new you.

Leaving the Cocoon

Suppose we could observe a caterpillar turning into a butterfly. We watch a caterpillar make its cocoon. We know that inside that cocoon the caterpillar is developing into something beautiful, lovely, multicolored.

Do you know the beautiful thing about it? Inside that cocoon is developing something that can fly. But have you ever seen a caterpillar trying to get around? He has all those legs, but he's barely making it. That caterpillar is like a lot of people. "How are you doing?"

"Oh, you know, trying to make it."

That's how we were. We were caterpillars, trying to make it. Well, one day we met Jesus, and the Holy Spirit spun a cocoon around us and started painting us beautiful colors. He gave us wings and said, "Fly!"

But many of us said, "But what about this cocoon?" Well, that cocoon is meaningless now because we are way beyond it. We can fly!

But you say, "I've never flown before. I don't know how to fly."

What you need to hear is, "But you don't understand. All you have to do is leave the cocoon and you will fly. You don't have to try to fly. Just leave the cocoon. If you do that, you will fly!" Why? Because butterflies are made to fly. A butterfly just has to be a butterfly.

But as long as that butterfly is tied to its old life in the cocoon, as long as it has a caterpillar mind-set, it will never fly even though everything it needs to fly has been stitched into its nature.

If you're not flying in your Christian life, maybe it's because you are used to your old cocoon. You've become comfortable in that cocoon and you say, "I can't fly. I can't break these habits. I hear what you're saying, but I can't apply it to my life."

That's because you are looking at who you were before the cocoon, not at who you are now in Christ. If you think you're a caterpillar, you won't fly. Caterpillars aren't made to fly.

But if you look at who you are in Christ, there's no reason you can't fly. Look in the mirror. You'll see wings. Believers should never say, "I can't," where God has said, "You can!"

Biblical Thinking

Now, that may sound like nothing more than the power of positive thinking, but it isn't. It's the power of biblical thinking. As we saw earlier, the power of biblical thinking is, "I can do all things through Him who strengthens me" (Philippians 4:13). Notice it isn't all things, period. It's "all things through Christ."

What does Christ have to do with it? He propels my wings. He strengthens me. Christ is my enablement to leave the cocoon. Once I emerge from that cocoon, I can fly.

So whatever the habit, whatever the struggle, whatever the problem, you say "I can overcome it in Christ" if indeed God has said you can. So if we're going to return to our first love and put Christ back in His rightful place, we need to think with the new mind He has already given us.

PLUGGED IN AND PROGRAMMED

One of the amazing things about computers is the way they can track down information in fractions of seconds. The computer's "mind" has been programmed so that it can sort through mountains of information and zero in on exactly what is needed.

You and I have been given the mind of Christ. God has let us in on His very thinking processes so that we can track down His mind on our earthly situations. Thus we can actually think in time what God has determined in eternity.

But a computer only works properly if it is both plugged in and programmed. An unplugged but programmed computer does not work. Neither does a plugged-in but unprogrammed computer.

Some Christians are in church every time the door is open. They can quote Scripture, they take notes on the sermons, and they have marked-up Bibles. But somehow they are still "walking like the Gentiles walk." They have a plug problem. They need to get plugged in to the power source.

Other believers are always shouting, "Praise the Lord! Thank you, Jesus!" They seem fully plugged in, but they've got a programming problem because every time a problem comes up, they cave in and ask, "What am I going to do?"

The answer is to be plugged in and programmed. Programmed means you learn the Word of God so that you have the divine data stored and ready to draw from in the time of need. Plugged in means you are walking in dependence on the Holy Spirit so that the power line is well established between you and heaven.

If you are both programmed and plugged in, then all the data necessary to live Christ's life in this world is available to you. You have the mind of Christ working on your behalf. Draw on it. Think with it.

RETURNING TO YOUR FIRST LOVE

We must apply the mind of Christ by taking off the old life, saying no to it, and putting on the new life, saying yes to it by realizing who we are in Christ: brand-new creatures. When you're faced with "walking as the Gentiles walk," remember who you are and act on who you are. These ideas will help:

1. If you are going to cultivate and think with the mind of Christ, you are going to have to say no to a lot of activities, even harmless ones, in order that you might say yes to your new life. To keep in practice, say no to at least one thing that may be OK in itself but is not helping you toward spiritual maturity.

2. Since your mind absorbs whatever is put into it, you must also deal with any negative influences that may be affecting your mind. Some are pretty easy to deal with: Turn off the TV, close the magazine, stop going to that place. Avoiding people who pull you down may be a little harder, but if you know God wants you out from under their bad spiritual influence, ask Him to show you His "way of escape" (1 Corinthians 10:13).

3. A lot of people are afraid to be alone and quiet because they have never learned how to think and meditate on the important things. Part of developing your new mind is spending time alone with the Lord so that He can communicate His mind and heart to you. As soon as possible, find some time to get alone and get quiet before the Lord. Listen for the "still, small voice" of the Spirit.

4. As a visible reminder that you have taken off the old life and put on the new life, find the oldest, most tattered, most worn piece of clothing you own and put it out where you'll see it every day for a while. Every time you look at it thank God for the new you!

CHAPTER SIXTEEN

MAKING GOD'S KINGDOM A PRIORITY

It almost goes without saying that if someone is really your first love, you'll find out what that person cares about the most and you'll care about it the most too.

Well, what Jesus cares about most is the kingdom of God, so that's what we had better find out and care about. The kingdom is Jesus' top priority. While He was on earth, He pursued a program that was being dispensed from heaven rather than simply a momentary activity that had no eternal purpose.

Jesus' earthly ministry was all about building God's kingdom. So therefore, it follows that we as Christians ought to make building God's kingdom the highest priority in our lives. In fact, if God's kingdom is not your priority, you'll find out that your life will not be what God meant it to be.

Now, Jesus was a very practical Person. He lived in a real world with real people. When He wanted to make real points, He used real illustrations. When it came to our priorities, one of the illustrations Jesus used was how we handle our resources.

This is not because money or property were Jesus' primary concerns, but because people's attitudes toward their possessions is a reliable gauge of their spiritual condition. And Jesus knew that finances would be something everyone could relate to in understanding what He had to say about priorities. Let's open our minds and hearts so He can teach us.

MAKING KINGDOM INVESTMENTS

Jesus says, "Do not lay up for yourselves treasures upon earth" (Matthew 6:19). The words *lay up* and *treasure* have the same root. So Jesus is saying, "Do not treasure for yourselves treasures." What does He mean? Should we not bother with a savings account? Is He saying don't invest in Wall Street, don't have any money put aside for tough times that may come?

That can't be what Jesus is saying, because the Bible applauds saving. The book of Proverbs is full of verses that commend the wisdom of laying something aside for the future (see Proverbs 6:6–11).

The Wrong Priority

Jesus' point is captured in the phrase "upon earth." His concern is not what you are laying up, but why you are laying it up. His concern is stockpiling for earth rather than stockpiling for heaven. His concern is that even Christians can become so messed up in their priorities they spend their time accumulating stuff for themselves and doing nothing for the glory of God.

Many of us have wonderful bank accounts, but our spiritual account is bouncing checks because what we have stored up, we have stored up for ourselves. That is, it has little eternal value.

The question in how you handle your money or property is, how does the kingdom of God benefit from it? If God's kingdom doesn't benefit from your income, your investments, your home, or whatever you have, then you are just storing up for yourself.

According to Jesus, there is a fundamental problem with such storage. You don't want to put your stuff "where moth and rust destroy, and where thieves break in and steal" (Matthew 6:19b). When you do not make God's kingdom your priority, you are investing in something that has a very short life.

In Jesus' day, this thing of moths and rust was a very real problem, because they didn't have the storage capabilities and protective materials we have today. Remember the clothing situation we talked about in chapter 15? A person in that day might have only three or four garments in a lifetime.

Citizens who were fairly wealthy back then would buy woolen garments. The only problem was that these garments were very susceptible to moths. And since they didn't have moth balls and cedar-lined closets, moths would eat holes in the garments.

You get the picture. Even though a person might spend a lot of money for a garment, it would have no long-term value because it would get eaten up. It's the same in the spiritual realm. Anything you do that cannot be measured in terms of eternity is lost. Anything accumulated for self has no lasting value.

The Right Priority

If storing up for ourselves is the wrong priority, what's the right one? Jesus gives it to us in verses 20–21:

Lay up for yourselves treasures in heaven, where neither moth nor rust destroys, and where thieves do not break in or steal; for where your treasure is, there will your heart be also.

Jesus is saying that your heart follows your treasure. If you are investing on Wall Street, for example, you probably take the *Wall Street Journal* and read it religiously, because where your money is, there your heart is. Where your investment is, there your heart is.

That's why Jesus wants you to invest so heavily in His agenda. When you do that, you won't have any trouble making Him your first love, because your heart will follow right along.

Now I didn't say there was anything wrong with investing or reading the *Wall Street Journal*. The issue is your priorities.

This is very critical. Jesus is explaining that when you live for yourself, the issue isn't money. Money only illustrates the issue. The issue is priorities. When you live for yourself, when you are concerned only with your kingdom and your agenda, and not with God's kingdom and His agenda, then your investments will be short-lived.

Now I must clarify something else here. Jesus is not just concerned about time. He also cares about location. Let me show you what I mean. Jesus is not saying, "Lay up treasures in heaven now so you can have them later when you get there." That's a time focus: Live now, go to heaven later.

Instead, Jesus is concerned about *where* your treasure is located, not just *when* you get it. Some Christians say, "I'll live for me now and for heaven in eternity." No, Jesus is concerned that you live for heaven now. God is concerned that His kingdom be your priority now so that whether it's your time, talent, or treasure, you measure it by its eternal value.

Obedience

Let me say a word or two here about obedience. When Jesus commands us to pray that God's will might be done on earth as it is done in heaven, that's exactly what we should pray and should seek to do. God is not into suggestions. He's only into commands. So obedience is not an option for us.

God has given us many good reasons to obey Him. He has been incredibly good to us. That's what Matthew 6 is all about, His grace in giving us the things we need when we love Him first and put Him first.

We ought to obey also because God's commands are not burdensome. When God tells you to do something, it's to help you, not hurt you. That means obedience takes faith. You have to believe that God has your best interest at heart when He tells you to do something, especially if it's not your preference.

It's hard sometimes to get my children to see that I have their best interest at heart in the things I tell them to do. Their perspective is that if I really cared about them, I would never ask them to do that. So I say to them, "Just trust me. In time you will see my good purpose worked out in your life."

This is the goal of obedience: to see God's plan work out in your experience. You can't see that if you're doing your own will. Jesus said He came to do His Father's will, not His will (John 6:38). Put that together with John 8:29, where Jesus said His Father was always with Him because He always pleased the Father, and you find something interesting.

The way to get close to God is obedience. Not church attendance (though that is part of obedience), not the little religious things we do every week, but obedience draws us close to God. So if you want to chase the material things Jesus talks about here in Matthew 6, know that it will cost you dearly. It will cost you the intimate presence of God.

HAVING A KINGDOM PERSPECTIVE

Since I'm making the assumption that you don't want to let things come between you and your first love for Jesus Christ, you must ask yourself whether you are using the things God has given you to build eternal value.

This is important because, if you are a Christian, He did not give you those things for your personal enjoyment only. They are not your "private stash."

Our Resources

Now don't get me wrong. If God has given you a home, He wants you to enjoy it. If He has given you a nice wardrobe, He wants you to enjoy it. If He has given you a bank account, He wants you to enjoy it. If you are legitimately successful, my goal is not to make you feel guilty.

My job is to urge you and teach you to view your success from a kingdom perspective. Paul says in 1 Timothy 6:17:

> Instruct those who are rich in this present world not to be conceited or to fix their hope on the uncertainty of riches, but on God, who richly supplies us with all things to enjoy.

Paul is not condemning those who have. He is condemning those who keep what they have for themselves and give no thought to God's kingdom. Paul is concerned that you develop a kingdom orientation to life, not a selfish orientation.

Otherwise, you will always be talking about what you want, what you need, and what you demand instead of what God wants, what God needs, and what His glory demands. For selfish people, God's concerns do not come up in the conversation.

An Illustration

Jesus illustrates what He means with the human eye:

> The lamp of the body is the eye; if therefore your eye is clear, your whole body will be full of light. But if your eye is bad, your whole body will be full of darkness. If therefore the light that is in you is darkness, how great is the darkness! (Matthew 6:22–23)

As light comes into your eye, the eye focuses on it, and, as a result, you can see. Therefore, your whole body can function properly, because when you can see, you can get where you want to go and do what you have to do without needing special assistance.

But if your eyes go dark, you are in trouble. I remember once in the shower I got soap in my eyes. I reached for the towel, but it wasn't there. I couldn't look to see where it was. So I reached back over, but the soap dish was sticking out and I bumped my lip against it. Blood starting coming out of my mouth.

I tried to bend down another way, but I misjudged the soap dish and bumped my forehead. So I tried moving back. But I slipped on the bar of soap and went down. I was in a mess.

Jesus' point is that when the eyes go, everything else is messed up too. When you lose your kingdom perspective because you've lost your spiritual eyesight, the result is not just that you don't see things spiritually. The rest of your life is messed up so that you won't be able to handle anything properly.

When your spiritual eyesight goes, the rest of you is very dark. And many Christians are in darkness because they are not looking at life from the perspective of God's kingdom.

Choices

Many people don't have time for God's program. They can talk on the phone, but they can't share their faith. They can watch television, but they can't read the Word. They don't focus on God's kingdom, but they make time for their kingdom. So Jesus concludes this section with Matthew 6:24:

> No one can serve two masters; for either he will hate the one and love the other, or he will hold to one and despise the other. You cannot serve God and mammon.

That word *master* means slave owner. *Mammon* means property, and it was used generally of money or material possessions. No one can serve two slave owners. Either this one is "Massa" or that one is "Massa." But not both. You can't love two masters either.

You must make a choice. Jesus didn't say you couldn't have money. He said you can't serve it. What does serving money mean? Serving money means it determines what you do. It calls the shots.

Does God tell you what to do with the things you have, or do you go ahead and make those decisions independently of Him? Does God direct your life, or do you do it yourself? That's His concern. His concern is about priorities.

When the spiritual light is gone, choices can only be made in the darkness. That was God's complaint in Malachi 1. The people of Israel were giving God their leftovers. They did not prioritize Him properly.

It's like the farmer who had two prize-winning calves. He was so excited that he told his wife, "Honey, I'm going to let the Lord know that I recognize these calves are gifts from Him. We are going to give one calf to the Lord and keep the other."

A few weeks later, he came in dejected. His wife said, "What's wrong?"

"Honey, the Lord's calf just died."

It's always the Lord's calf that dies, isn't it? When we have to make choices, the Lord loses because we do not prioritize His kingdom and His glory.

The Real Payoff

The concern of Christians who are growing in their faith is that they make kingdom investments. Let me tell you something. Kingdom investments pay better interest than earthly ones. Kingdom investments appreciate. Earthly investments depreciate.

Many people have invested in success, but don't have peace. Many have invested in homes, but they don't have a family. That's poor interest.

It's a poor return on your investment to have a home and be miserable at the thought of going there. It's poor interest to be president of the company, but be unable to sleep at night.

But when you live your life in terms of the kingdom of God, it pays high interest. God says He will meet your needs (Philippians 4:19). He'll show you His will and give you direction in life (Romans 12:2). He'll give you wisdom in making your decisions (James 1:5). That's a high return, and it only comes with kingdom investments.

ELIMINATING ANXIETY

Are you a chronic worrier? Then keep reading, because Matthew 6:25 is for you. Jesus says, "Do not be anxious." He even repeats it twice (vv. 31, 34). This has the force of "Stop being anxious. Cut it out!"

You can spiritualize it all you want, but worry is a sin. If you are a worrying Christian, you are a sinning Christian. It doesn't carry much weight to tell Jesus that He's your first love, then act like you can't trust Him to look after you.

No Allowance

The Bible makes no allowance, no excuse, for worry. Then why do we worry? Because we don't think kingdom. It's the absence of a kingdom mentality that produces anxiety or worry.

Remember Jesus has just said, "You can't serve two masters. You are either going to give Me your complete devotion, or you are going to be devoted to your other master."

Serving two masters is like trying to have two lovers. If you want to know where that mess leads, review chapter 14. But the disciples are hearing this and saying, "Hold it, Jesus. There's a risk involved in being completely devoted to You." They were worried about the risk, and you may be worried about it too.

The Risk

You may be saying, "I'm not sure I'll make it going Jesus' way. I'm not sure I'm going to get ahead if I adopt a kingdom mentality. This is a dog-eat-dog world. You have to play politics and pull strings to make things happen. No one is going to give you anything. If I do this kingdom thing and serve God completely, I might get left behind. God can have my Sundays."

But remember, the choice isn't between having a master or being your own master. As Bob Dylan once sang, "You gotta serve somebody." And anyone familiar with slavery knows you don't serve your master one day a week. You are lucky to get one day a week off.

Jesus knew the disciples were worried about that level of commitment, just like many Christians today. But the failure to go all the way with Him is the reason people can't get their lives together. Jesus says:

> Do not be anxious for your life, as to what you shall eat, or what you shall drink; nor for your body, as to what you shall put on. Is not life more than food, and the body than clothing? (Matthew 6:25)

Indicting God

Worry is a hideous sin to God because it is an indictment against Him, a slap at His love. If my children worried about whether I was going to feed and clothe them, I would feel pretty bad about the way they thought of me as a father. They indict me when they worry.

When you worry, you are saying, "God, I don't really know about You. I'm not sure You are a caring God. I'm not sure You are a providing God. You are good for church on Sunday, but I'm not sure about You. So I've got to take care of this myself."

But Jesus says, "If you are going to worry, at least worry about something important, such as your life." We worry whether we are going to have enough to eat. Jesus says we'd better worry about whether we are going to be alive to chew.

"Is not life more than food?" Jesus asks. In other words, "If I'm going to wake you up tomorrow, I'm going to feed you. Now which is easier? Feeding you or waking you up?

"Don't worry about breakfast tomorrow. Worry about whether your heart is going to stop tonight. Worry about whether I'm going to keep your brain working and your heart pumping. If you are determined to worry, worry about that."

Now most of us don't worry about stuff like that. We assume when we go to bed at night that we are going to wake up the next day.

But Jesus isn't done with us yet. "Isn't the body more than clothing?" is His next question. We are big on clothes. We're into fashion and designer names and designer jeans, and we want to look good. "I can't go to church today. I don't have a new suit. I don't have a decent dress."

See, you're worried about the wrong thing. You'd better worry that you can still lift your arm to put it in the sleeve. Isn't your body more important than what you put on it? Then why are you worried about what you wear rather than whether your body keeps working so you can get dressed? The issue is priorities.

The Futility of Worry

Now Jesus takes this a little further:

> Look at the birds of the air, that they do not sow, neither do they reap, nor gather into barns, and yet your heavenly Father feeds them. Are you not worth much more than they? And which of you by being anxious can add a single cubit to his life's span? (Matthew 6:26–27)

Jesus says, "Worry doesn't add anything positive to your life." This is such practical stuff, and we know it so well, that we miss the value of what He is saying. These verses are so familiar to many of us that if we're not careful we react, "Yeah, yeah, I know all that. Tell me something new."

Check out the Birds

The cure for that kind of indifference is to do what Jesus said in Matthew 6, verses 26 and 28: "Look. Observe." If we would observe nature we would learn more about God than we currently know, and we just might worry less.

But most of us don't look at life theologically. That is, we don't look at the world around us in the context of the truth about God. Take the birds, Jesus says. Birds never worry about what they are going to eat tomorrow. They assume that if they get up tomorrow, there is going to be a worm tomorrow. So robins go out hunting for a worm without stopping to worry whether God might have run out of worms.

We've been talking about how our worry indicts God.

But notice Jesus' indictment of our lack of faith in verse 26. The Father who feeds the birds is *our* heavenly Father, not the birds' heavenly Father.

So what, you say? Well, worrying about whether God will feed us is like my kids worrying about whether I'm going to feed them while I'm feeding the dog. If I'm feeding the dog, I'm going to at least give them some Cheerios. If I'm taking care of the dog, am I not much more going to take care of my kids?

See, birds know instinctively that God owns the ground the worms are in and knows how to bring them to the surface at the right time. The birds know how to go where the worms are hanging out because God is in control, and He gives them the instincts to show up at the right place at the right time.

The person who observes life theologically, who understands the sovereignty and the sufficiency of God, says, "Lord, things look bad economically. But I know You are my heavenly Father. And You told me that as long as You keep me here, You will provide for me. I don't know how You are going to do it, but thank You in advance for the food that I'm about to receive."

Check Out the Flowers

Jesus gives us another lesson in observing nature in Matthew 6:28–29:

> And why are you anxious about clothing? Observe how the lilies of the field grow; they do not toil nor do they spin, yet I say to you that even Solomon in all his glory did not clothe himself like one of these.

If you want to see God clothe the flowers with beauty and color, come to Texas during wildflower season. Jesus says that even the magnificent wardrobe of Solomon, who was a multi-billionaire by today's standards, can't compete with God's flower garden.

Now, how does God provide for the flowers? They come up already clothed. Birds have to go out and catch worms. But flowers come up clothed.

Jesus is saying that sometimes God provides for us by leading us to where the provision is, by giving us the ability to work and generate an income so we can put life's necessities on the table. But at other times, He does for us what He does for the flowers. He brings it to us while we're just sitting there.

But either way, God provides. So what are you worried about? Peter, who knew a few things about worry, tells us, "[Cast] all your anxiety upon Him, because He cares for you" (1 Peter 5:7). When you cast your cares on Jesus, leave them there. Don't take them back. Say, "Jesus, this is Your problem."

When my kids ask me about something and I say, "I'll take care of it," do you know what that means? It means they don't have to think about it anymore. Jesus is telling us, "Why are you still worried about it? Didn't I say I would take care of it?"

We often tell our children when they pester us, "Didn't I say I would take care of it?" That means it's a done deal. God says He will take care of you if you make His kingdom a priority.

REFLECTING A HEAVENLY PERSPECTIVE

Now Jesus starts to draw out the implications of God's care for us and the kind of response we should have to it:

> But if God so arrays the grass of the field, which is alive today and tomorrow is thrown into the furnace, will He not much more do so for you, O men of little faith? Do not be anxious then, saying, "What shall we eat?" or "What shall we drink?" or "With what shall we clothe ourselves?" . . . for your heavenly Father knows that you need all these things. (Matthew 6:30–31)

This is very important. It is a sin to call God our Father and question whether He's going to meet our needs. That's having "little faith," and that's a serious problem. You say, "How do I know if I have little faith?"

The Wrong Questions

Look at the questions you are asking. Let's bring verse 31 up to date. Here's how we ask those questions today: "How are we going to make it? How are we going to get by? Where's the next payment going to come from? What if one of the kids gets sick? What if the car breaks down?"

We fret and pace and stew, and God looks down from heaven and says, "O, you of little faith."

Have you ever stopped to think that the only reason you can ask "How are we going to get by?" is because you have gotten by to this point? If you had not gotten by to this point, you wouldn't even be around to ask the question.

God's heart is hurt when we are so kingdom-insensitive that we forget the King of the kingdom is also our "Abba," our "Daddy." He wants us to have a perspective that reflects that. Instead, we worry. But worrying is like shoveling smoke. You are not any better off when you're done. Like a rocking chair, worry produces activity but takes you nowhere.

Let's get it straight. We are not just worrying. We are sinning. Satan can bring worry to us, but we are the ones who keep it.

The Wrong Example

If we needed a further reason not to worry about things like food and clothing and shelter, Jesus provides it in verse 32: "For all these things the Gentiles eagerly seek."

We know from our study in the previous chapter that "the Gentiles" are the unsaved. We learned in chapter 15 that God doesn't want us to think like them. Here Jesus tells us not to act like them either.

That word *seek* means to strain for something. The Gentiles break their necks trying to get things. They connive. They scheme. They work double and triple overtime, when those of us who know God can cool out and say, "Lord, I've done all I can do for one day. It's in Your hands now. You make up my lack."

What a relaxed attitude. The Gentiles can't do that. Why? Because they don't have a heavenly Father to look after them. They've got to look after themselves. They have no God to supply their needs, so they have to supply their own needs. They don't have anyone worrying for them, so they must worry themselves.

The Right Focus

Christians worry by choice, not because they have to. If you have a kingdom perspective, it changes everything. If you really love Jesus as your first love, it makes all the difference.

At least four times in the Gospels, Jesus indicted people for having little faith. Each time, the disciples or someone else was whining because things didn't look good.

Once He and the disciples were on the Sea of Galilee headed to the other side (Mark 4:35–41). There was a storm, and Jesus was asleep in the boat. The disciples came and said, "Teacher, do You not care that we are perishing?" (v. 38). They were saying, "We are getting ready to drown, and You are snoring? We are about to go under, and You are asleep?"

Jesus got up, rebuked the wind, and said, "Why are you so timid? How is it that you have no faith?" (v. 40). In other words, "How many times do I have to go over this? Since I know that we're going to make it to the other side, it doesn't matter what happens in the middle of the lake. I'm going to sleep. You stay up and worry if you want."

Then there are those people who get mad if you don't worry with them. They say, "Oh, I'm so worried!"

You say, "Didn't Jesus say that God loves you more than the birds or the lilies? Didn't He say He's going to meet all your needs if you make His kingdom your priority? What are you worried about? Go home and go to sleep."

They come back, "I'm tired of those spiritual answers."

But people lay in bed tossing and turning, taking sleeping pills and going through all that because they have little faith. God says, "Don't worry, I'm up. Trust Me and go to sleep."

HAVING OUR NEEDS MET

We talked about this back in chapter 12 when we looked at the subject of rewards, so once again I just want to review here. Jesus says in Matthew 6:33: "But seek first His kingdom and His righteousness; and all these things shall be added to you."

The order here is all-important. But we reverse it. We say, "Lord, I'm going after all these things and whatever I have left over, I'll use to seek Your kingdom and Your righteousness."

Putting God First

But God says, "No, no. Seek first My kingdom. Put Me first. Put Me first in your resources. Put Me first in your time. Put Me first in everything. Make Me your first love."

In other words, in everything you do ask this question: "What would please God in this situation?" That's putting Him first. When you do that, God says, "I will honor that and meet all your needs."

Now there's something to put your heart at rest. There's something to give you peace. There's something to cause you to relax. Your heavenly Father who controls this universe says, "If you will put Me first, you can leave the rest to Me."

Jesus concludes His teaching in Matthew 6 by saying: "Therefore do not be anxious for tomorrow; for tomorrow will care for itself. Each day has enough trouble of its own."

His Supply of Grace

The problem with worrying about tomorrow is you never run out of tomorrows. How can you be worried about tomorrow when you haven't fixed the mess in your life today?

You and I must learn to live life one day at a time. God only gives us the help we need for today. He doesn't give us tomorrow's help today. So don't worry about what you are going to do tomorrow, because when you get to tomorrow, God's grace will be there to meet you and give what you need.

We worry today about how we are going to make it tomorrow, next week, and next year. Jesus says, "When you get to tomorrow, My grace will be there for you. When you get to next week, My grace will be there waiting for you. When you get to next year, you'll find My grace is still there. I just want to get you through this day." God's supply of grace is inexhaustible. That's high interest!

How can we not love a Savior who loves us and cares for us like that? How can we not care about what He cares about? How dare we not make His kingdom our first priority? If we'll just get our first love in order and do the "first works" God has called us to do, He'll take care of the rest.

RETURNING TO YOUR FIRST LOVE

The key to making this thing work is simply this: You only get this when you give priority to God's kingdom. If you don't make His kingdom your priority, you will be like the heathen: seeking and struggling and worrying and breaking your neck. But if you put God's kingdom first, He will help you prioritize your life. Here are some ideas to get you started:

1. Since the tug of the world is still real, how do you know if something you want is good for you in terms of building God's kingdom? Submit your desire to these questions:
   (1) How much money, time, etc., will it take to get it?
   (2) How might it change you if you get it?
   (3) How will it affect your walk with Christ?
   If your desire fails the test, give it up and go on.

2. Here's another test of whether your focus is a kingdom focus or a worldly one. Write down your three most valuable, most important, or most irreplaceable possessions. Now look at your list and ask what would happen if God took one or all of them away from you? Would you get mad at Him or get bitter? Think about it—and make sure you hold your earthly possessions in an open hand in case God decides He needs to take them.

3. Spend the next five minutes listing all the things that are bothering you right now. And when your list is complete, turn it over to Jesus Christ and thank Him that He has promised to worry about it for you if you'll keep your focus on Him.

4. When it's all said and done, the final question is, where is Jesus Christ *second* in your life . . . and what are you going to do about it?

CHAPTER SEVENTEEN

CARING FOR GOD'S PEOPLE

W e all must be born again individually. There is no question about that. But having been born again we become part of the church, members of the body of Christ. The church is also called in Scripture the family of God and the household of faith. Members of this family call each other brothers and sisters. God is our Father, Christ our elder Brother.

There's a very good reason the Bible uses this kind of family imagery to talk about the church. It's because we are to have the same kind of care for one another that the members of a family have for each other. We're to look out for and help each other the way loving family members look out for each other. And when necessary, we are to exercise the same kind of discipline that exists in a healthy, properly functioning family.

In fact, most of the commands in the New Testament that are related to how believers should act are given in the context of the body. That's also in line with our primary text in Revelation 2, which Jesus Christ spoke to the entire church at Ephesus.

We saw earlier in the case of the church at Corinth that an entire church can lose its first love, just as an individual believer can. So as we return to our first love, we want to bring other believers in the body with us.

With this in mind, I want to widen the spotlight in this final chapter and focus on the church as a family. We are going to talk about the ministry of caring for each other, another of the "first works" we are called to do when we put God back in His rightful place in our lives and in the church. We'll deal with this subject under six primary headings.

CARING ENOUGH TO COMFORT

The first of these caring ministries we are called to exercise toward each other is caring enough to comfort, to be available when a brother or sister needs a shoulder to lean on. Paul says in 2 Corinthians 1:

> Blessed be the God and Father of our Lord Jesus Christ, the Father of mercies and God of all comfort; who comforts us in all our affliction so that we may be able to comfort those who are in any affliction with the comfort with which we ourselves are comforted by God. (vv. 3–4)

The Source of Comfort

We need to understand that comfort begins with God. That's where Paul starts. He says God takes pity on us. That's the idea of the word *mercies.* It means to hurt inside because you feel what other individuals are going through. Their pain becomes your pain and their agony becomes your agony.

Now if God is a spirit, how can He feel what we feel? Spirits can't feel what human beings feel. That's why the first half of verse 3 is so crucial. God is "the Father of our Lord Jesus Christ." And Jesus knows what it is to be rejected, to be slapped around, to be misunderstood, to be tempted. He knows what it is to go through the struggles of life.

So does the Father who is spirit understand how we feel? The Son explains it to Him. Right now, Jesus is in the presence of the Father acting as our intercessor, providing the Father with all the experiential data He needs about what it's like to be human.

The Bible says in Romans 8:26 that the Holy Spirit gets in on the comforting too. Sometimes we hurt so badly that when we bow our heads to pray, we can't get any words out.

But the Bible says that's OK because the Holy Spirit takes the confusion of our pain, organizes and arranges it, and delivers it to the Son. The Son enters into our pain because He is our High Priest who can "sympathize with our weaknesses" (Hebrews 4:15).

The Holy Spirit delivers the facts. Jesus delivers the touch. He understands how it feels. He says, "This is how it feels," and the Father says, "We have to do something about it."

So God is not only the Father of mercy. He's also the "God of all comfort." He knows how to soothe the pain. He knows how to enter in and help with your affliction. He knows how to walk alongside and give support in the need.

So we have One who not only feels what we feel, but can address the problem. That's important, because as these verses remind us, the source we draw from to comfort others is the comfort we ourselves have drawn from God.

So if you are hurting in any way because you are putting God first, making His kingdom your priority, I've got good news for you. Comfort is on the way, because Paul says God comforts us in all our afflictions.

Passing It Along

The idea is that God will meet you in your distress, showing you His mercy and bringing you comfort so that you might turn around and comfort another brother or sister who is in pain. When you see a fellow believer hurting, you are to remember how you were once the "comfortee" and become the comforter to a new comfortee.

God is growing a group of people who are so in touch with Him and with one another that comfort is an automatic result. So now God has the option either to bring comfort directly to a hurting saint or to call on one of the comforters in His body to be the agent through which His comfort is delivered.

Isn't that what family is all about? Isn't that what families are supposed to do? If you're a member of the family of Christ, you ought to be about comforting other family members.

As Christians minister to one another in their pain, Paul says in 2 Corinthians 1:6 that the comfort we render to each other is "effective in the patient enduring of the same sufferings which we also suffer." He assumes that we as believers will suffer. That's not even at issue. The issue is that we care enough to comfort each other.

Now, not everyone will tell you that Christians are going to suffer and will need comfort. Some people present the gospel like this: If you accept Jesus as your Savior, your problems will be solved. I mean, it's money in the bank. You won't be lonely anymore, you won't be afraid anymore, you won't struggle anymore, you won't feel rejected anymore.

What they're describing is what heaven will be like. But here on earth, it just isn't so. Paul says we will suffer, and we need to endure it patiently. When do you get comfort? You get comfort when you hang in there with the suffering.

That's what Paul means here. You are a candidate for God's comfort when you receive from your suffering the lesson He is trying to teach you in your suffering.

And when you hang in there and experience God's comfort, you're equipped to come alongside other believers who are undergoing trials and comfort them so that God's work in them will have its perfect result (James 1:2–4). That takes caring.

CARING ENOUGH TO STIMULATE

You and I are living today in a very impersonal world where people have lost the art of caring. How many times have you found yourself saying, "I don't care"?

How different it's supposed to be among God's caring community, the church. Look at Hebrews 10:24–25:

> Let us consider how to stimulate one another to love and good deeds, not forsaking our own assembling together, as is the habit of some, but encouraging one another; and all the more, as you see the day drawing near.

People who don't care don't stimulate each other. But for us as Christians, it's part of the divine strategy.

I say that because the word *consider* has the idea of strategizing or planning. What are we to strategize about? Ways to "stimulate one another to love and good deeds." *Stimulate* is a strong word. It means to provoke. Have you ever had people in your life who provoked you?

We usually think of this as a negative, but that's not how it's used here. See, God is invisible, yet this God has given us visible instructions. The question is, how does this invisible God energize us, remind us, and provoke us to keep on keeping on? One way is through each other.

God's Provokers

You and I are God's provokers. We are the ones who take the divine data and infuse it with provocation so that we are doing what we are supposed to be doing for the kingdom. We are to come up with strategies to provoke each other. That's our job.

The writer of Hebrews says we should stimulate one another to love. Biblical love, of course, is that love which seeks the highest good of another even if it's inconvenient for me. Was it inconvenient for Jesus to die on the cross of Calvary? I don't even need to answer that. Do you know what stimulating other believers does? Besides helping them stay on track, it helps the provoker by forcing him to forget himself and focus on someone else. So we need to ask how we can stimulate other believers to love and good deeds.

Gather Together

The writer answers that at least in part in verse 25, a very familiar passage we have already come across in our study. His point is as powerful as it is obvious: A body of people can only stimulate one another by getting together on a regular basis.

There is power in a group that you do not get by yourself. This is why the New Testament's design is to get the group, the church, to act as a unified body. Not only is there power, but when a group of caring and committed people come together, they stimulate one another in a way that no one member could ever be stimulated sitting at home in front of the television.

This is why it is wrong for us as the body of Christ, the family of God, to forsake our assembling together. The writer says that some in his day had already developed the habit of not assembling. Things haven't changed much, have they?

But when you pull away from God's family, when you leave the caring environment of your local church, you are risking the loss of any dynamic presence of God in your life. Then, when you really need Him, you wonder where He went. He didn't go anywhere. You're the one who left.

See, we don't understand what the church is. The church is not where you come just because everything is right. The church is where you come when something is wrong and you need a family who understands. The church is where you come when you need a group of caring people who won't put you down, but will stimulate you to keep the faith and have an encouraging word for you.

And the great thing is, it works both ways. There will be times when you're on the stimulating and encouraging end of the stick, and that's uplifting too. But you can't help anyone else if you hide out alone. As we pointed out in an earlier chapter, you don't come to church just because you care about you.

No, you come to church because you care about your brothers and sisters. You ask God to use you to stimulate them even as you need stimulating sometimes. We need to make this work in the church, because when the world tears you up, it won't turn around and help you. And the world isn't getting any better as "the day" approaches.

Have you ever gotten up on Sunday and felt like skipping church? But you got dressed anyway and dragged yourself in the door. You know, "I'm here. That's about all I can say." But all of a sudden, the soloist that day has a word from God for you. It sounded like it came from heaven. Then the Word is opened, and every verse seems written just for you. By the time you leave church you are stepping high, on fire, everything is OK.

Why? Because you assembled yourself together with other believers, and the electricity of the Holy Spirit moving through the body stimulated you. That's what church is supposed to do!

CARING ENOUGH TO SHARE

Another part of taking care of each other as God's people is learning the joy and the responsibility of sharing.

We have a wonderful model of this sharing in the book of Acts. You may recall that as Acts opens, we have the risen Lord Jesus commissioning His apostles and then ascending back to heaven. Then in Acts 2–3, we see a dynamic church born on the Day of Pentecost in Jerusalem and growing rapidly as thousands of people are added in a short time.

All Things in Common

These believers are meeting together in harmony and unison, and they are having all things in common. This is further illustrated for us in Acts 4:32, where we encounter an interesting arrangement:

> And the congregation of those who believed were of one heart and soul; and not one of them claimed that anything

belonging to him was his own; but all things were common property to them.

Now, I'm sure that reading this rubs a lot of modern-day Christians the wrong way. I mean, this gives you the idea that my house became "our" house, my car was "our" car, and my clothes became "our" clothes. You get the picture of somebody coming over to your house at any time, walking in, and saying, "I think I will wear this today."

Well, it wasn't quite like that. It was much stronger. Those who had houses sold them and gave the money to the apostles (vv. 34–35)! I mean, what these believers had was available to the body. They had become such a close-knit community of Christians that what God provided to them was responsibly made available to the church. They were willing to share.

I said above that we live in a very impersonal world. We also live in a very selfish world. People need an oasis of caring, a place they can go where they know somebody is going to care enough to share. A place where people are willing to pay the price of sharing, because sharing requires an investment of time, energy, and resources.

The willingness of the Jerusalem saints to share had a powerful effect on the church. Unity in the pew provided power in the pulpit. The apostles had great power in the proclamation of the Word because the church was unified (v. 33).

This ministry of sharing also brought provision from heaven: "For there was not a needy person among them" (v. 34). To use a contemporary idiom, these believers put their money where their mouths were.

Sharing Today

Now when we read this today someone always asks, "How can I meet all the needs around me today?" The answer is, you can't. It's impossible for you to meet all the needs.

So you say, "Which needs do I meet?" The biblical answer is, the needs that cross your path. There are two things you should guarantee: one, that your immediate family is taken care of; and two, that your local church family is taken care of. Of course, if your resources allow you to meet needs beyond those, you should do so. But these come first.

The Bible teaches that you and I are just managers of God's property. We don't really own anything, and the proof of this is that one day we will leave it all behind. This means that what we have is available to the kingdom.

We have a great illustration of this attitude in verses 36–37 of Acts 4. This is where we first meet Barnabas, the "Son of Encouragement." Barnabas owned a piece of land, which he sold for the benefit of the body. He brought the money from the sale and gave it to the apostles, just like the other believers did.

Now Barnabas must have been at least somewhat well-to-do. We don't know how much he had, but obviously he was doing all right. But then he found out that there were needs in the body. Remember, there must have been about ten thousand believers in Jerusalem by now (see 2:41; 4:4). They had all kinds of needs, so Barnabas shared what he had.

Why do we share? Because we recognize that God has been faithful to us, and that is the only reason we have something to give. Nobody is going to sell a piece of land he owns and turn all the money over to the kingdom unless he realizes and believes that God actually owns the land and he's just the steward.

See, the reason I can open my home to a ministry or to the young people at church is that God has been faithful to me. You can use your car to help others because God has been faithful to you.

As the family of God, we need to care enough to share what He has given us. Some of us have more of one thing, others have more of something else. As we share what we have and pool our resources, needs are met and God is glorified. One way you know that your love for Christ is in its rightful place is that you are willing to share with His people.

CARING ENOUGH TO CONFRONT

The first three categories of caring are easy to talk about. Who doesn't want to comfort, stimulate, and share with others?

But if your family is going to be a real family, everyone has to do his part. If the husband is doing his thing for his goals, the wife is doing her thing for her goals, and the kids have their own agendas, you are headed for trouble.

You often hear people say, "I want to let him be himself," or "I want to let her be herself." We fail to understand that in a family, the caring thing to do is not to let one person destroy the family's unity. The caring thing to do is to ensure that each individual member operates on behalf of the whole.

In the family of God, we as believers are accountable for what happens to the whole family. If we fail to function properly, we hurt the family. That can't go on unchecked, so sometimes we have to care enough to confront an erring Christian.

A Serious Matter

Now I want to show you from the Bible how serious a matter this is. In Matthew 5:23–24, Jesus says that if you are sitting in church and you remember that your brother has something against you—notice, not that you have something against him—don't give your offering and don't continue with your worship until you go confront that brother about the problem and settle it.

Why is this so important? God won't deal with you if you are not dealing with your brother because we are talking family.

In Matthew 18:15–17, Jesus says if your brother sins, go and reprove him in private. If he listens to you, you have won your brother. If he does not listen, "take one or two more with you, so that by the mouth of two or three witnesses every fact may be confirmed" (v. 16).

Paul tells us in 1 Thessalonians 5:14 to "admonish the unruly." He gets more specific in 2 Thessalonians 3, where he says to "keep aloof" from the unruly (v. 6) and

take special note of them that they "may be put to shame"
(v. 14).

You may not have realized church was that involved.
Maybe you thought it was a suit, a dress, a hat, and a sit-
down. That does not a church make. If we are going to
return to our first love, we must confront what's wrong
and set it right.

Preferences

If we are supposed to confront each other when the
need arises, we had better find out what deserves confrontation.

The key here is preferences versus absolutes. Principle number one is that you and I have no right to impose
our preferences on each other. There is freedom in God's
church for personal preferences in things like clothes,
hairstyles, music, or anything else that is not a criterion
for Christian unity.

The problem is not that God's people have preferences. The problem comes when we try to force everyone
else into our mold. We are not obligated to each other's
preferences (Romans 14:5).

Absolutes

But while we have freedom related to our preferences, we do not have freedom related to God's absolutes.
Principle number two is that where God has spoken, it
does not matter what we prefer, we think, or we like.

We are to confront each other when someone is acting in opposition to divine truth. You can encourage
someone regarding your preferences. But you can demand
when it comes to God's absolutes. God is not into asking,
He is only into telling.

See, if you go around trying to please everyone, you
are never going to get God's work done. As a pastor, I had
to learn that. I was trying to please this person and that
person, and what this person wanted was opposite of
what that person wanted.

I got to the point where I said to the Lord, "I don't
want to get an ulcer, Lord, so I'm going to please You and

trust You to work out the rest of it." Whenever people become the defining point for your actions, you wind up pleasing people while God is still waiting for you to turn Him on.

Why should we care enough to confront each other? Because the truth not only affects us, it affects other people we affect. I've said before that there are other people in the family besides ourselves whom we need to consider.

How to Confront

How do you confront? Jesus gave us the procedure in Matthew 18. This guards against someone being accused based on a rumor or because one person has a grudge against another.

Paul gives us the spirit in which to confront. We are to do it by "speaking the truth in love" (Ephesians 4:15). If you care, you confront, and if you confront, let it be known in your confronting that you care. You don't hedge on the truth, but you don't deliver it with a hammer. As we'll see below, the goal of confrontation is restoration, not destruction.

What if the person being confronted responds, "Mind your own business"? What if he rejects you or gets angry at you? The Bible says that's not your problem. Even if you don't win your brother or sister back, you win God's approval.

CARING ENOUGH TO WITHDRAW

Confronting a sinning believer isn't necessarily easy. This next step of caring is a little more severe. But don't forget our context. We're talking about returning to our first love, giving God back His rightful place in our lives and in the church. You don't do that by closing your eyes to wrong.

Instead, God calls us to cut a straight line spiritually. If we don't, the believer who is walking out of line with the truth will tempt other members of the family to join in. If it appears that one member is getting away with sin, someone else will think, "Hey, if Joe can get away with that, I can too."

Besides causing other believers to stumble, a sinning Christian also gives those outside the faith an excuse not to get serious about God. Someone will always say, "The reason I don't go to church is because it's full of hypocrites."

Now we know that this doesn't excuse the unbeliever. Hypocrisy only proves that there's a real thing out there somewhere. Unbelievers are still responsible before God for the real thing, but failing to deal with problems in the church certainly doesn't help in drawing lost people to Christ.

The Need to Withdraw

For this category of caring I want to go back to a passage we touched on above, 2 Thessalonians 3:6:

> Now we command you, brethren, in the name of our Lord Jesus Christ, that you keep aloof from every brother who leads an unruly life and not according to the tradition which you received from us.

We know that Paul had already urged the church to deal with the unruly (1 Thessalonians 5:14), but evidently some of these people had not taken heed. They were not walking their new walk.

Paul was following Jesus' instructions in Matthew 18. He had brought the matter to the attention of these unruly believers, telling the Thessalonians to go to those who needed it and confront them. But when confrontation does not work, the next step is to bring the matter to the church.

So Paul does that here. Notice this is an apostolic command. He's drawing on his authority to tell the church the next step to take. Verse 14 of 1 Thessalonians 5 lets us know he's bringing this to the whole church, because he tells them to mark out those who were unruly for the next step of discipline: withdrawal.

Don't misread this. Paul is not saying withdraw from somebody who blows it one time. He is speaking here of one who has adopted disobedience as a lifestyle, who is living in deliberate, unrepentant sin. So Paul says to withdraw, "keep aloof from," an unruly brother. Why? First, so you don't get caught up in his sin, so his lifestyle does not rub off on you. Second, so that people don't associate you and the unruly believer as best friends, so they don't get the idea that you approve of this lifestyle.

Withdrawing from a sinning Christian doesn't mean you don't ever talk to this person. Paul is saying you relate to the erring brother or sister from a distance.

Unruly Living

What is unruly living? It is any habitual way of life that is not commensurate with the teachings of Scripture. Unruly living is deciding you will do what you want regardless of what God's Word says. It is deciding that you do not want to seek the glory of God, but the satisfaction of your flesh.

We've already seen a couple of reasons that it's important to do what the Bible says and identify such people. Let me give you another one from verse 13 of 2 Thessalonians 3: "But as for you, brethren, do not grow weary of doing good."

What's the point? Paul realizes that the Thessalonian believers who were doing right might get discouraged if the ones who were doing wrong felt free to keep on doing it and seemed to get away with it. The ones who were working and providing for their families might say, "I may as well quit too if these others are going to sit around and do nothing."

Paul said no, you folk who are living disciplined lives, who are doing what God wants you to do, keep doing it. Don't let the people who are living unruly lives stop you from walking right. What a powerful reason to deal with the unruly!

Verse 14 is stronger than verse 6 because it is a formal declaration of non-association. This brother or sister can no longer receive the benefits of the local assembly. Now, withdrawing can ultimately lead to excommunication where the rebellious brother has to be removed from the membership and placed under the judgment of Satan (1 Corinthians 5:5).

Why does God do this? So that His family can function like a family and not have renegades living in the house. Notice, however, withdrawing, keeping aloof from, is not done in anger or hatred (1 Thessalonians 5:15). The goal is to win the person back, which brings us to our final category of caring.

CARING ENOUGH TO RESTORE

In a loving family, if one of the members is caught in a trespass the goal is to restore him or her, not hurt the person further. We'll look at Galatians 6, beginning with verse 1:

> Brethren, even if a man is caught in any trespass, you who are spiritual, restore such a one in a spirit of gentleness; each one looking to yourself, lest you too be tempted.

We've come across this verse before. You may recall that the word *restore* means to set a broken bone, to put it back together.

The Problem

Let's consider some important things about this passage. Notice the brother is "caught" in a sin. In other words, this is not if you think someone is doing something, or you hear about it, or the person looks like he'd do it if he had half a chance. No, that's not the criterion.

What's a "trespass"? It's the idea of someone who was on the right path, but veers off. So we are not talking about a determined lifestyle of sin. That person needs to be disciplined. We are talking about someone who is on the right road, but takes a wrong turn and does something wrong.

When that happens, you set the broken bone. You try to help fix the fracture, not compound it. One of the reasons hurting people don't want to come to church is that they do not view the church as a place for healing, but as a place where people will jump on their broken bone and break it again.

The Restorers

That's the problem, but who are the restorers? "You who are spiritual." Since not everyone in the church is spiritual, not everyone qualifies to be a restorer. So we have to ask what it means to be spiritual.

Paul defines a spiritual person in 1 Corinthians 2:15–16 as one who possesses the mind of Christ. So if you want to know whether you are spiritual, ask yourself if you look at life from the divine perspective.

When it comes to a person who needs restoration, are you going to give him God's perspective or "I think . . ."? You see, an erring brother doesn't need any more ideas. It's ideas that got him in trouble in the first place. He needs some answers from God's Word.

How do you restore someone? In a "spirit of gentleness." You massage the wound, not rub salt in it. Gentleness is a fruit of the Spirit (Galatians 5:23). It's tender loving care. Who exhibits the fruit of the Spirit? Those who are spiritual.

Spiritual people can restore others in this spirit because they know they can also be tempted and fall. See, only an immature believer would think he or she is above sin. That's an attitude of pride that says to the sinning Christian, "How in the world could you do that? I'd never fall for that." That's not what a spiritual restorer says.

BURDENS AND BACKPACKS

Notice in Galatians 6:2 that Paul widens the focus to talk about our mutual ministry. I want to close by looking at verses 2–5 and leaving you with a final word of challenge and encouragement.

What is a burden? It's something you are carrying that is too heavy for you to handle alone. Are you helping to bear somebody else's burden? You can't always *take* another's burden, but you can help him carry it. Restoring a fellow believer doesn't mean you take his consequences for him, but you can help him bear any consequences that may be involved in his restoration.

Why should you bear another's burden? "For if anyone thinks he is something when he is nothing, he deceives himself" (v. 3). Do a little self-analysis. The moment you start thinking you are really something, God has something to tell you about yourself. You aren't hitting on anything. It's like I said above about the immature Christian who thinks he's got it together and couldn't possibly stumble. Watch out! Don't fool yourself. Better "examine [your] own work" (v. 4) before you start bragging.

Paul closes this portion of Galatians 6 by saying, "For each one shall bear his own load" (v. 5). Is that in contradiction to verse 2? No, what we have is simply two different Greek words.

As we've already indicated, verse 2 is talking about a heavy load, one that's too big for one person to carry alone. The word in verse 5 means basically a backpack, like the one soldiers used to wear to carry their garments as they marched. Paul says don't ask your brother or sister to carry your backpack for you.

That is, don't expect someone else to meet your responsibilities for you. You have to carry your own backpack. So the question is, are you carrying your own backpack? Are you meeting your responsibilities before the Lord in your personal life, family life, and church life? My friend, we have got to get beyond lazy Christianity and start caring for one another!

RETURNING TO YOUR FIRST LOVE

There's not a lot left to say, except let's get busy with the business of caring for each other. Here's an application idea for each of the categories of caring we talked about:

1. Is there someone in your fellowship who you know is hurting and needs someone to lean on? Our tendency is to draw back from people like this because we're afraid we'll mess up and say or do the wrong thing. Don't do that. Reach out a hand of comfort, depending on God to touch that friend through you.

2. If you'd like to be a Christian who stimulates others to get it together, do a little self-evaluation. Look at your strengths. Are you using them to the full in the body of Christ? What about your weaknesses? Do you have a plan for improving them? Get those things going, and you'll motivate someone else!

3. Sharing starts as an attitude. For instance, does your schedule include time for others, or would God have to crack your day wide open to get you to share your time? Ask the same question about your finances, your home, and all the other stuff God has so freely shared with you. The answers should tell you whether you have a sharing spirit.

4. We've talked about confrontation before, and it's a tough one. At this point I encourage you to pray that God will make you sensitive should the need arise to confront a fellow believer. Pray that you will have the discernment to know whether the issue is a preference or a biblical absolute.

5. When it comes to the need to withdraw, if you don't follow biblical guidelines you could be unwittingly helping to grease the skids for a sinning Christian. If there is a Christian you know whose lifestyle is an embarrassment to God, make sure you are not doing anything to help it along: e.g., pretending like nothing is wrong, continuing to fellowship with this person, or dodging the issue when it comes up.

6. Restoration is a good note on which to end the book and these steps. To help prepare yourself to be a restorer, ask yourself how you'd want to be dealt with if you were caught in a trespass. Then determine that you will deal with an erring brother or sister the same way when the need arises.

EPILOGUE

I pray that the Holy Spirit has used something I've said in this book to motivate you to return to your first love for Jesus Christ and serve Him faithfully. Just knowing how much He loves us ought to be enough to make us want to love and follow Him (see Romans 5:8).

And as if that isn't enough, Christ has also promised us a reward at His judgment seat based on how we loved Him and served Him. Paul said, "I see a gold medal at the end of this race, and I want to go for the gold."

What does it take to get the gold? It takes a winner's attitude: "Run in such a way that you may win" (1 Corinthians 9:24). I want to cross the finish line at the end of my life saying I won, and I want you to be right beside me!

Paul made it unmistakably clear he was in the Christian race to win. If you and I are going to come out as winners—that is, receiving God's approval both in time and in eternity—it will be because we learn to say no to things that take away from the accomplishment of that goal.

I like what Paul says in 1 Corinthians 9 because he is talking to the whole church. He is saying, "All of you are in the race, so go ahead and run!" (v. 24).

Then he says in verse 26, "I don't know about anyone else, but I am running to win!" My final challenge to you is that you might make loving and serving Christ and seeking His approval the dominant goal of your life. That you might go for the gold that He will one day award to everyone who loves Him supremely.

Let me change illustrations and tell you about a father who was on his way to work one morning. He was running late, but he knew he had to catch the 8:05 train because he had a major presentation to make that day. This was to be his big day. But it was now 7:45 and he was running around the house trying to get his stuff together. His little boy kept getting in his way, so he told him, "Go outside and play!"

It had rained the night before, so the ground was muddy. Well, as the father rushed out the door, there was his son having a great time playing in the mud. He had mud all over him. The dad hollered to his wife, "Honey, please come get him!" But his wife was somewhere in the back of the house.

So the father said to his boy, "I can't fool with you now. I've got to go!" But as he sprinted across the lawn, he slipped and went down on his knees in the mud. His freshly-pressed suit now had mud on it. But he had to catch the 8:05.

So he brushed off his pants and briefcase as best he could and took off. He had mud and grime on him, but he had to catch the 8:05. All the time, however, his son sat playing in the mud, content to be covered in the muck because he wasn't going anywhere.

Some Christians are like that little boy. They are in the mud and love it. They keep slopping unrighteousness all over their faces and smearing their bodies in sin, having a grand old time. But other Christians are in the mud only because they slipped. They want out. They want to get clean.

The way you know which kind of Christian you are is whether you are willing to get up out of the mud and catch the train. Jesus Christ bids you to come aboard the 8:05.

You say, "But my knees are dirty."

That's OK. Get aboard with dirty knees if you must, but don't miss the 8:05.

You say, "But my elbows are dirty."

Bring those dirty elbows, but don't miss the 8:05.

You say, "But my friends are still playing in the mud."

Yes, but they're going to miss the 8:05.

You say, "My family is in the mud."

But they are not catching the 8:05. Don't hang around with your friends who are having fun in the mud when you can put your muddy self on the 8:05 because the train has a bathroom with soap and water. You can clean yourself up.

Like the prodigal son, you can get up out of the mud, catch the 8:05, and come home. So come on home to full commitment to Jesus Christ. Whatever it takes, put your love for Him back in first place where it belongs. If you get that fixed up right, everything else will take care of itself.

SUBJECT INDEX

SCRIPTURE INDEX